CHIEF STANDING BEAR IN FULL REGALIA

LAND OF THE SPOTTED EAGLE

BY
LUTHER STANDING BEAR

FOREWORD BY RICHARD N. ELLIS

University of Nebraska Press
Lincoln and London

First Bison Book printing: 1978

Library of Congress Cataloging in Publication Data

Standing Bear, Luther, Dakota chief, 1868–
  Land of the spotted eagle.

  1. Teton Indians.   2. Teton Indians—Government relations.   3.
Indians of North America—Government relations.   I.   Title.
E99.T34S7   1978   970'.004'97   77–14062
ISBN 0–8032–0964–9
ISBN 0–8032–5890–9 pbk.

Bison Book edition published by arrangement with Albert L. Cole

Manufactured in the United States of America

FOREWORD

It is this loss of faith that has left a void in Indian life—a void that civilization cannot fill. The old life was attuned to nature's rhythm—bound in mystical ties to the sun, moon and stars; to the waving grasses, flowing streams and whispering winds. It is not a question (as so many white writers like to state it) of the white man "bringing the Indian up to his plane of thought and action." It is rather a case where the white man had better grasp some of the Indian's spiritual strength. I protest against calling my people savages. How can the Indian, sharing all the virtues of the white man, be justly called a savage? The white race today is but half civilized and unable to order his life into ways of peace and righteousness.

Luther Standing Bear, "The Tragedy of the Sioux," *American Mercury* 24, no. 95 (November 1931): 277.

In 1931, after an absence of sixteen years, Luther Standing Bear returned to the Pine Ridge Sioux Reservation in South Dakota. In preceding years conditions on the reservation had worsened, and Standing Bear was shocked by the physical and mental status of the reservation Sioux. If his visit did not serve as a catalyst for the writing of his third book, *Land of the Spotted Eagle*, it undoubtedly confirmed and strengthened previously formed opinions about the impact of federal Indian policies and convinced him of the need to educate the American people about the strengths of traditional Sioux culture. While he wrote about the Teton Sioux, his people, he also offered more general comments about the importance of native cultures and values and the status of Indian people in American society.

Although Standing Bear describes himself as an Oglala, one of the subtribes of the Teton, or western, Sioux, he may have been a Brulé.[1] He was probably born in the mid-1860s, in the month "when the bark of the trees cracked" in the year of "breaking up of camp." His father, Standing Bear the first, was probably a Brulé band leader on the Rosebud Reservation, which was just to the east of Pine Ridge. Plenty Kill, as young Standing Bear was named, was raised in the traditional Sioux manner, although Sioux freedom was being restricted by military campaigns and government policies, and traditional culture was also undergoing change.

During the 1850s the American army appeared in force in Sioux country, and in 1855, following an army attack on a

Brulé camp at Ash Hollow in southwestern Nebraska, Spotted Tail, a legendary Brulé warrior and rising political leader, was held for a year at Fort Leavenworth, Kansas Territory. The decade of the 1860s saw increasing conflict as the army campaigned against the Sioux in the Missouri Valley and to the west in 1863 and 1864 and in the large-scale Powder River campaign of 1865. Brulé leaders were present at the Fort Laramie treaty councils in 1865 and 1868 and agreed, under pressure, to reside on a reservation. Ultimately their territory became the Rosebud Reservation. The military campaign following George Custer's defeat at the Little Big Horn in 1876 resulted in enforced reservation life and subjected the Teton Sioux to government policies designed to eradicate the old culture and replace it with the culture of white America, for the goal of federal Indian policy was to assimilate Indian people into white society.

Young Plenty Kill, while trained to be a Sioux warrior, lacked the opportunity to fulfill that training. Instead, his life was influenced by the tremendous pressures placed upon Sioux life. He entered Carlisle Indian School in Pennsylvania as a member of the first class, and it was there that he was given the name Luther Standing Bear.

Carlisle opened its doors in 1879 and became a model for government Indian schools. It was dedicated to education and culture change; and at Carlisle, Luther Standing Bear became acquainted with itchy red flannel underwear, tight shoes, stiff collars, and the prohibition on the use of native languages. When his father came for a visit, he had to ask permission so that he could communicate in Lakota.

Standing Bear learned tinsmithing, a trade that was useless on the reservation; so when he returned to Rosebud he became an assistant teacher at a reservation school and later an agency clerk, storekeeper, assistant minister, and rancher. Some of these jobs were at the Pine Ridge Reservation, and Luther and his brother, Henry, took their allotments at Pine Ridge after the Dawes Act of 1887 was applied to the Sioux.

Standing Bear also became involved in show business in 1902, when he became a member of Buffalo Bill's internationally famous Wild West show. The troupe performed before the king of England. Standing Bear rejoined Buffalo Bill the following year, but a train wreck in Illinois, which killed some members of the group, left him seriously injured. Ultimately Standing Bear moved to California, where he joined the lecture circuit and became a member of the small group of Indian actors in Hollywood. Late in life he wrote four books, *My People the Sioux* (1928), *My Indian Boyhood* (1931), *Land of the Spotted Eagle* (1933), and *Stories of the Sioux* (1934).

Luther Standing Bear had led a full life and had a broad range of experiences by the time he wrote *Land of the Spotted Eagle*. His experiences at Carlisle and life in the East and his observations of the administration of federal Indian policy on the reservation made him very critical of government treatment of Indian people. He had first-hand experience in dealing with the federal bureaucracy and knew how difficult that could be. As an educated Indian who had received an allotment of land, he could receive title to that land and American citizenship when he was judged competent to manage his own affairs. Until then his land was held in trust by the government. The process, which should have been simple, was made difficult, and Standing Bear eventually went to Washington, D.C., saw the secretary of the interior and commissioner of Indian affairs, and remained in the city until he received the appropriate documents. He later wrote that the day he received his papers and thus his freedom "from the iron hand" of the Indian agent was one of the greatest days in his life.[2]

Standing Bear used his freedom to leave the reservation. In 1931 in an article in the *American Mercury*, he wrote that he left "because I was no longer willing to endure existence under the control of an overseer." He had tried reservation life and attempted "to adapt myself and make readjustments to fit the white man's mode of existence," but failed. "I developed into a chronic disturber," he wrote. "I was a bad Indian, and the agent and I never got on. I remained a hostile, even a savage, if you please. And I still am. I am incurable."[3]

Standing Bear's pride in his ability to abandon the security of reservation life and make his way in the white world was justified. In a sense he had beaten the system, although he had done only what the government and reformers supposedly wanted all Indians to do. The goal of federal Indian policy was to assimilate Indian people into the broader society, to Americanize American Indians, but in practice administration of Indian policy consisted of a system of controls over the lives of

Indian people, controls that did nothing to prepare these wards of the government for full participation in American life, either as individuals or as a people.

When he returned to the reservation in 1931, Standing Bear was aware of the dichotomy between the goals and effect of federal Indian policy, and he was critical of the system and the underlying attitude toward Indian people. What he saw at Pine Ridge caused him to write the article for the *American Mercury* and undoubtedly influenced the subsequent manuscript, *Land of the Spotted Eagle*. "I found the destruction of my people continuing," he wrote; "I found conditions worse than when I left them years ago."[4]

Standing Bear found the reservation economy in terrible shape. The Sioux suffered from hunger and ate horse meat because beef was unavailable. "Food! Meat! Everyone wanting meat! Yet the Sioux live in the finest cattle country in the land," Standing Bear protested. "The white farmers scattered liberally all through their reservation have fine-looking cattle, as well as pigs, chickens, turkeys and horses. But not the Indian; he is poverty-stricken!"[5] The Sioux cattle industry had all but disappeared, and when Standing Bear attempted to purchase a steer for a feast, he bought it from a white man because he could not find an Indian who owned cattle. "The country is manifestly a cattle country," said Standing Bear, echoing similar comments made previously by those familiar with the climate of South Dakota. "The Sioux are not farmers. They can raise cattle and if given a chance will become independent. The logical procedure is to give back their reservation to them. Remove the white man entirely," he suggested. "Fence the reservation if necessary. Stock the land with cattle and let the Sioux do the rest."[6] Others had offered similar suggestions, but they fell on deaf ears at the Bureau of Indian Affairs in Washington, D.C.

With their lives controlled by the Bureau, with the economy disintegrating, with continued change in tribal culture because of government policies, and with little participation in decision making, the old Indians were "pictures of lost hope." Standing Bear found a spiritual as well as a physical deterioration. "Incentive is gone," he wrote. "Old and young are meek to the point of docility, obeying every command of the agent. They settle no questions for themselves; their overseer decides everything. The system has crushed them; they are nonentities."[7] Standing Bear observed the impact of the system upon reservation Sioux, and he became reacquainted with it personally when he was summoned by the agent to identify himself and explain why he was on the reservation. All visitors to the reservation were under surveillance while they walked "on the ground of this government prison," he complained.[8]

When Standing Bear wrote his protest of government treatment of the Sioux for the *American Mercury*, his article joined a long list of other attacks on federal Indian policy. The previous decade had witnessed a growing movement for reform. Leading magazines printed exposés on Indian affairs; such diverse organizations as the Indian Rights Association, the American Indian Defense Association, and the General Federation of Women's Clubs joined the movement, and investigations were conducted. Reform began during the administration of President Herbert Hoover and accelerated with the election of Franklin D. Roosevelt and the appointment of John Collier, leading critic of Indian affairs, to the office of commissioner of Indian affairs.

Houghton Mifflin Company published *Land of the Spotted Eagle* near the end of the protest movement and about the time that the Indian New Deal began. Luther Standing Bear considered this his most important book, an assessment with which many modern readers concur. Today it appears on reading lists for college courses in anthropology, literature, and history.

Standing Bear's first book, *My People the Sioux*, written with the assistance of E. A. Brininstool, author of a number of books on western history, is largely autobiographical. In it he presents some cultural material, particularly in the area of child rearing, but he emphasizes certain aspects of the first thirty or forty years of his life such as the Carlisle years, the Ghost Dance, and his position with the Wild West show.

Land of the Spotted Eagle is quite different. Assisted by Melvin Gilmore, curator of ethnology at the University of Michigan, and Warcaziwin (spelled Wahcaziwin by Standing Bear), who later wrote a number of articles on Indian affairs, Standing Bear described traditional Sioux life. He was concerned because whites viewed Indians as ignorant savages without redeeming virtues. "White men," he wrote, "seem to have difficulty in realizing that people who live differently from themselves still might be traveling the upward and progressive road of life."[9]

Approximately 80 percent of the book is ethnographic in nature, with chapters on child rearing, social and political organization, the family, religion, and manhood. The culture described is that of the Teton Sioux, and the text is highlighted by personal reminiscences, anecdotes, and humor. While the book is not tremendously detailed and is rather loosely organized, it did reach a broad audience that was generally unfamiliar with the publications of anthropologists and others who had studied Sioux culture. Standing Bear presents a very positive view of Sioux life, but occasional errors exist and some statements remain controversial. Recipients of Sioux attacks, for example, reject claims that the Sioux were not aggressive and did not fight to gain territory or to conquer others.

An equally important difference between *My People the Sioux* and *Land of the Spotted Eagle* is in the nature of Standing Bear's evaluation of federal Indian policy. He was mildly critical in the former, much more critical in the latter. Indeed, the last two chapters, which include his views on Indian affairs and his suggestions for the improvement of Indian-white relations, form an important part of the latter book. Criticism centered on the effort of whites to remake Indians in their own image. The effort to strip away everything that was Indian resulted in disaster. "Everything that was natural and therefore healthful, was displaced with things unsuitable, foreign, and unfitted." The Sioux and other Indians were "degraded by oppression and poverty into but a semblance of their former being," he wrote.[10]

He was confident that whites would resist any similar effort to remake their culture. He wrote, "Had conditions been reversed and the white man suddenly forced to fit himself to the rigorous Indian mode of life he might now bear the stigma of 'lazy' if, indeed, he were able to survive at all."[11] He echoed the view of Big Eagle, a Santee Sioux, who, commenting on events leading to the Santee uprising of 1862, said, "Then the whites were always trying to make the Indians give up their life and live like white men—go farming, work hard and do as they did—and the Indians did not know how to do that, and did not want to anyway. It seemed too sudden to make such a change.

If the Indians had tried to make the whites live like them, the whites would have resisted, and it was the same way with many Indians."[12]

Standing Bear's recommendations to improve the condition of Indian people have a remarkably modern sound. He believed that Indians should be trained to be teachers, engineers, doctors, and lawyers for employment on reservations, and he favored bilingual education and the incorporation of Indian history into the curriculum.

As an Indian author with four books to his credit, Luther Standing Bear deserves more recognition than he has received. His publication list is a remarkable accomplishment for an individual whose formal education was limited to a few brief years at Carlisle. That there were so few Indian authors in the nineteenth and early twentieth centuries adds to his significance in American literary history.

A small but active group of highly educated Indians existed in the United States during this period. Among them were anthropologist Arthur Parker, attorney Thomas Sloan, the Reverend Sherman Coolidge, Carlos Montezuma, who was a physician and editor of the newsletter *Wassaja*, Henry Roe Cloud, a minister and educator, and Charles Eastman, a physician and author. Luther Standing Bear was not of that group and lacked the advanced education of these and others. They were individuals in professions quite remote from Standing Bear's, and they moved in different circles. Standing Bear was acquainted with Thomas Sloan, who helped him in his quest for citizenship, and he undoubtedly knew Charles Eastman, for they both lived at the agency at Pine Ridge in the early 1890s. There is no evidence, in Eastman's correspondence, however, of any continued contact between the two men.[13] That Eastman or Parker wrote books and articles is notewothy but not surprising. That Luther Standing Bear wrote four books, two of which are still of interest and value today, is a distinctive achievement.

RICHARD N. ELLIS
University of New Mexico

NOTES

1. See Richard N. Ellis, Introduction to Luther Standing Bear, *My People the Sioux* (Lincoln: University of Nebraska Press, 1975), pp. xiv–xv.

2. Standing Bear, *My People the Sioux*, p. 282.

3. Luther Standing Bear, "The Tragedy of the Sioux," *American Mercury* 24, no. 95 (November 1931): 273.

4. Ibid., p. 274.

5. Ibid., p. 275.

6. Ibid., p. 276.

7. Ibid.

8. Ibid.

9. Luther Standing Bear, Preface to *Land of the Spotted Eagle*.

10. Ibid., pp. 67, 167, 226.

11. Ibid., pp. 168.

12. Quoted in Roy W. Meyer, *History of The Santee Sioux* (Lincoln: University of Nebraska Press, 1967), p. 116.

13. Raymond Wilson, "Dr. Charles Alexander Eastman (Ohiyesa): Santee Sioux," (Ph.D. diss., University of New Mexico, 1977), is an excellent study of Eastman's career.

PREFACE

IN THIS book I attempt to tell my readers just how we lived as Lakotans — our customs, manners, experiences, and traditions — the things that make all men what they are. There are reasons why men live as they do, think as they do, and practice as they do; hence, there were forces that made the Lakota the man he was.

White men seem to have difficulty in realizing that people who live differently from themselves still might be traveling the upward and progressive road of life.

After nearly four hundred years' living upon this continent, it is still popular conception, on the part of the Caucasian mind, to regard the native American as a savage, meaning that he is low in thought and feeling, and cruel in acts; that he is a heathen, meaning that he is incapable, therefore void, of high philosophical thought concerning life and life's relations. For this 'savage' the white man has little brotherly love and little understanding. From the Indian the white man stands off and aloof, scarcely deigning to speak or to touch his hand in human fellowship.

To the white man many things done by the Indian are inexplicable, though he continues to write much of the visible and exterior life with explanations that are more often than not erroneous. The inner life of the Indian is, of course, a closed book to the white man.

So from the pages of this book I speak for the Lakota — the tribe of my birth. I have told of his outward life and tried to tell something of his inner life — ideals, religion, concepts of kindness and brotherhood; of laws of conduct and how we strove to arrive at arrangements of equity and justice.

The Lakotas are now a sad, silent, and unprogressive

people suffering the fate of all oppressed. Today you see but a shattered specimen, a caricature, if you please, of the man that once was. Did a kind, wise, helpful, and benevolent conqueror bring this situation about? Can a real, true, genuinely superior social order work such havoc? Did not the native American possess human qualities of worth had the Caucasian but been able to discern and accept them; and did not an overweening sense of superiority bring about this blindness?

These questions may be answered in the light of the reader's sense of justice and quality of imagination. As for myself I risk this indulgence and say: Of my old life I have much to remember with pride. There were among us men of vision and humane ideals; there were great honesty and loyalty; beautiful faith and humility; noble sacrifice and lofty concepts. We were unselfish and devout. In some instances we attained notable success, and we were on the way. On the whole, we succeeded as well in being good and creditable members of our society as do many of the dominant world in being good members of their citizenry.

Nevertheless, Indian life has been enriched with fine and understanding white friends, and one such, a man of true nobility, has been of inestimable value to me in reading my manuscript and offering suggestions — Professor Melvin Gilmore, Curator of Ethnology for the University of Michigan, Ann Arbor, Michigan, himself an author. As a botanist of recognized standing he made valuable suggestions, and his keen technical knowledge refreshed my memory that had become somewhat dimmed through a broken contact with the land of my birth. To Professor Gilmore I express my sincerest appreciation, not only for his assistance in this particular work, but for his fidelity in portraying the Sioux people in his published works.

My last word is to give credit to my niece and secretary, Wahcaziwin, who now assists me in writing and editing.

All former difficulty has been eliminated, since my hardest work came in making myself understood in all the details and intricacies of Indian thought and life. But Wahcazi-win has a broad and complete understanding of her own, and when I speak she fully understands.

CHIEF STANDING BEAR

EXPLANATORY NOTE

LAKOTA is the tribal name of the western bands of Plains people now known as the Sioux, the eastern bands calling themselves Dakotas. The word Sioux is not an Indian but a French word, and since the author is dealing with the tribal customs of his people, he chooses to use the ancient tribal name of the band to which he belongs.

CONTENTS

ILLUSTRATIONS

INTRODUCTION

I HAVE often thought it a great pity that our people, the European race, should have burst in upon this land of America and spread ourselves over it as we did in the manner of unsympathetic aliens instead of introducing ourselves as prospective friends, desiring to become fully acquainted with the native features of beauty and of interest in the land, and with the admirable qualities of its people. The native people were able, willing, and ready to be our guides, and to put us at ease in the land which was their home, and to make us feel at home in it also. But we preferred to begin, and to carry on, so far as possible, the removal and destruction of all the belongings of this home and to substitute for them, whether fitting or not, the belongings of our former home in Europe. So we proceeded to destroy instead of adapting and enriching America. We began merely to try to build a New Spain, a New France, a New Netherlands, and a New England. Instead of accepting the good gifts of this new land and people, and adding to them desirable gifts from our own store, thus completely furnishing a really new and handsome home, we spurned them, and our endeavor has resulted in destroying untold native beauty and desirable character, in place of which we have succeeded in establishing a second-hand establishment, furnished out with many of the belongings of the old home to which we were accustomed, but lacking here their proper sense of fitness and independence. We have destroyed and driven out many delightful native birds and in their place have introduced such pests as the starling and the house sparrow. We have changed the landscape, and over extensive areas have destroyed all the native vegetation, and instead of exquisitely beautiful and richly varied native flowers appearing in continually successive waves of color throughout the round of the seasons, both in forest and prairie, we now have burdock, mullein, dandelion, and wild carrot and other boisterous intruders.

Meantime the native people of America could only look on at this devastation in inarticulate and sorrowful amazement. Whereas they had always lived on terms of friendliness and accord with nature, they saw our people ever set themselves in intentional antagonism with set purpose of 'conquering nature,' often simply for the sake of conquest.

It is strange that the people of European race coming into possession of this country never did make themselves acquainted with the native people of America. Instead of accepting them simply as one among the human races of the world, endowed with the powers of thought, with emotions and sentiments similarly as are all other races, they have preferred always to view them either in a hazy and spectral light or else in an equally unreal lurid light. Strangely enough, our people have refused to look upon the native people of America as people who had to adjust themselves to their natural environment and to reclaim their necessary food, clothing, and shelter, and to satisfy the demands of their æsthetic nature from among the natural gifts of this land.

Being so constantly misunderstood, the native people of America have been unable to give themselves true expression in the patterns of thought and feeling of the alien race, and hence have been for the most part mute or inarticulate. But now some representatives of the native American race are succeeding in some manner and degree in portraying the thought and feeling and the life of their people to the understanding of the alien race. In this undertaking THE LAND OF THE SPOTTED EAGLE does fairly delineate the old native life in such manner as should be grasped with facility by the intelligence and the common human feeling of all persons. If the following paragraph from this book might be extensively and understandingly read by all our people it should go far to correct many false notions:

'We did not think of the great open plains, the beautiful rolling hills, and winding streams with tangled growth, as "wild." Only to the white man was nature a "wilderness" and only to him was the land "infested" with "wild" animals and "savage" people. To us it was tame. Earth was bountiful and we were surrounded with the blessings of the Great Mystery. Not until the hairy man from the east came and with brutal frenzy heaped injustices upon us and the families we loved was it "wild" for us. When the very animals of the forest began fleeing from his approach, then it was that for us the "Wild West" began.'

MELVIN R. GILMORE

UNIVERSITY OF MICHIGAN

LAND OF THE SPOTTED EAGLE

. .

CHAPTER I

CRADLE DAYS

As a babe I was cared for and brought up in the same manner as all babes of the Lakota tribe. Wrapped in soft warm clothing made from buffalo calf skin I lay on a stiff rawhide board when not held in my mother's arms. This board was slightly longer than my body, extending a few inches below my feet and above my head. It was without spring, hard and unbending, but it kept my tender back straight and allowed my neck to grow strong enough to hold up my head.

Special attention was given to the head of every Lakota babe, for a smooth round cranium was considered very pretty, and the Lakota mother, in common with all mothers, wished her child admired and praised. Accordingly, it was the custom to make for a newborn babe a strong but soft and pliable cap of deerskin or of buffalo calf skin. This garment fitted smoothly, but was made to let out as the child grew in size. For six or eight months, or as long as the bony structure was soft, the child wore this cap to keep the head from becoming misshapen.

When night came I was taken from my cradle and my body given further attention. I was stripped of my clothing and placed upon a soft bed by the fire where I was warm and comfortable. My entire body was thoroughly rubbed and cleansed with buffalo tallow. I was allowed to kick my legs, swing my arms, and exercise my muscles. My little brown body got the air and grew used to being without clothing. It was the aim of my mother gradually to get me used to all kinds of temperature, for she knew my health depended upon it. So, soon after birth and even in the coldest months, this training was carried on. It became a ritual that was regularly and religiously kept and I was never put to bed until I had been cleansed and massaged. After a time all Lakota babes became, as the Chinaman said, 'All face.'

This thoughtful care was taken of me for the sake of keeping my growing body healthy and well formed just as it was at birth. It was intended that I should become an erect and a straight-limbed man without marks or blemishes. My muscles must be supple and I must use them with agility and grace. I must learn to run, climb, swim, ride, and leap with as much ease as most people walk.

Manhood was thus planned in babyhood. My mother was raising a future protector of the tribe. When the days of age and weakness came to the strong and active, there would have to be those to take their places. I was being fitted to take one of these places of responsibility in the tribe.

For the first six years of my life, mother's thought was so largely centered on me that she sacrificed even companionship with my father in order to give me her full time. A weak or puny baby was a disgrace to a Lakota mother. It would be evidence to the tribe that she was not giving her child proper time and attention and not fulfilling her duty to the tribe. More than that, it was evidence that she had not used proper social discretion and defied an age-old tradition. It was a law with the Lakotas that for the first six years of a child's life it should have the unrestricted care of the mother and that no other children should be born within the six-year period. To break this law was to lose the respect of the tribe and both father and mother suffered the penalty. A fine, healthy child was therefore a badge of pride and respect and healthy babies were the rule.

As for crippled or deformed babies, I have never known one to be born so. Occasionally, however, a child was born with a blue or red mark on the body, but this caused no concern having nothing to do with the health of the child. Among adults a cripple was so because of some accident of life or war. Now and then a man or woman would become afflicted with a crooked mouth or one that drooped at the corner. The explanation for this condition was that the person so troubled had at some time spoken unkindly or maliciously of another who had passed on to the land of the ghosts. The spirit of the injured one returning in the state of resentment would come close to the offending one and startle him with a quick whistle. The offender in his fright would turn quickly in the direction of the sound and the side of his face would be drawn down at the corner. No innocent person could hear the whistle of the ghost, but the guilty one hearing would be marked for life. Guilt was thus betrayed. So it became bad form for one Lakota to speak harshly of another, and the habit of speaking slowly and carefully with guarded words became the polite custom.

The stiff piece of rawhide on which I was kept most of the day was not at all uncomfortable with its soft padding of buffalo hide. Being so simple in construction, it enabled my mother to carry me about with her while busy with her household tasks. My head reclined on the board and could not bob backwards as she walked or moved about at her work or rode her pony. This cradle was not meant to be attractive, but was just an everyday utility article. For dress-up occasions I was carried about in a lovely cradle made of smooth rawhide boards covered with the softest of buckskin. The hood was also of buckskin decorated with porcupine quills dyed in the brightest of colors. To this gayly colored hood there were fastened tassels of eagle feathers also dyed in bright colors. It was kept perfumed with 'wahpe waste mna' or sweet leaves.

For six or eight months I spent a good deal of time in one of these cradles. When camp was moving, mother put me on her back and wrapped me to her with her blanket. Sometimes she placed me on the travois for a journey, but not often. If she rode her pony, she first mounted, then I was handed to her. With her blanket she fastened me securely to her. When I became old enough to sit up, she put me astride the horse in front of her. I cannot, of course, remember the first time I rode this way, but neither can I remember learning to ride by myself.

Most of mother's work was performed while carrying me in my cradle on her back. She packed and unpacked her horses and even put up her tipi while carrying me in this fashion.

When working in the tipi she often leaned my cradle against something so that I stood in an upright position. In this way I could look around and, no doubt, I watched mother's movements as she worked, listened to her as she talked or sang little songs to me. If I fell asleep she took me out of the cradle and I slept while she watched.

Most of the time a Lakota infant was lightly and simply dressed, but a great deal of time and care went into the making of the material for garments. Mothers preferred a light-weight buckskin or unborn buffalo calf skin for such purposes. When properly tanned, no manufactured material can equal these skins in richness of texture and quality. When the process of tanning is complete, these skins are exquisitely white, richer in sheen than fine broadcloth, and softer than velvet. The Lakota woman washed these garments in water and by rubbing brought them back to their original softness and whiteness. Garments for dress wear were trimmed with fringe, quillwork, and paintings.

For sanitary purposes the down from the cottonwood tree pods was used. Also in the fall of the year cattails furnished a soft airy down, but the cottonwood down was preferable. No like article manufactured in mills can equal this down in silky fineness, so light it floated in the air on a still day. Besides, the supply was plentiful and the women kept it stored in large deerskin bags. For sanitary purposes finely powdered buffalo chips were also stored away and was most effectual in its intended purpose.

As the Lakota child continued to develop, it had the constant companionship of an elder; if not father or mother, then aunt, uncle, or one of the numerous cousins of the band. Children were always welcome charges of all who were older. Every child not only belonged to a certain family, but also belonged to the band, and no matter where it strayed when it was able to walk, it was at home, for everyone in the band claimed relationship. Mother told me that I was often carried round the village from tipi to tipi and that sometimes she saw me only now and then during the day. I would be handed from relative to relative and someone was constantly amusing me.

A large portion of the care of a child fell to its grandmother, and in some respects she was as important in the child's life as the mother. The interest of the older women became centered on the welfare of children, and, possessing both experience and wisdom, they were much depended upon. This wisdom concerning the lore of taking care of little ones gave grandmother a superior position, especially with the younger women and mothers. It made a place for her as teacher and adviser in her band. It was, too, lighter work than carrying wood and water and tanning skins, these tasks being taken care of by the younger and stronger women.

Grandmothers became skilled in preparing food for children, and most of them had a host of little ones running after them all the time. When children became hungry, they nearly always ran to grandmother first for food and she was never found lacking in a supply. Nor were children ever refused in their request for food. There was

a special delicacy which took time and patience to prepare
and of which all children were fond. This was *wasna* and
it was grandmother's job to make it. *Wasna* was made
of dried meat and dried choke-cherries pounded together,
seeds and all, until it was a fine meal. This meal was
thoroughly mixed with and held together in loaves or
cakes by the fat skimmed from the boiled bones of the
buffalo. It was not only a delicious food, but a health
food good for young children beginning to eat solid food.
No one claimed grandmother's official job as *wasna*-
maker.

Grandmother took care of all our toys. Our winter
toys she stored away in the summer. When winter came
she stored away the summer toys. She made pretty bags
in which she laid away our marbles, tops, and other toys.

Most grandmothers seemed to be happiest when caring
for a number of little ones. And I especially remember one
grandmother for her fondness for children. This grandmother — I have forgotten her name — belonged to the
band of my grandfather, Chief One Horse. This old lady
lived to a great age, but before her death became stricken
with blindness. With all this handicap she could not
give up caring for her charges. One day she called all the
children together and began painting their faces. This
was a daily task for someone and it was her way of helping. The children all grouped about her, each waiting his
turn. Her bags of paint were near and soon all the children were fixed up. But pretty soon the children began to
feel a queer drawing sensation of the face as if it was being
all puckered up into one spot. They began to look at one
another and found that each little brown face was speckled
with white and withered in places. Then curious mothers
began to look their children over. It was soon discovered
that grandmother had got her bags of salt mixed up with
her bags of paint and each child was generously salted
instead of painted. This incident became a great joke in

the village. Everybody laughed, including grandmother herself. The joke became history, for her band was thereafter called *Mini skuya ki cun*, or, 'The band that paints their faces with salt.' It is so called to this day.

When I became old enough to walk, I spent much time in the tipi of my grandmother. If mother and father were going out for the evening and I did not care to go, I went and slept in grandmother's tipi and I was always welcome. I remember my grandmother as a patient and tireless worker. She went on long walks gathering fruits and plants, and sometimes she took me with her. When I grew old enough to understand, she told me many things about their nature and usefulness. Much of her simple knowledge would be of value today.

In learning to talk, Lakota children were encouraged and helped, beginning about the same time as children of the white race. But there was no 'baby talk' for them. All speech in their presence was full and complete.

And so the days of my infanthood and childhood were spent in surroundings of love and care. In manner, gentleness was my mother's outstanding characteristic. Never did she, nor any of my caretakers, ever speak crossly to me or scold me for failures or shortcomings. For an elder person in the Lakota tribe to strike or punish a young person was an unthinkable brutality. Such an ugly thing as force with anger back of it was unknown to me, for it was never exhibited in my presence. For this nobility alone I sing the praises of the Lakotas — this thing alone denotes them a brave people.

Mother was a comely woman, not very large but plump and rounded in form. Her face was soft in outline and her features were good. Her skin was light in color and fine in texture. Her long black hair she wore in two braids which hung one on each side of her face after the fashion of the women of her tribe. When she was a child she was quite pretty and possessed a sweetness of disposition.

She was called Wastewin, or Pretty Face, and since it turned out that she became a belle in her tribe she was well named. Her name signified grace and goodness as well as good looks, and my mother possessed both of these qualities.

As soon as I could walk steadily, my training in obedience began. I was asked to do little errands and my pride in doing them developed. Mother would say, 'Son, bring in some wood.' I would get what I was able to carry, and if it were but one stick mother would in some way show her pleasure. She had a way of saying 'Son' that expressed great affection for me. It was in doing this very errand for her that I met with my first childish mishap. I was a very small child, but I came into the tipi with some sticks for the fire and in my eagerness I stumbled and fell headlong. One of my hands went into the live coals and I have the scars to this day.

I not only obeyed mother, but I just as readily obeyed father, grandmother, and grandfather. This, no doubt, helped in keeping peaceful relations in the family group.

But lessons in obedience were not the only ones to begin at an early age. I was taught kindness to grandmother and to all old people. I saw my mother give frequently to them and I was allowed to give at the same time. I learned truthfulness, respect for the rights of all people, order, and like virtues. So each day, with a brightening mind, I learned by examples of kind action. Just as the tiny roots of a plant silently absorbed the earth food, so my childish consciousness absorbed the influences which surrounded me, especially the silent, subtle influence of my mother.

Lakota babies cried very little, as has often been noted and commented on by white writers. This habit of being quiet was not due to punishment but to training. It was, no doubt, dangerous in olden days to allow a child to cry, especially at night or when the camp was on the march.

Children were told, 'Be quiet, a witch might hear you.'
This is the only way in which Lakota children were
frightened, so far as I know, until the white man came
among us, and then mothers often said, 'Be quiet, child,
a white man may be near.' So the white man was used to
frighten little Indian children into silence. Indian women,
and as might be expected, Indian children, were much
frightened at the first white man they saw. Many times
a white mother has said to her child, 'Be good or a terrible Indian will get you.' But just as many Indian mothers have quieted their children with the dread thought
that a white man might be near. We with mature minds
might ponder on this and see what we have really done
to children with these foolish statements. We can see,
if we are fair with ourselves, that much unnatural fear and
hatred may have been bred in this way.

Now and then twins were born to a Lakota woman,
but not often. In our tribe they were regarded as very
mysterious beings. Twins were people, it was believed,
who had lived with the tribe at some past time and had
come back again to live life over. They were therefore
regarded as old people and not young people. I have
seen twins with ear-holes for earrings and this was proof
that they had lived before with us. The spirits of little
twins would hover about a tipi, lifting up the curtains
and peeking in. They were then looking for a place in
which to be reborn. They were visible only to certain
people and when the person who saw them shouted or
called for some one else to look, the twins disappeared.
These little twin spirits always appeared about the tipi
tied together with a rope.

The twins who were born among us had habits and
characteristics that boys and girls born singly did not
have. They were always doing things that ordinary boys
and girls did not do. Though it was forbidden for Lakota
brothers and sisters to speak and joke freely with one

another, twin brothers and sisters were the closest of companions and often stood apart from the others, holding whispered conversations; and it would never be known what the whispered talk was all about. There were ties between twins that did not exist for the rest of us and they broke social laws that we were not permitted to break. Another strange thing was that if one of the twins died the other scarcely ever lived. Marriage sometimes brought about a break in companionship if the twins were brother and sister. However, if the twins were of the same sex the companionship usually continued. From the mother's standpoint, twins were as well liked as other children and there was never any difference in the treatment of them.

As a child I was of just as great importance to my warrior father as I was to my attentive mother. He found it a great pleasure to provide for us both and much of the time he was away on the hunt procuring food and clothing. Whenever he was about the tipi we spent much time together. Indian fathers seem to enjoy their sons, and mine played often with me. It was a pastime with him to lie on the ground on his back and with his legs crossed toss me up and down on one foot. It was his delight and mine also to 'play horse' this way. Father sang to me, too, but not the childish songs and the lullabys that mother sang. He sang the brave or warrior songs, so I grew up loving the songs of my people and learning them as soon as I could speak.

Since father was training me also, the lessons that mother began were kept up by him. When I became sturdy enough to run he would tell me to bring his pony close to the tipi door so it could be bridled. One thing that I ran after more than anything else was the village whetstone. Usually there were but one or two of these useful articles in a village, so it was much in demand. Whenever father wanted to sharpen his arrows he sent me for the 'izuza' or rubbing-stone. I went from tipi to tipi until I had found the much-used article.

Father gave me my first pony and also my first lesson in riding. The pony was a very gentle one and I was so small that he tied me in place on the pony's back. Not that I would suffer fright, but so that father could lead the pony about slowly while I got used to the sway of the animal's motion. In time I sat my horse by myself and then I rode by father's side. When I could keep pace with him and my pony stayed side by side with him, that was real achievement, for I was still very small indeed.

Such expressions as 'I can't,' and 'I don't want to,' found no place in my mind. I did not have to listen to long speeches on 'how to be like father.' A lesson, in fact, did not imply much conversation on either side. But since I was to learn to do the things that he did, I watched my father closely.

Certain ceremonies are considered very important in the life of a Lakota child and to these father attended. Of course, the morning of my birth, father had a man cry the news to the village and gave away a horse. But my first real ceremony took place a few days later. This was my naming ceremony. There are two other important ceremonies in the life of a Lakota child, and I, being the son of a chief, received them all.

The morning of my naming ceremony the singing of praise songs announced to the village that the ceremony was to take place. The singers stood by our tipi door and sang songs of praise for my father. When the people of the village had assembled, a praise singer called out, 'Hear All! Hear all! The son of Standing Bear will be named. Hear all! Hear all! His name will be Plenty Kill.' Mother came out of the tipi holding me in her arms. In the meantime father had selected an old man who was to receive the horse to be given away in honor of the event. Some one led the horse up and the end of the rope about its neck was placed in my tiny hands. He took the rope from my hands and extending his arms toward me said, 'Ha-ye-e-e, Ha-ye-e-e,' which meant both thanks and blessings for me. He led the horse away while the singers still sang songs of praise.

About nine months after my birth the second ceremony took place. At this time my ears were pierced and it was a much more impressive ceremony than the first. It was held during the sun dance when many bands were gathered together. It was customary to hold many minor ceremonies of various sorts before the actual Sun Dance began. There was much singing and much dancing by groups of performers. Also there was a great deal of giving and receiving of presents.

The ceremony began, as usual, with the singers announcing the ceremony. Then mother walked to the center of the large circular enclosure carrying me in her arms and leading two splendid spotted horses. They were lively and spirited and pranced about a good deal while different groups took up the singing. An old man, considered an expert in piercing ears, came and stood beside mother. He carried instruments of bone, sharp and fine as needles. Father then came, and last of all the needy man who was to have the two spotted horses. There was more singing while the old man thrust my ears with the sharp instrument and father placed something in them which he had prepared for the purpose. For several days mother watched my ears carefully and soon they were ready for rings. The two holes in my ears cost father two valuable spotted horses.

CHAPTER II

BOYHOOD

WITH the coming of boyhood, life became more lively and exciting and gradually my activities took me further away from the care and influence of the tipi. I still continued to learn, however, in the same manner in which I had learned as a babe — by watching, listening, and imitating. Only I watched my mother less and began to observe the ways of my father more. In time too, I took to watching the older boys and whatever they did I tried to do.

In Lakota society it was the duty of every parent to give the knowledge they possessed to their children. Each and every parent was a teacher and, as a matter of fact, all elders were instructors of those younger than themselves. And the instruction they gave was mostly through their actions — that is, they interpreted to us through actions what we should try to do. We learned by watching and imitating examples placed before us. Slowly and naturally the faculties of observation and memory became highly trained and the Lakota child became educated in the manners, lore, and customs of his people without a strained and conscious effort. I have known children to become very apt in learning the songs they heard. One singing would sometimes suffice and the child would have the words and tune so well in mind that he could never forget it.

This process of learning went on all the time. There was no period in the life of the Lakota child such as that referred to by some as the 'playtime' of life, when the child is growing only in body size and not in mind. Body and mind grew together. No one would be able to say how much can be learned through great keenness of sight and hearing unless, having possessed them, they were suddenly deprived of them.

But very early in life the child began to realize that wisdom was all about and everywhere and that there were many things to know. There was no such thing as emptiness in the world. Even in the sky there were no vacant places. Everywhere there was life, visible and invisible, and every object possessed something that would be good for us to have also — even to the very stones. This gave a great interest to life. Even without human companionship one was never alone. The world teemed with life and wisdom; there was no complete solitude for the Lakota.

Such living filled one with a great desire to do, to be, and to grow. In my boyhood, and in actual childhood, I was filled with the desire to be a brave and this desire urged me to constant activity. I was overjoyed when at the age of ten years my father arranged for me to accompany him on a war party. I was not the least bit afraid and was only sorry when for some reason we were forced to come home without having met the enemy.

The way in which Lakota children were trained caused them to regard with admiration all those of wisdom and experience. All yearned for wisdom and looked for experience. For myself, I felt that if I grew wise, my people would honor me; if I became very brave, I should be like father, and if I could become a good hunter, it would please my mother. And so I thrived upon the thought of achievement and approval and I do not think that I was an unusual Indian boy. Dangers and responsibilities were bound to come, and I wanted to meet them like a man. I looked forward to the days of the warpath, not as a calling nor for the purpose of slaying my fellowman, but solely to prove my worth to myself and my people.

One lesson to learn was to be strong in will. Little children were taught to give and to give generously. A sparing giver was no giver at all. Possessions were given away until the giver was poor in this world's goods and had no-thing left but the delight and joy of pure strength. It was a bounden duty to give to the needy and helpless. When mothers gave food to the weak and old they gave portions to their children at the same time, so that the children could perform the service of giving with their own hands. Little Lakota children often ran out and brought into the tipi an old and feeble person who chanced to be passing. If a child did this the mother must at once prepare food. To ignore the child's courtesy would be unpardonable. But it is easy to touch the heart of pity in a child, so the Lakota was taught to give at any and all times for the sake of becoming brave and strong. The greatest brave was he who could part with his most cherished belongings and at the same time sing songs of joy and praise. It was a cus-tom to hold 'Give-away-dances' and to distribute presents that were costly and rare. To give is the delight of the Lakota.

Such an education could not be confined to a certain length of time nor could one be 'finished' in a certain term of years. The training was largely of character, beginning with birth and continued throughout life. True Indian education was based on the development of individual qualities and recognition of rights. There was no 'system,' no 'rule or rote,' as the white people say, in the way of Lakota learning. Not being under a system, children never had to 'learn this today,' or 'finish this book this year' or 'take up' some study just because 'little Willie did.' Native education was not a class education but one that strengthened and encouraged the individual to grow. When children are growing up to be individuals there is no need to keep them in a class or in line with one another.

Never were Lakota children offered rewards or medals for accomplishment. No child was ever bribed or given a prize for doing his best. No one ever said to a child, 'Do this well and I will pay you for it.' The achievement was

the reward and to place anything above it was to put unhealthy ideas in the minds of children and make them
weak. Neither were lessons forced upon a child by an attitude of threat or by punishment. There was no such thing
as the 'hickory stick,' and any Lakota caught flogging a
child would have been considered unspeakably low. I have
never heard of a child in my tribe leaving home on account
of discontent or to escape parental rule. There could be no
greater freedom elsewhere. Neither have I ever heard of
young people committing suicide over studies or duties imposed upon them. Lovers occasionally planned death for
themselves, but never children.

In the course of learning, the strength of one small mind
was never pitted against the strength of another in foolish
examinations. There being no such thing as 'grades,' a
child was never made conscious of any shortcomings. I
never knew embarrassment or humiliation of this character
until I went to Carlisle School and was there put under the
system of competition. I can never forget the confusion
and pain I one day underwent in a reading class. The
teacher conceived the idea of trying or testing the strength
of the pupils in the class. A paragraph in the reading book
was selected for the experiment. A pupil was asked to rise
and read the paragraph while the rest listened and cor-
rected any mistakes. Even if no misakes were made, the
teacher, it seems, wanted the pupils to state that they
were sure they had made no errors in reading. One after
another the pupils read as called upon and each one in
turn sat down bewildered and discouraged. My time came
and I made no errors. However, upon the teacher's question, 'Are you sure that you have made no error?' I, of
course, tried again, reading just as I had the first time.
But again she said, 'Are you sure?' So the third and
fourth times I read, receiving no comment from her. For
the fifth time I stood and read. Even for the sixth and
seventh times I read. I began to tremble and I could not

see my words plainly. I was terribly hurt and mystified. But for the eighth and ninth times I read. It was growing more terrible. Still the teacher gave no sign of approval, so I read for the tenth time! I started on the paragraph for the eleventh time, but before I was through, everything before me went black and I sat down thoroughly cowed and humiliated *for the first time in my life* and in front of the whole class! Never as long as I live shall I forget my futile attempts to fathom the reason of this teacher's attitude. Out on the school grounds at recess I could not join in the games and play. I was full of foolish fears.

What would happen the following Saturday night at what we called, 'Chapel meeting'? Every Saturday night the entire school gathered for a meeting in the chapel at which assembly various school matters were discussed. General Pratt, the superintendent of the school, usually gave a talk, urging us to be good pupils and instructing us in the ways of good behavior. Reports were given by the teachers and the roll-call held. Also any boy or girl who had broken any of the rules during the week were given the opportunity to report themselves and say they were sorry and would in the future attempt to do better. If they did not do this, they stood a chance of being reported by some other student or by the teacher. This was a splendid rule, but, of course, not pleasant, and I had never had a bad report handed in.

Saturday night came and the building was full of students and teachers. I was filled with anxiety and could not keep my mind from that reading lesson. I was, I thought, to be reprimanded before the entire school for having a poor lesson.

Soon General Pratt was on the platform, talking about the value of possessing confidence. He said he always wanted us to do our best and never to be afraid of failures. If we did not do well at first try over and over again, and as he said this he struck the table with his fist to emphasize his idea. Then he told the students that the class of Miss C. had received a reading test and that Luther Standing Bear had read his lesson eleven times in succession and correctly every time. My heart lightened. I truly liked General Pratt and words of praise from him meant a good deal to me. But in spite of the praise that I received that day and the satisfaction that I have had in all these years in knowing that I was a good student, I still have the memory of those hours of silent misery I endured in childish misgivings.

We were to learn that according to standards of the white man those not learned in books are not educated. Books were the symbol of learning, and people were continually asking others how many books they had read.

The Lakotas read and studied actions, movements, posture, intonation, expression, and gesture of both man and animal.

When the first white teachers came among us to take charge of the day schools, they were schooled and could read books. But they were unlearned in the ways of our country. Many things they did showed that they were not adjusted to the surroundings, and were amusing to us. I remember well one of the first men teachers sent out to take charge of the district schools. He was furnished a wagon and team but not being acquainted with teams, a driver was furnished also. For a while the driver took him from district to district until he felt able to handle the team himself. One day this teacher came to a place in the road that sloped down very abruptly. He neglected to put on the brakes and the horse began running down the hill. The driver, thoroughly frightened, thrust his leg out between the spokes, thinking to stop the wagon. Of course his leg was broken. Soon after he was again well, this man left his team to follow a flock of prairie chickens. When he returned to the road where he had left the wagon and horses, he found they had gone. Some time later he was picked up all fagged out and apparently lost in his sense of direction.

In teaching me, father used much the same method as mother. He never said, 'You have to do this,' or 'You must do that,' but when doing things himself he would often say something like, 'Son, some day when you are a man you will do this.' If he went into the woods to look for a limb for a bow, and forked branches for a saddle, I went too. When he began work I was sure to be close by, quietly observing with the keenest interest.

The most important thing for me to learn, father must have considered, was how to make and use the bow and arrow. For the making of these two articles was the first thing he taught me. There were trips to the woods which both of us enjoyed. I learned that ash was the preferred wood for a warrior's bow. A hunter would use a cherry or cedar bow. The wood of the cedar made a very strong bow, but it cracked easily. As for myself, I started with willow wood. It was easy to work with and quite strong enough for me. Hickory does not grow in the country of the Lakotas, and so was not used until the white people brought it to the plains in their wooden yokes. If a discarded yoke was found, it furnished material for two good bows.

A bow looks to be a very simple weapon, but sometimes a great amount of skill is used in its making. A bow in the rough does not look like much, but when it has been smoothed on a rough surfaced rock, heated and bent to shape over a fire, and polished, it looks very little like the limb of a tree. The Lakota bows were short and strengthened with sinew, the man behind the bow deciding the strength. When the bow was shaped, small flattened strings of wet sinew were pasted lengthwise on the back until it was covered. The ends of the strings did not meet flush, but each extended, wedge-shaped, past the other, thus adding strength. The tips of the bow were then covered with sinew and the weapon placed in the shade to dry slowly. When thoroughly dry, the hard edges of sinew were rubbed smooth and tassels of dyed horse hair added as decoration. A bow of this description was good for many years' use, and a warrior armed with such a weapon and plenty of arrows in his quiver felt pretty safe. The bow was strictly a man's weapon, and I have never known a woman of my tribe to even try to use one.

For arrows we used the slender limbs of a shrub which we called the 'early berry,' but which the white people called the wild currant. In the spring, masses of pink, red, and almost black berries appeared so it was aptly named *wicakanaska* or early-berry bush. The limbs of this shrub grew straight up from the ground and had very small hearts or cores. Arrows made from them were heavy and could not be wind-swept. Feathering correctly was quite important too. The best specimen of Lakota hunting arrow had three feathers finished with a fluff of down that came from under the tail feathers of the bird. Two red wavering lines, the symbol of lightning, were painted from the feathered end halfway to the arrow tip, but grooved the rest of the way to the tip so as to allow the blood to flow freely from the body of the animal, thereby hastening death.

Every warrior wore his quiver as he wore his clothes — it was a part of his attire. Ordinarily the quiver was worn at the back, but in case of quick action it was thrust under the belt of the warrior or hunter in front where his right hand reached the head of the arrows with scarcely a movement. A skilled man shot with great rapidity when necessary, doing so automatically. At night the warrior's bow and quiver hung on the tripod at the head of the bed, so that it was close at hand.

A boy's first bow was not a weapon; it was a toy made of a twig so small it could be used in the tipi. The arrow was of slough grass. Shooting was a game called *cunksila wahinkpi*. As I grew larger and older I always had a bow to suit my age and size. Unconsciously my bow became a part of my body, as it were, and I used it as I did my feet, hands, or arms.

At the age of eight I was considered expert enough to be included in a party of youths who went on a hunting trip. A deer was killed, and though I was in no way responsible for it I brought home my first piece of meat. Father at once gave away a horse. I was a very proud boy and my longing to become a good hunter increased. I wanted to bring my family more meat.

Just as unconscious skill came to me in the use of my bow and arrow, so it came to me in riding. When I was on my horse I might have been a part of him, for nothing but force could unseat me. When too small to leap to his back, I ran and climbed up his foreleg like a squirrel and was on the go while climbing; for small chance a slow horseman would have getting away from a rapid firing arrow expert. Always we kept in mind the skill of the enemy. But being a rider did not mean being a complete horseman. Father taught me how to make saddles of cottonwood and elm, ropes of rawhide or twisted buffalo hair, blankets, and halters. I learned to look after my horse when he was troubled with sore feet, and how to make horse-shoes of buffalo hide; and, too, how to recognize horse sense and intuition. The horse is continually giving signs of what he sees, hears or smells. In the daytime the Lakota horseman watched his horse's tail and ears. With these he indicated the presence and direction of animals or people. At night he snorted at any unusual smell or sound. My father once had a horse which was as good as any watchdog. At the slightest cause he would snort his distrust or displeasure, then run straight to father. For this reason father used him in his journeys, as he could lie down at night feeling sure that nothing would get near without a warning from his friendly sentinel.

Father had a great sense of the rights of animals and was

a true humanitarian. His ideas along this line would meet with the approval of any humane society in the land and I am sure it would be hard for him to tolerate some of the brutalities one sees on a city street. Father inculcated in me a feeling of interdependence toward my horse something like one would feel towards a companion. The dog had been the age-long companion of the Lakota woman, assisting her in household duties and the care of children, but the horse was the Lakota man's most trusted friend in the animal kingdom.

In order to see that my ponies were well fed and kindly treated, father once said to me, when presenting me with a fine pony, 'Son, it is cowardly to be cruel. Be good to your pony.' So in the winter I never turned him out to forage as best he might. I placed him in the cottonwood groves for protection. There was a grass that grew in damp places or bordering streams and that stayed green all winter. Our horses were very fond of it and father had me cut bundles of it to carry to my pony. In the summertime when I went to the stream, it was suggested that I should take my pony and throw water on him; and if we found deep water we swam together, my hand grasping his mane.

When I grew to be a young man I possessed a great pride, just as had my father in his youth, in riding a fine horse. When, as a young brave, I went out on parade, I brushed my horse until he shone, wove wreathes of sweet grass for his neck, and tied eagle feathers to his tail and mane.

All this was in accordance with the Lakota belief that man did not occupy a special place in the eyes of Wakan Tanka, the Grandfather of us all. I was only a part of everything that was called the world. I can now see that humaneness is not a thing which can be ordered by law. It is an ideal to be lived.

It was at councils, feasts of the lodges, and ceremonies that children learned a great deal concerning social con-

duct and manners. Social custom was closely observed
and many ceremonies, both social and religious, were performed according to strict form. The men, especially the
warriors and councilors, were quiet and dignified in manner. The women were quiet too, and very retiring. Loud
talking and exaggerated or boisterous actions were considered very unseemly for either man or woman. The
speeches were short and spoken without affectation. The
dancing was done mostly by the warriors, and the singing
by groups who were trained for such occasions. The women, dressed in their best, sat around the circle watching
the scene with interest. When food was served everybody
joined.

These gatherings were for all members of the band, so
whenever my parents attended I was allowed to go.
Children were never put to bed to be got out of the way,
never given some work to do, nor pushed off to play. My
father and mother enjoyed my presence; of that I am sure.

There was much dressing for these festivities and whenever my parents dressed up I was dressed in my finery too.
It seems to me that father must have considered me a very
valuable boy, or else his pride in me was more than ordinary, for he was always dressing me up. Of course, it may
be that I, like all small boys, found it very disagreeable to
be dressed in fine clothes. Anyway, I well remember that
father made for me a very long, heavy ornament for my
hair. I disliked very much to wear this headpiece, for it was
made of six or eight silver disks, graduated in size, and
strung on buckskin. It was a very wonderful ornament to
be sure, but its weight was something to be appreciated and
furthermore it was tied to what white people are pleased
to call the 'scalp lock.' Now when father dressed for some
festivity he would paint my face, smooth my hair and tie
my confirmation plume at the left side of my head at the
top, and tie the silver ornament so that it hung down the
back of my head. I always went as father dressed me and

never told him how uncomfortable I felt. But I would wait my chance, and when he was occupied and could not see me, I slipped over to mother, told her of my discomfort and that I could not play well. Like all mothers she knew well how little boys like to play, so, saying nothing, she would slyly remove the ornament from my head. Mothers have a way of doing things for little boys and girls without disturbing father's feelings about them.

There was another ornament that father made for me and which no boy could wear with comfort. This was a breastplate made of imitation bone beads some three or four inches in length and put together with small brass beads. It covered my small chest and extended beyond my shoulders in such a way that I could not lift anything from the ground, nor could I shoot my bow. Such an ornament was considered very elegant and I may have looked very imposing in the eyes of my father, but how could any boy get joy out of life if he could only carry his bow in his hand?

It was at these councils that we listened to wisdom and learned to regard it with esteem. Parents instructed the young to be quiet and respectful and soon they felt the importance of their tribal gatherings. The old warriors retold stories that had become tribal history. Some of these stories had been told many times, but yet were never old. There were always the young to tell them to, and, besides, the people lived over their lives through the memory of great events. The young warriors, some of them just back from their first big hunt or war-party, told their stories in song and dance. Some may have come home badly wounded, while some may have been fortunate and killed many of the enemy without meeting with mishap. A mark of special bravery was to rescue from danger a friend who had either been wounded or lost his horse. Every young brave who was entitled to do so, wore his decoration indicating his deed. If he had been wounded, he painted his wounds with red, and likewise his horse if it had been wounded. One young man — I forget his name — told a thrilling story of his attack on a buffalo. He was returning home from a war-party. He carried his gun, for it was after the coming of the white man, but he was out of ammunition. His only weapon was a knife. He became very hungry, for he had been without food for several days, and game on the plains had been very scarce. At last he came upon a small herd of buffalo and seeing one lying on the ground and apart from the others conceived the idea of killing it with his knife. Getting on the leeward side of the animal, the young warrior crept close enough to spring upon its back. Grasping the long hair upon the neck, the brave plunged his knife into the infuriated animal. The charging buffalo was unable to throw him off and finally the kill was made. The young man had his meal and continued his journey homeward.

At these ceremonies, praises were sung for all our braves and it was there that the boys determined to be braves themselves some day. They wanted to be men of courage and to merit praise and honor. Within me, I can still feel the force of those stirring songs.

The Victory ceremonies centered about the young warriors and everyone was very proud of them. This was because the young hunters and warriors were the protectors of the tribe. To them everyone, young and old, looked for protection. Lives, food, property, and fireside were in their keeping and the cost was theirs even to giving up their lives. For this reason, mothers and sisters joined happily in honoring the braves at these big celebrations.

Mother further interested me by sometimes talking about the braves. She would tell me what they had done and why they were honored. Men in council were there because of merit. A man might be poor in goods, own few horses, and live in a small tipi, but he would sit with the council. Riches brought no man power and though he might have many horses he could not buy a seat with the wise ones. Mother tried, I believe, to develop in me a spirit of fair dealing and also the wish to appraise people justly.

Father liked the company of braves very much and he sometimes invited a number of them to come to his tipi for a good time. He arranged for these parties beforehand by asking mother to prepare a nice meal. When the friends arrived, there would be plenty of food to serve. While the feast was being enjoyed, the braves related experiences of the hunt, of war, of their vigils and of *wico oyake*, which is the only word in Lakota denoting the history of the tribe. These talk fests usually ended with the braves telling jokes on one another and there was much merriment. I was sure to be about somewhere sitting very quiet and where I would not be easily observed but seeing and hearing everything. So brave in their hearts were these warriors that they sat and told the most thrilling and hair-raising experiences as if they were everyday happenings. It was a great sight and I am glad that I have this picture of my Lakota forbears.

Lakota children, like all others, asked questions and were answered to the best ability of our elders. We wondered, as do all young, inquisitive minds, about the stars, moon, sky, rainbow, darkness, and all other phenomena of nature. I can recall lying on the earth and wondering what it was all about. The stars were a beautiful mystery and so was the place where the eagle went when he soared out of sight. Many of these questions were answered in story form by the older people. How we got our pipestone, where corn came from, and why lightning flashed in the sky, were all answered in stories. The springs were *wiwila* or living things. But all things lived and were good for the Lakota. Even the spider came to the brave on the mountain top with a message of friendship.

A Lakota brave was once holding his vigil and fasting.

In his vision there came to him a human figure all in black. The person in black handed to the brave a plant and said, 'Wrap this plant in a piece of buckskin and hang it in your tipi. It will keep you in good health.' When the brave asked who was speaking to him, the figure answered, 'I can walk on the water and I can go beneath the water. I can walk on the earth, and I can go into the earth. Also I can fly in the air. I am smaller than you, but I could kill you in a moment. I can do more work than any other creature, and my handiwork is everywhere, yet no one knows how I work. I am Spider. Go home and tell your people that the Spider has spoken to you.' This happened long ago, but the Lakotas still use the Spider's medicine.

These stories were the libraries of our people. In each story there was recorded some event of interest or importance, some happening that affected the lives of the people. There were calamities, discoveries, achievements, and victories to be kept. The seasons and the years were named for principal events that took place. There was the year of the 'moving stars' when these bright bodies left their places in the sky and seemed to fall to earth or vanished altogether; the year of the great prairie fire when the buffalo became scarce; and the year that Long Hair (Custer) was killed. But not all our stories were historical. Some taught the virtues — kindness, obedience, thrift, and the rewards of right living. Then there were stories of pure fancy in which I can see no meaning. Maybe they are so old that their meaning has been lost in the countless years, for our people are old. But even so, a people enrich their minds who keep their history on the leaves of memory. Countless leaves in countless books have robbed a people of both history and memory.

When I was about nine years of age I had the third and last ceremony of childhood — the Confirmation ceremony. This event is the most important one in the life of a

Lakota child. In it the confirmed one accepts trusts and obligations that are forever kept and vows are taken that are never broken. In exchange for consecrating one's life to service the tribe places the one who takes the ceremony in the highest social position and bestows upon him the right to wear the white eagle plume. Those who wear this feather sit at the feasts and take part in ceremonies at which others may only look on.

The Confirmation ceremony is deep and serious in meaning. In nature it is social, religious, and ethical. It is social, for the life of the child will be devoted as much as possible, or as much as wealth will allow, to the service and welfare of other members of his band. Throughout life the confirmed one must stand ready at all times to help the needy and distressed. It is a great honor to be asked by those in want to share your food, clothing, horses, or any comfort of life. By the same rule it is considered a breach of etiquette for one in need to go to another band for help when there are those in his own band consecrated to the work.

The ceremony is ethical in nature, for the practice of all virtues — kindness, generosity, truthfulness and service — are placed above gain and personal profit. The saying, 'It is more blessed to give than to receive,' is literally and practically observed. One really becomes his 'brother's keeper' and selfishness is utterly destroyed. For one to shrink from meeting the duties implied in the Confirmation ceremony is to lose face and standing.

The religious import of the ceremony is profound, for the child is given into the guardianship of the invisible powers of goodness. With solemn ceremony and before the sacred altar of earth, the Spirit of the Great Mystery is felt and acknowledged. Through song and prayer His power is begged to remain and guide the child throughout life, that it may walk only in righteous ways. When at last the pipe has been smoked, the pact with the Great Mystery is made.

My two sisters and myself were confirmed at the same time. We wore the finest clothing we had ever worn and enjoyed the richest feast ever prepared for us. Our godfather provided the feast and furnished the clothing for me and my sisters. As for father, it cost him as many of his best horses as he could spare from his herd. When all was over, father and godfather were poor men, but it was worth the sacrifice to enjoy the honor for the rest of our lives.

The father wishing to give his child the benefit of the Confirmation, first takes stock of his wealth. He counts his horses and decides the least number that he can possibly get along with. The rest of the herd he will contribute as presents the day of the ceremony. The father then chooses a man whom he knows to be trustworthy and most fitted to be the godfather of his children. A friend is asked to carry the information to the man chosen to be godfather. It is considered a great honor to be asked to be a godfather and I have never known a man to refuse such a request. To be able to stand the sacrifice willingly and gladly is a mark of strength and quality.

The godfather at once begins preparations. He selects the singer of the sacred songs and two dancers to perform the Confirmation or Corn dance. These songs and dances are given on no other occasion. Godfather makes the rattles, drums, and wands which are sometimes highly decorated. Sometimes the small children are carried in buffalo robes. Godfather gets the robe and selects four women to carry the four corners. All the women relatives are called together and asked to help in making the garments for the children. Everything worn by the child must be new, and no effort is spared to make each one look its best. All the art and skill of the maker is applied, and sometimes there is much vying in having one set of garments outdo the garments of another ceremony. Some of the articles of dress made for Confirmation are very valuable when decorated with painting, porcupine-quill work, and elk's teeth. A tipi is set up in some convenient place in the village to house the beautiful garments until they are to be worn. Then there is the feast to think of, and godfather furnishes the food for this and selects the cooks, helpers, and waiters. Last of all, godfather builds the sacred altar of earth. It is square and at each corner there stands a stick at the top of which is tied a little bag of tobacco. In the center of the altar is placed a buffalo skull and around are spread fresh boughs of sagebrush. Close to the altar the pipe is placed, leaning upright against a small rack of boughs or limbs.

When all these details have been completed, godfather sets the day of the ceremony and so notifies the father of the children. The father gathers his horses in from the plain so as to have them handy to give away on the appointed day. Horses being very valuable property they, of course, form the greatest sacrifice on the part of the father.

On the day of the ceremony the procession begins at the tipi of the godfather and goes to the tipi of the father. It is led by a virgin carrying a lovely and perfect ear of white corn on a slender wand. From the tip of the ear of corn there waves a white eagle plume. Next come two dancers carrying rattles in their right hands and wands in their left hands. The wands are decorated with a fan-shaped ornamentation of eagle feathers, a fluff of green neck feathers of the duck, and some owl feathers, all symbolic. They are further decorated with paint, and tassels of dyed feathers. After the dancers follows a group of singers keeping time to the beat of the drum. They sing:

To kte tipi so
Ha eya he ye e ya he ye ye ye
Ha eys he ye e ya he ye ye ye
Ha eya he ye e ya he
He eya he ye e ya he

Le hunka ya ya ya
Le hunka ya ya ya
Le hunka ya ya ya
Le hunka ya ya ya
Eca tu kte tipi so
Le ya hunka

E ya we ya he ya ha ya e ya
E ya we ya he ya ha ya e ya
E ya we ya he ya ha ya e ya
E ya we ya he ya ha ya e ya

The entire thought of the first stanza is given in the first line, the only one that can be translated. This line says, 'Where are the children whom we seek?' The rest of the verse implies that the children are being sought, for something of importance is to take place.

The first line of the second verse says that the *Hunka* or Confirmation is to take place. The word *Hunka* means the whole ceremony — songs, dances, and speeches. The chorus of the song is merely an arrangement of syllables to carry the tune.

When the procession reaches the tipi of the father, there they find the child, or children. The women who carry the buffalo robe put the child in it, and each woman to a corner, join the procession. The singing continues, and in the same order of march, the child is taken to the tipi where the godfather has placed the new clothing and where he has built the altar. The child is taken in and the old clothing which it has been wearing, signifying the old life, is removed. New garments, signifying a new life, replace the old. The child is now ready for instruction from the wise man who has been brought there for that purpose. The old man offers thanks to the Great Holy before the sacred altar. He instructs the child in its duties to the tribe. The old, weak, or disabled must be looked after and the child must never refuse to help those who ask. He must live righteously, always speak truthfully, and fill his daily life with usefulness. When the wise man finishes, he paints a black line across the forehead and down the bridge of the nose of the child. He then ties a white-eagle fluff to the hair at the left side of the head. This fluffy plume, which symbolizes a prayer, completes the robing of the child. The wise man smokes the pipe while all is silent. When he puts the pipe once more upon the earth the tomtom beats are sounded in quick rhythm. The singers begin the song once more and the beautiful Confirmation dance is performed. When it is ended the ceremony is over and the solemnity of the occasion has passed. Feasting and fun begin and there is much giving away of presents.

The older boys as a rule had a group of younger ones following them and as I was now a good marksman with the bow and an expert horseman I joined this group of followers, too. In everything the little fellows were imitators, and no matter what the game or sport, they tried to meet the pace. The nice thing about it was that the older boys never seemed to regard the younger ones as nuisances. They took time to look after us and, in fact, all seemed proud to share in this responsibility.

There was a custom among the Lakotas often followed by young men whereby an older boy voluntarily adopted as a special charge some younger boy. The older one appointed himself as guardian and helpmate to the younger, the obligation to last throughout life; and through war or peace, in times good or ill, the brotherhood was to exist. If the two went with the same war-party, the older boy gave up his life if necessary to save that of the younger. The ties assumed could have been no stronger had they been actual blood ties. This trust we put in older companions was never questioned, not even by our parents, and my mother never worried when I was with my caretakers.

When the contests of the older boys became too much

for us little fellows, then we watched them. It was natural for me, and I suppose it was the same with the other boys, to pick the best one to imitate, whether in work or in games. So strong with us was the idea of example that the boy who played ball better than all the rest was the one who became the example. If a boy in the group was outstanding as a rider, then I practiced riding, hoping that I might be as good. There was always one, or a few in every band, who swam the best, who shot the truest arrow, or who ran the fastest, and I at once set their accomplishment as the mark for me to attain. In spite of all this striving there was no sense of rivalry. We never disliked the boy who did better than the others. On the contrary, we praised him. All through our society, the individual who excelled was praised and honored.

On the hunts we younger boys carried the blankets and the extra arrows for the older boys. We made ourselves useful in exchange for our welcome. In following them we boys got our first hunting lessons. Woods hunting was easier than plains hunting, so we hunted first in the woods. When we had reached the haunts of the animal we sought, we began to look and listen. Animals are clever and we had to match their cleverness by reading their obscure signs. We not only watched the path ahead of us and the paths to the side, but kept watch of the path back of us. A good hunter watches all animals, for one often betrays the presence of another. Some of the signs we watched for were bits of hair, grass, broken sticks, the bark of trees, birds in the air, foot prints and overturned stones. Then, too, we depended much upon our sense of smell. Some of the animals that we could most readily scent were the porcupine, badger, bear, and skunk. A beaver-dam could also be smelled for some distance. Whenever signs grew scarce and our leaders stopped to survey the landscape and search for new signs, we did the same and tried to see the things they saw.

Rabbit-hunting was great fun even for the older boys, and we never refused to join one, for we little fellows got the tails. The fluffy tips were dyed in pretty colors and we wore them for hair ornaments. The skins we saved to make into winter hunting caps. Furs being usable, skinning was something else to be learned. When a porcupine was skinned, the quills, hair, and tails were saved — the quills to be dyed by the women for their decorative work, the hair for head roaches, and the tails for hair combs. The fur of the skunk was cut into strips and used for neck ornaments, while the entire hide was esteemed by the old men for tobacco pouches. The scent bag of this animal was carefully preserved, too, and the liquid kept for disinfectant purposes. A drop mixed with paint and smeared on the body kept away ailments. Skins of the raccoon made fine hunting caps and most hunters preferred a cap of fur to a bare head, for it helped in concealment. The tail of the raccoon we boys used to tie on the necks of our ponies. The furs of the otter and the beaver were most prized by the young braves, but these animals were wary and only the older boys hunted them. However, by the time we boys were ten or twelve years of age we were quite wise in trailing, stalking, covering, disguise, and all the arts of a good hunter. Some of the lads before their teens joined the men in their hunt for big game. At an early age physical strength was developed from long-distance walking, running, and climbing. Even long hours of crawling or walking in a stooped position had to be endured, for much of the hunting was on the low-shrubbed and grassy plains country.

Even the games which boys played put their strength to test, for most of them called for strenuous action. One of these games was called *canhuyapi*, meaning 'wooden leg.' White boys have this game, calling it stilts. *Canhuyapi* was a follow-the-leader game, the strongest boy being the leader. Through deep water, mud, snow-banks, brush thickets, and high grass, the leader took his followers, testing to the utmost their strength and courage. It was great fun, but when it came to going up and down steep banks or rocky places, the ones who tumbled were many, and, once down, one was out of the game.

Contests for strength were played in the water and the divers would search for a rock or root of a tree to hold, in order to see who could stay below the surface the longest. In winter the contestants plunged into the icy waters to see how much cold they could endure.

All boys did not have equal enthusiasm for all games, but one thing they all tried to do was to mount while their horses were running full speed. Running a few steps by the side of the horse, then grasping its mane and springing in the air, the rider was lifted by the motion of the animal. Another quite necessary thing to learn was to mount at the back of a rider who was going at full speed. In case of a battle, if a warrior were unhorsed, another could save him by riding swiftly by. The one on foot grasped the tail of the horse and leaped to the back of the rider and to safety. This was hard to do, but easily practiced with gentle ponies. Such training developed skillful horsemen.

A riding and shooting game was *hanpa kute*. A pole was planted in the earth and a moccasin placed on top of it for a target. Riding by as fast as possible, we shot an arrow at the moccasin. In order to be fair the rider must go by the target at full speed. If he slowed his pony down as he neared the pole he was ruled out of the game.

Back of all this physical attainment was the further objective of tenacity and poise. In play we imagined ourselves in the midst of the enemy in all sorts of conditions — on foot, surrounded, wounded, and without weapons — and with bullets and arrows flying toward us. The tighter the place in which a warrior found himself, the more resourceful he needed to be. Nerve, pluck, and quick action were necessary. These saved a warrior's life when the odds were against him. So one never gave up. It was fight to the last, and that spirit saved many a brave. But even this was not all. Sometimes odds were too heavy, and circumstances were not to be overcome with physical strength. There was then the power of medicine and the protection of faith. Over and over the thought was repeated in the mind, 'No arrow will strike me, no wound will kill me.' Stronger and stronger grew the faith within until actual belief became established. A warrior could go into battle believing that his enemy was powerless to harm him, for there was no wound nor hurt that he could not withstand.

All Lakota boys were supposed to join one of the numerous lodges when they became old enough. The one we favored was the one we paid most attention to by imitating its members, trying to dress like them, and singing their songs. Only we made play of it and not work. My choice was the Fox lodge, and I remember when I was only six or seven years of age, calling a council of playmates of like age and holding a feast. At that time we had received some white man's flour, so mother gave me some and we boys went off by ourselves to hold our feast. We cooked what we thought was a very fine dish of flour, sugar, and water, its sumptuousness added to by contributions of *wasna* and dried meat. Many times we played at being Fox lodge men and when doing so we tried to arrange our dress like that of the lodge members, who wore long trails of painted buckskin down the back, decorations of feathers on the hair, and who carried short clubs like policemen's billies. These clubs were decorated with feathers, were sometimes painted, and a whole fox skin hung from the handle. In solemn manner we elected a leader and chose one to play the tomtom. We used a small pole for the brave staff; and from memory we repeated the songs and danced the steps of the Fox dance.

In most of our games and strenuous sports we were not

joined by the girls. They never rode, hunted nor swam with us; neither did they play such rough games as *canhuyapi* with us. There was, however, a fine relationship between boys and girls, the boys always assuming the position of protectors. Every brother was supposed to look after his sister. I remember well an accident that proved the value of this training in me. One day a number of us were playing some distance from the village. We all had our ponies but had dismounted to gather chokecherries. Suddenly one of my sisters (she was the daughter of my aunt according to the white man's relationship) screamed in fright, thinking she had seen an enemy warrior peeping at us. We ran for our ponies and I, frightened, ran with the rest. But all the while I could not allow myself to be the first one away — I was determined to let the girls go first and be the last boy at that. When my sisters had a good start for home, I whipped my pony, staying a little behind them, however, in order to see them safe at home. I never denied my fright, for I was only about seven years of age, but my training told me that my first duty was to the girls.

The ties of sentiment between brother and sister were strong; nevertheless, no Lakota boy ever spoke directly to his sisters or girl cousins. This rule of conduct a Lakota boy dared not violate, for to do so was showing the utmost disrespect for them. If a number of boys and girls were playing a game together, and a brother wished to tell his sister something, he would either ask some of the playmates to carry his message for him or else shout it so all could hear. He would not speak to his sister and say, 'Come, sister, we must now go home,' but would address all by saying, 'Sister and I must now go home.' Even today, when in the home of my sister, I speak to her through her husband, though I receive letters from her directly.

Lakota children in their play, either alone or in groups, roamed far and wide over the countryside. They grew up without a sense of restriction and confinement. Their faculties became accustomed to space and distance, to skies clear or stormy, and to freedom in its full meaning. The 'Great Out-doors' was reality and not something to be talked about in dim consciousness. And for them there was perfect safety. There were not the dangers that seem to surround childhood of today. I can recall days — entire days — when we roamed over the plains, hills, and up and down streams without fear of anything. I do not remember ever hearing of an Indian child being hurt or eaten by a wild animal.

Every now and then the whole village moved ten or fifteen miles to a grassier spot, but this was not considered much of a job. It was less trouble than moving a house from the front to the back of a city lot. Miles were to us as they were to the bird. The land was ours to roam in as the sky was for them to fly in. We did not think of the great open plains, the beautiful rolling hills, and winding streams with tangled growth, as 'wild.' Only to the white man was nature a 'wilderness' and only to him was the land 'infested' with 'wild' animals and 'savage' people. To us it was tame. Earth was bountiful and we were surrounded with the blessings of the Great Mystery. Not until the hairy man from the east came and with brutal frenzy heaped injustices upon us and the families we loved was it 'wild' for us. When the very animals of the forest began fleeing from his approach, then it was that for us the 'Wild West' began.

CHAPTER III

HUNTER, SCOUT, WARRIOR

IN THE natural course of events every Lakota boy became a hunter, scout, or warrior. It was necessary that every boy should choose one of the three callings and by the time he had reached early manhood he was ready, by training, to follow the one for which he seemed most fitted. The selection was his.

Not every young man became all three — hunter, scout, and warrior — in one. The bravest warrior was not always the best scout nor was the best scout necessarily a good hunter. Some men possessed special ability as scouts and followed scouting almost exclusively. Then there were men who developed into expert hunters and rode fearlessly into a herd of buffalo in mad flight, yet when it came to facing an enemy in battle they were not the foremost.

Most young men at some time in their lives tried to become medicine-men. They purified themselves and held the vigil hoping for direct communion with spirit powers, but in this few succeeded.

To become a great brave was, however, the highest aspiration. At the same time it imposed upon the young man the greatest efforts. Not only must he have great physical bravery and fighting prowess, but he must meet the severest tests of character. The great brave was a man of strict honor, undoubted truthfulness, and unbounded generosity. He was strong enough to part with his last horse or weapon and his last bit of food. In conduct he never forgot pride and dignity, accepting praise and honor and wearing fine regalia without arrogance. To endure pain, to bear the scars of life and battle, to defy the elements and to laugh and sing in the face of death, a man had to possess the prime requisite of a Lakota brave — courage. And only the brave could hope to become a chief.

When but a mere child, father inspired me by often saying: 'Son, I never want to see you live to be an old man. Die young on the battlefield. That is the way a Lakota dies.' The full intent of this advice was that I must never shirk my duty to my tribe no matter what price in sacrifice I paid. Yet in serving my tribe I was serving myself. If I failed in duty, I simply failed to meet a test of manhood, and a man living in his tribe without respect was a living nonentity. My ancestors had been brave men. There was not an enemy they feared — not even did they fear death. So if I were not afraid to die I would then dare to do whatever came for me to do.

Among surrounding tribes both friendly and otherwise, the Lakotas were known as fearless fighters. Not because they looked for trouble with their neighbors, but because they determinedly kept their territory free from enemy tribes who now and then invaded their grounds. Certain areas were recognized as the homeland of the Lakota, and when the scouts discovered an enemy band near, the warriors went out and drove them back. Now and then a war-party went out to avenge the death of a fellow tribesman, but most of our troubles were over boundary lines or hunting grounds.

Contrary to much that has been written, warfare with the Lakota was not a tribal profession. They did not fight to gain territory nor to conquer another people. Neither did they fight to subject other tribes to slavery. They never kept captives nor exacted tribute from those subdued, and there was no institution that remotely resembled a prison. As a matter of fact, the philosophical ideal of the Lakota was harmony, and the most powerful symbol was that of peace. So powerful was this symbol that the wise men or chiefs had but to present it to the war-

riors and they obeyed its mandates, no matter how reluctant they might be.

The people who troubled us most were the Pawnees and
the Crows. One of the biggest fights the Lakotas ever had
over a hunting ground is within my memory, though I was
too small to take part. The Lakotas were moving south
on their own territory to reach a herd of buffalo when they
ran into a band of Pawnees who were shooting the animals
and driving them off. A fight ensued, in which about
three hundred Pawnees were killed. A few prisoners were
brought to our village after the fight. We fed them and
made friends with them, but soon sent them back wearing
our best clothes and riding our best horses. In the group
of Pawnees was a boy probably out with his first war-
party. We played together about the village in the friend-
liest way until he went home. A few years later we met
again at the Carlisle School.

The Lakota warriors were proud of their fighting ability
and were fully aware of their reputation as good fighters.
They took pride in wearing a fine headdress and regalia
into battle, even though it made them conspicuous. It
was a mark of bravery and a challenge to the foe.

The reputation of the Lakotas as fighting men spread
among the white people, though not even with them was
warfare sought until realization came to the people of the
plains that they must fight or disappear as had the buffalo.
Then their cause became a righteous one for the preservation of the race. For this the Lakotas have been put down
in history as the 'most warlike of all tribes.' It was the
French who called us the 'Sioux,' or 'Enemy People,' and
other references have been made to the tribe such as the
'Mighty Sioux and the 'Fighting Sioux.' On account of
the love for fine dress and haughty and dignified manners,
Catlin's characterization of the Lakotas was that they
were the 'aristocrats of the plains.' But for the name

'Sioux' which the French gave us we might still be called the Lakotas.

It is said that Nature makes the man to fit his surroundings. If that be the case, then a description of the land partly, at least, describes the people. Our homeland was proportioned on a big scale. There seemed to be nothing small, nothing limited, in our domain. Our home, which covered part of North Dakota, all of South Dakota, and part of Nebraska and Wyoming, was one of great plains, large rivers and wooded mountains. So wide were the prairies that the sun seemed to rise out of one distant edge and in the evening to set in the opposite distant edge. The weather was extreme. The winter was cold with sleet and ice and the temperature often below zero. The winds were so strong they made us feel their strength. The summers were hot and violent with color. At times the skies were as blue as Lakota blue paint and as far as the eye could see the earth was a deep green, while the sun set in red as dazzling to the eye as the white of midday. The rain fell in streams and the storm warriors threw their lightning sticks to earth and shook our tipis with their thunder. We grew used to strength, height, distance, power.

Nature dealt vigorously with the Lakota and they with bodies almost bare became vigorous. What the body was fitted for the mind was fitted for also, and physical hardihood was matched with spiritual hardihood. There was little fear within. The mental reaction of the Lakota was one of unity with these tremendous forces, and rather than terror many times the attitude was a welcoming defiance. I have seen a brave, without uttering a word, strip himself to breechclout and walk out into a rain falling so heavily in sheets that a few paces from the door his form was lost to sight. He went out to be alone with Rain. That is true love of Nature.

Surroundings were filled with comforts for the body and beauty for expectant senses. Every morning the sun was received by each individual in a moment of silent reverence; and in the evening the sunset was watched, for it held the secret of the next day's weather. The springs and trees inspired songs and stories which we wrote in our minds and framed in our consciousness.

Of all our domain we loved, perhaps, the Black Hills the most. The Lakota had named these hills *He Sapa*, or Black Hills, on account of their color. The slopes and peaks were so heavily wooded with dark pines that from a distance the mountains actually looked black. In wooded recesses were numberless springs of pure water and numerous small lakes. There were wood and game in abundance and shelter from the storms of the plains. It was the favorite winter haunt of the buffalo and the Lakota as well. According to a tribal legend these hills were a reclining female figure from whose breasts flowed life-giving forces, and to them the Lakota went as a child to its mother's arms. The various entrances to the hills were very rough and rugged, but there was one very beautiful and easy pass through which both buffalo and Lakota entered the hills. This pass ran along a narrow stream bed which widened here and there but which in places narrowed so that the tall pines at the top of the cliffs arched their boughs, almost touching as they swayed in the wind. Every fall thousands of buffaloes and Lakotas went through this pass to spend the winter in the hills. *Pte ta tiyopa* it was called by the Lakotas, or 'Gate of the buffalo.' Today this beautiful pass is denuded of trees and to the white man it is merely 'Buffalo Gap.'

Two lovely legends of the Lakotas would be fine subjects for sculpturing — the Black Hills as the earth mother, and the story of the genesis of the tribe. Instead, the face of a white man is being outlined on the face of a stone cliff in the Black Hills. This beautiful region, of which the Lakota thought more than any other spot on earth, caused him the most pain and misery. These hills were to become prized by the white people for reasons far different from those of the Lakota. To the Lakota the magnificent forests and splendid herds were incomparable in value. To the white man everything was valueless except the gold in the hills. Toward the Indian the white people were absolutely devoid of sentiment, and when a people lack sentiment they are without compassion. So down went the Black Forest and to death went the last buffalo, noble animal and immemorial friend of the Lakota. As for the people who were as native to the soil as the forests and the buffalo — well, the gold-seekers did not understand them and never have. The white man will never know the horror and the utter bewilderment of the Lakota at the wanton destruction of the buffalo. What cruelty has not been glossed over with the white man's word — enterprise! If the Lakotas had been relinquishing any part of their territory voluntarily, the Black Hills would have been the last from the standpoint of traditional sentiment. So when by false treaties and trickery the Black Hills were forever lost, they were a broken people. The treaties, made supposedly to recompense them for the loss of this lovely region, were like all other treaties — worthless. But could the Lakota braves have foreseen the ignominy they were destined to endure, every man would have died fighting rather than give up his homeland to live in subjection and helplessness.

How long the Lakota people lived in these mid-west plains bordering the Black Hills before the coming of the white men is not known in tribal records. But our legends tell us that it was hundreds and perhaps thousands of years ago since the first man sprang from the soil in the midst of these great plains. The story says that one morning long ago a lone man awoke, face to the sun, emerging from the soil. Only his head was visible, the rest of his body not yet being fashioned. The man looked about, but saw no mountains, no rivers, no forests. There was no-

thing but soft and quaking mud, for the earth itself was
still young. Up and up the man drew himself until he
freed his body from the clinging soil. At last he stood
upon the earth, but it was not solid, and his first few steps
were slow and halting. But the sun shone and ever the
man kept his face turned toward it. In time the rays of
the sun hardened the face of the earth and strengthened
the man and he bounded and leaped about, a free and joyous creature. From this man sprang the Lakota nation
and, so far as we know, our people have been born and
have died on this plain; and no people have shared it with
us until the coming of the European. So this land of the
great plains is claimed by the Lakotas as their very own.
We are of the soil and the soil is of us. We love the birds
and beasts that grew with us on this soil. They drank the
same water we did and breathed the same air. We are all
one in nature. Believing so, there was in our hearts a great
peace and a welling kindness for all living, growing things.

In appearance, the Lakotas were large and strong with
well-defined features. Both body and face were usually
well proportioned. The eyes were not large, but they were
bright and steady in gaze, and I have never seen a Lakota
who was 'pop-eyed.' In color the eyes were black or
brown from dark to very light. The skin light brown and
for all the weather never black. It was fine in texture, and
though age and weather tended to wrinkle the skin it
never seemed to coarsen.

In physique the Lakotas were strong and powerful.
Legs, lungs, eyes, and arms were developed to a high degree. For centuries the Lakotas had hunted on foot, walking and running down their game and killing it with the
strength of their right arm. Even after they became expert
horsemen they sometimes preferred traveling on foot.

Favorite sports of the Lakotas were the ball and running
games which everybody attended. The young players
stripped to their breechclouts and painted their bodies,

showing to best of advantage their wonderful muscles. The display these young fellows made in the agile and graceful use of their bodies was a sight to see. These games were pure sports held for the exhibition of skill. Health and strength were such natural and common conditions that such a thing as beauty and strength contests were not thought of. No doubt prize-giving for the slenderest leg, the prettiest back, or the handsomest face would have been considered very foolish amusement.

The Lakotas believed that their bodies were nourished not only by food — meat, fruit, and plant — but that wind, rain, and sun also nourished. All things that helped sustain the body — food, pure air, water, and sun — were medicine. When doctoring the sick the medicine-men sometimes sang the song of the sun:

> *Wanka tan han he ya u we lo*
> *Wanka tan han he ya u we lo*
> *Mita wi cohan topa wan la*
> *Ka nu we he ya u we lo*
> *Anpe wi kin he ya u we lo*
> *A ye ye ye yo*

These words were supposed to be those of the sun delivering his power to the medicine-man to be used for the sick, and he reminds the medicine-man that the power of the sun reaches to the four corners of the earth. The sick were sometimes carried out into the sun and those who were recovering from wounds sat in the sunshine. The skin of the Lakota absorbed any amount of sunlight without blistering or reddening. Newborn babies were sometimes quite fair, but with gradual exposure to the sun became light brown in color.

The Lakotas did not worship the sun, nor did they pray to it. They merely recognized the bearing it had upon all life, manifesting as it did the universal powers of the Great Mystery. So when the Lakota prayed or sang songs of praise, the sun carried them direct to Wakan Tanka.

Every day for the Lakota began with a salute to the sun, and as a bringer of light, it was recognized, whether its face was visible or whether it was hidden by a clouded sky. It was habit and custom to receive the sun by awaiting its coming. For a moment, silently and erect, the sun was faced. There was no kneeling, no words were spoken, and no hands were raised, but in every heart was just a thought of tribute. No assembly ceremonies were held in the morning, each and every person on his own account holding his moment of worship. Even if alone, the Lakota never forgot this moment of worshipful silence. The only time an assembly worship was held was when the tribe was on the move. It was the rule to be on the march before the break of day, but just as soon as the rays of the sun were visible, the old men who carried the pipe halted the caravan and made ready to hold the ceremony. As fire was carried, it was but a few moments till a small flame burned on the earth; then with every face turned to the sun the pipe ceremony was performed.

Further recognition was given the sun by the erection of the villages with every tipi door facing the east. Ever since the first man came from the soil with his eyes on the morning sun, the Lakotas had built their homes with doors facing the east. The medicine-lodges, the Sun Dance enclosures, the sweat-bath houses and all ceremonial tipis were built with doors opening to the east. Only occasionally, to face away from a storm, a high bank or cliff, or some other natural obstruction, was a tipi placed with door opening toward any direction but east. The main exception was the tipi in which the watchers kept the fire burning for the return of the scouts. The door of this tipi opened toward the direction which the scouts had taken and by which they would return.

The only time the sun injured was after a snowstorm when snow blindness might occur, but the hunters prevented this by rubbing charcoal around their eyes and down the bridge of the nose. Persons who became afflicted were treated with snow bandages. Snow was placed on the eyes and held there with a bandage, three or four hours being long enough to cure. There was no treatment for sunstroke, for it was unknown. The hottest summer sun on a bare head brought no complaint from a Lakota, for weather in any form was never a topic of conversation. Such complaints as, 'It is too hot today,' or 'It is not warm enough,' were never heard. To complain against the weather would be denying the praise offered to the Great Mystery each morning for the day and all it held. However, the evening sun was watched for a forecast of weather, and if a ring appeared around the sun a storm was looked for soon.

Time of the day was kept by the sun — hunter, traveler, and home-keeper — all watching its movements. Hours were not kept but there were terms for morning, for noon and for evening. All time up till noon was before noon and all time thereafter was afternoon. Children were taught to watch the sun and were often asked to come home when the sun was in the 'middle,' meaning, of course, noon.

In the arts of design and drawing the sun was often used, being a favorite subject with the men. Occasionally the women used it as a symbol in their beadwork, but more often it was painted on the tipis and war shields of the men. Women often chose a sun name for their children, such as *Wi he napa*, meaning Rising Sun, or *Wi sapa*, meaning Black Sun.

The sun was a very important symbol in the Sun Dance of the Lakotas, which was in reality a religious ceremony. The sunflower, which grew in great abundance on the plains before they were upturned by the white man's plow, was the symbol of the sun and for this reason was used a great deal in ceremonial decoration. The Lakotas adored this flower for its golden beauty, remindful of the sun, and because its face was at all times of the day turned toward the sun. The Sun Dancers wore sunflowers made of rawhide and painted yellow. The buffalo also was a prominent symbol in the Sun Dance, for it was a beautiful woman in the guise of this animal who brought to the Lakotas this wonderful thanksgiving ceremonial. And strange it is, but the buffalo loved the simple and odorless sunflower just as did the Lakota. These great beasts wandered through the sunflower fields, wallowing their heads among them. Sometimes they uprooted the plants and wound them about their necks, letting sprays dangle from their left horns. So the sunflower and the buffalo were two beloved symbols of the Lakota.

So first, last, and throughout existence, the Lakota knew that the sun was essential to health and to all life. In spring, summer, and winter its rays were welcome. In the spring its warmth brought forth new grass; in the summer its heat cured the skins, dried the meat, and preserved food for storage; and in the winter the Lakotas bathed their bodies in the sunshine, stripping themselves just as they did to bathe in the streams. Without these life-giving rays all would be death, so when the Lakota arose each morning to meet the sun he met a personality — the emissary of Wakan Tanka.

As the Lakota looked at the sun, he drew in great breaths of pure morning air. With bare feet upon the earth, breathing was done consciously and deeply. The air was considered more bracing and more exhilarating before the sun had thoroughly warmed it, which was another cause for early rising. The person who would not get up and drink in the morning air with the first rays of the sun lacked zest for the day's adventures. Morning was the only time in which to energize body and nerves and the morning air the only stimulant to awaken senses. There were no herbs, roots, drinks, nor rich food to urge one to greater activity. The morning air supplied all that was necessary to create appetite and send the blood healthily on its course.

Not only did the Lakota like the air, but the wind as
well. It was considered a friendly force and a carrier of
messages. In the world of the Lakota nothing could be
useless nor futile, so the whirlwinds filled their mission by
hurrying here and there with messages. The good intentions of the wind were acknowledged by the naming of one
of my sisters Wamniomni, or Whirlwind.   Sometimes
the wind came and sent the dust from the buffalo wallows
circling high in the air and clouding the sky when otherwise the air would have been clear, for grass covered most
of the ground. But when the dust blew, the Lakotas said
the air was being cleaned for them, for when the wind sub-
sided the days seemed brighter and clearer. Neither wind
nor hail storms sent the Lakota braves to shelter, for it was
then that they held walking contests to see who could travel the fastest against the force of the storm.

The tipi was perfectly ventilated and the air at all times
fresh.   Night and day and all seasons of the year we
breathed pure air.   Smoke and soot from the fire and bad
air rose up and out of the tipi, and our throats and lungs
were not filled with ashes and other impurities. The only
time that smoke settled in the tipi was when a sudden whirlwind caught the wind flap in a wrong position, but this was
only for a few moments. When the whirlwind had passed
on, the smoke from the fire started at once to ascend. The
wood generally used — elm, cedar, and cottonwood —
made very little smoke at any time. The Lakota thought
of air much the same way as the white man does of water
— something cleansing, something to bathe in.   Our
bodies bathed in air, and breathing was not only conducted through nose and lungs but with the entire body.
As a result the changing seasons brought no readjustments
to the body and there were no such things as 'colds,' 'in-
fluenza' and 'grippe' epidemics. We were rewarded in full
and in plenty for our love of nature.

The use of water was part of the Lakota's morning ritual, just as was prayer or breathing, and never was a mouthful of food eaten until a long drink had been taken. But no water was swallowed until first the mouth had been thoroughly rinsed. This was considered such an important health measure that children were instructed to follow the rule until habit had been formed. As the Lakota did nothing aimlessly, there were beneficial reasons, no doubt, for this habit.

After drinking deeply, the hands, face, and head were washed. In olden days water was kept in the paunch of the buffalo hung on a pole and so adjusted that the water-bag was easily tipped, letting the water run out freely. The water was always fresh and usually a few sprigs of mint floated on the top. There was no stinting in the use of water, for Lakota villages were nearly always located close to a stream. Early-morning or before-breakfast bathing was the rule with the men and boys in both winter and summer. Cold, frosty paths leading to the stream and ice-covered water did not weaken the hearts of the Lakota braves and I can remember seeing men and boys breaking the ice in order to have a plunge before breakfast. The women and girls generally bathed in mid-afternoon when all work was done and they had the village more or less to themselves. With them it was not a hasty plunge but they sported about quite a good deal. Water games were played and their laughter could be heard for some distance.

Though the Lakota lived near streams they had a special sentiment for springs and the purity of spring water. Springs were brought up by a living force or spirit called *Wiwila*. Whenever one lay down to drink from a spring, they said to it, 'Wiwila, have pity on me as I drink.' As boys we lay and watched the water bubbling up from the earth, feeling that it could not come up without some force back of it, so in it we saw the Great Mystery. So it was with a feeling of submission or human limitation that we whispered, 'Wi-wi-la, have pity on me as I drink.'

When a Lakota brave wanted a 'kick' he got it from a draught of water from some cool, dripping stream. It was customary to gather a spray of mint which grew by the edge of the spring and, laying it on the surface, draw the water into the mouth through the leaves. That was mint julip *à la Lakota*. The habit of drinking copiously of pure water was one that doubtless helped to keep the Lakota in splendid health, and the amount that some of them were able to drink at one time was astounding. I was once in a tipi where a medicine-man was giving a patient treatment. The medicine-man happened to be a Duck Dreamer, so, of course, the duck was helping him to find a cure for the sick man. The medicine-man asked me to bring him some water, so I brought him a vessel holding two quarts or more. He drank every drop and then quacked in perfect imitation of a duck. In a moment or so he called for more water and that he drank, too. I did not see how a human being could drink so much water at one time. The supposition was, of course, that the medicine which the duck furnished naturally grew in water, probably some root or water plant. Anyway, the patient recovered and the medicine-man did not drown.

A love for water was in the Lakota. Little children were fond of the rain, every shower being a bath for them; but their fondness and their resistance were not broken by constant warnings that it would injure them. Little fellows stripped and romped in the rain, and after it was over, or between showers, footraces were run. Courses were marked and a return point, say a hill, a mile or more away, was fixed. Before the start, each boy plastered a ring of mud on his chest to give him wind.

Night and hours of sleep for the Lakota were the same as for other creatures of the day and usually with the setting of the sun preparations were made for bed. Not all dances and ceremonies were held at night, many of them being performed during the day, so early retiring was the rule.

In lying down for the night the Lakota, either in the village or in the open, arranged his head toward the west if possible. Warriors were trained to awaken quickly, for if aroused at night it was usually for the purpose of going immediately into action. No matter, however, what the circumstances of the night, early rising was considered an aid in throwing off the lethargy of sleep. Only the sluggard or the ill was not up to meet the sun. For the latter there was excuse, but for the former there was none, and an able-bodied person who remained in bed after sunrise and the rest of the village astir was next to disgraced. When the village was on the move, it was imperative that everyone arise early and it was the custom for an old man to pass around camp before daybreak calling, '*Co-o-o! Co-o-o!*' at every tipi door. No one lingered after this call.

All the main rules of health being observed, it remained only for the Lakota to have good and nourishing food to keep him in good condition. Food was simple and alike for all — there being no rich man's and poor man's diet. Meat was the main article of food, the staff of life, eaten at all meals and in all seasons. If the scout carried food, which was seldom, it was usually a little meat dried or in the form of wasna.

The buffalo was usually cut up on the plain and brought in to the women. The Lakota huntsmen were expert cutters, but their method of dismembering differed from that of the white man. With only a knife the animal was separated at the large joints, muscles seldom cut throuhg. else the women could not handle them for drying. The long muscles of the back were never cut into, for it was from them the women took the sinew. If necessary, one hunter could handle an animal from skinning to packing by himself. There was a trick of turning the head of the animal and supporting the body by the horns in any position for conveniences of the hunter.

But little of the buffalo was not usable. Horns were

made into spoons, hoofs boiled for glue, ribs turned into sleds, toys, and games, the skull used for ceremonial purposes, the thick hide on the head dried and shaped into bowls and tubs, the large bones broken and boiled to skin for tallow and the hides used for innumerable purposes. The offal was left upon the plains. Fresh, untainted meat was an enjoyment of the Lakota as were pure water and air. Whatever was not consumed while fresh was dried, and meat preserved in this way kept wholesome for an indefinite time.

Whether meat was fresh or dry, it was usually boiled, for soup was the universal dish of the Lakota, being liked by young, middle-aged, and old. In olden days food was boiled in the paunch of the buffalo which was hung on a rack. Hot stones kept the food boiling until it was cooked. Meat roasted on an open fire was wholesome and the ashes which touched the outside not injurious but cleansing and stimulating to the system. Brains were used to thicken the soup, and tripe, either boiled or roasted, was a favorite dish. The intestines of the buffalo were thoroughly cleaned, looped over the end of a stick, and roasted to a crispy brown over a hot coal fire, or again, as if to make this good dish more enticing, the strips were braided or looped in chain-stitch before putting over the fire.

About once a week the Lakota ate a small piece of raw liver or kidney and considered it quite necessary to good health. The old folks said that they had always eaten the liver and kidney raw because it was good for them, and fed it to little children so that they would acquire a taste for it. Raw liver is now being recommended for use in the treatment of anæmic patients, but the Lakota discovered that long ago and there were no anæmics among them. The Lakotas were not habitual raw-meat eaters, but if for some reason hungry hunters thought it unwise or unsafe to build a fire, they ate, without cooking, the liver, kidneys, tripe, marrow, and spinal cord. The blood of animals was never drunk, with the exception of that of the deer, and this only occasionally and sparingly. Blood soup was sometimes made for the ill by pouring fresh blood into boiling water.

There were three main meals of the day — morning, noon, and evening. I remember a fellow in our village who was not considered as bright as most people. Three times a day before each meal hour this fellow climbed a little hill close by and sang a song in which he reminded the women that it was time to cook. In the morning he announced the rising of the sun by singing, 'Your grandfather is coming,' and telling the women that it was time for the first meal of the day. At noon he sang that the sun was in the 'middle' and that it was time for the body to be refreshed with good food. In the evening he sang, telling the women to put the water on to boil.

Though it was customary to serve food three times a day, children were allowed to eat whenever they felt like it and 'pieced' just like other children. Older folks also ate whenever their appetites prompted. Overeating by children was not allowed, and gormandizing was unknown until the white man came and eating habits changed. Previous to that time meat was cured and stored in sufficient quantities to last during the season when hunting was not easily carried on.

Breakfast, like all our meals, was a simple one, usually consisting of a single dish — meat or soup — but of which there was a plentiful supply. Tastes that were simple did not crave dishes of which they did not know and there were no dieting fads to follow.

Today an enormous amount of time is given to the preparation and eating of food. Not so long ago I sat at a dinner table close to a dancer. The young lady refused all meat during the meal, saying that she had some time since stopped using meat for the purpose of making her more spiritual. The lady was pale and rather thin. I understand since that dinner that there are a number of people who believe this same idea. If the eating of meat lessened the Indian's spiritual life, then how far could he have proceeded along spiritual lines if he had let meat alone, provided, of course, that this idea is correct. So far as I have observed, the humaneness of the Indian and his respect for the souls of beings has not been outdistanced by the white man. The white man has many cults and many isms, but he has numerous means of trying to prevent crime. Now meat was our staple food. Though we had both fruits and vegetables, it was meat that we most depended upon. Yet we were a society almost free from crime. We had one great faith, but no reform schools, no courts of justice, no jails, no judges, and no poor houses. We were a meat-eating people, yet peace was an ideal with us and the pipe of peace the strongest symbol of peace ever known. Therefore I believe this analysis all wrong, for the Indian proved his strength of thought and spiritual force in many ways.

Again in a newspaper some time ago I read the following statement by a famous physician, or medicine-man of the white race: 'The association of men with animals is unpleasant and dangerous for both.' Now that seems strange. The Lakota enjoyed his association with the animal world. For centuries he derived nothing but good from animal creatures. From them were learned lessons in industry, fidelity, and many virtues and much knowledge. Disease troubled us very little — neither man, bird, nor animal.

I have thought a good deal about what the white medicine-man has said. And it seems to me that the white race has come to fear nearly everything on earth — even his fellow being. The great physician went on to write that 'the most menacing disease is tuberculosis,' and blames the cows for it. Well, the Indians are not a milk-drinking people, yet, as soon as they are crowded together in the big government schools, they become afflicted with this dread disease. All I can say is that I am still thinking over what the medicine-man wrote.

The changing of fresh wild meat to cattle meat was a great trial to the Lakotas. The first cattle came to us looking thin and gaunt from the long drive across the plains and were then penned in corrals that could be smelled for miles. I remember when my father came home and reported to us that the white men had brought some 'spotted buffalo' for us to eat. We all got on our ponies and rode over to see the strange new animals and as we drew near there came to us a peculiar and disagreeable odor. So we stayed off some distance looking at these long-horned, 'spotted buffalo' and wondering how the white people could eat them for food. It was a long while before we could eat cattle meat, so for a time it was thrown away and the hides traded for goods at the trading posts. However, conditions were such as to force it upon us. Our buffalo had perished and we were a meat-eating people, so we succumbed to the habit which at first seemed so distasteful to us. We had, in the beginning, found the smell of the white man quite obnoxious, but at the first contact with his cattle we held our noses.

During the spring and summer our diet was varied with an abundance of fruit and vegetable life. *Tinpsila*, a root plant which when peeled was white-meated and looked something like a turnip, grew all over the plains and low foothills. These were eaten raw, cooked in soup, or dried and stored for winter use. The women and children gathered them, tied them in bunches, and hung them on racks to dry. Then there was *pangi*, which white people call Jerusalem artichoke, or tuberous sunflower. This plant has a tuber that rather resembles a potato and that is pure white when peeled. It was eaten raw or boiled in soup and seasoned with salt.

Quite clever were the storage places of the gopher and other small animals that made caches of food for winter use. Our women knew the likely places of these caches, usually near a low bank, and went hunting for them with a long, sharp-pointed stick. They poked in the ground until they came to a soft spot in the earth, and there, ten or twelve inches under the loose soil and carefully covered with fine dry shredded grass, would be a nice lot of vegetables lying in a heap as fresh as when gathered. Some of these caches would be three feet in diameter and would hold as much as one person could carry. They were models of neatness, too. There would be no sign of the tops and roots, both being cut clean from the vegetable, whereas when the women stored they left both attached, tying the bunches together by the long string-like roots.

The wild onion was a good and much-liked plant, but was quite strong, so was used only for flavoring. And still another root plant, similar to the Irish potato but smaller, grew in the woods. These were boiled, salted, and eaten with the fat of the beaver's tail, for we had no butter. Corn had come to us in a beautiful legend, but we did not grow very much of it. On the plains it would have been taken by the buffalo, so it was planted only in little spaces close to a stream where the ground was moist and rich. It was left uncultivated to grow by itself while the camp moved on, and when the camp came back the corn was gathered. Wild rice grew in places, but was not abundant in the Lakota country. The arrow-leaf furnished a tuber which we called *siptola*. Wild parsley and mints were used to flavor meats and soups. Then we had *cannakpa*, a mushroom that grew from the roots, stumps, and branches of the box-elder and elm trees. I never knew of a poison variety of this plant and I never knew it to grow on any but the box-elder and the elm. A food that had an interesting history for us was the tall plant that grew in the swamps, commonly called the bulrush. The duck, who brought many good plants and roots to the tribe, told the Duck Dreamer medicine-man about it and named it *psa*. In the early spring and summer we welcomed this plant, which was pulled up by the roots, and the white part eaten like celery.

The most welcome season of the year was the fruit season when the chokecherry, grape, plum, currant, strawberry, and gooseberry all grew plentifully in the woods along the streams. We feasted on these delicious fruits, sharing them with the bears, raccoons, muskrats, and beavers. The coyote even ate the wild plums that ripened and fell to the ground. The women gathered these fruits and dried them, putting them in storage for winter food. One of the first fruits of the year to ripen was the *wazusteca*, or strawberry, while very soon after came the wild currant. A splendid fruit of which we were especially fond was the buffalo-berry which grew on a thorny bush. Away from the woods grew the sand cherries on little low shrubs. Around and over sand hills, and patches so barren that not a blade of grass grew, these bushes flourished, yielding a luscious fruit which we were very careful in gathering. We picked this fruit only against the wind, for if we stood with our body odors going toward the fruit its flavor was destroyed. This was not the case with other fruits which we gathered. The fruit of the wild rose, which turned red in the late fall after the first frost, made a delicious food. It was very sweet either raw or cooked.

We had no sugar, but notched the box-elder and caught its juice in our horn spoons, drinking it like water. We had a natural taste for sweets, so when brown sugar was first brought to us we accepted it greedily. Later on, when we became rationed, we saw white sugar for the first time and called it *canhanpiska*, or white tree juice. I never saw an Indian who had to acquire a taste for candy, and since it was never included in our rations we always found something to trade for some at the stores. Another fruit that gratified our fondness for sweets was the prickly pear which grew on the plains. In late August and September this brilliant red fruit became very sweet and juicy, luscious and tempting on the bright green cactus.

The Lakotas had little need for medicine or cures of any sort, though there were plants that were used for curative purposes only. The most common remedy used by everyone and kept in the tipi at all times was the juniper berry. These berries were eaten off the tree or made into a tea mixed with the leaves of the sagebrush. The sagebrush itself was often used as a tea without combining it with other plants. Wounds, cuts, and like ailments were most usual, and for their treatment a small, single-stalked plant which we call *icahpe-hu*, and which white people call purple cone plant, was used. The long, slender black root of this plant, which grew abundantly on the plain, was chewed and applied to the injured place. Though not pleasant to taste, it eased pain and almost magically cured cuts and bruises. On the plain also grew a small-leafed, low-growing plant which was valuable in treating horses when they became afflicted with distemper. To the Lakota it was *sunka hohpapi pejuta*, or 'dog medicine.' Since we called our horses *sunka wakan*, or 'holy dogs,' this medicine was 'medicine of the dog.' From the water came a medicine, a sort of sedge grass with long, jointed roots. The root was dried in the sun, then disjointed in sections of four or five inches, and eaten for nervousness. Though very bitter, this medicine was a favorite with the women, who often wore a piece of it around their necks. It was also carried by the Duck Dreamer medicine-man, for it was one of the secrets imparted to him by the duck.

The Lakotas were blessed with good health, but this was natural, observing as they did all the rules that appertain to health. And as far as I can remember there was no such thing as a contagious disease. But when our mode of life changed and we began to eat 'spotted buffalo' and learned to eat bread, sugar, candy, and canned goods, we then realized the meaning of disease, particularly so when students returning from school came weakened and undermined in health, many of them to die in young manhood and womanhood. I can remember grandfather, old when I was just a child, deploring the situation, saying there was a time in his memory when people did not speak of disease. It was not a subject of conversation, not being an experience in life of any importance.

The most serious cases calling for treatment were those of wounds, cuts, or broken limbs, occasioned by events of a vigorous life or from battle and in the winter time severe cases of freezing, but withal blood-poisoning never resulted. Father lost a toe by freezing, but it healed without any treatment whatever.

When a young man, Standing Bull, a cousin of my father, was shot through the body by soldiers; the bullet entered the middle chest just above the stomach and came out in the back. The wound never healed completely, but he lived thirty years or more without any interference with his activity. Standing Bull liked to decorate himself for dances by painting a black spot over the wounds on his back and chest and long red stripes simulating flowing blood down from the wounds and his mouth and nose. Apparently his strength was not impaired, for he rode, hunted and danced just as ever, though he lost his sense of smell and coughed continually.

Injured legs and limbs were never taken off and recuperative powers of the body were marvelous. Little Moon came home from a war-party so badly shot in the left leg that the limb swung loose from his body as he rode into the village on his horse. He jumped to the ground and hopped into his tipi without assistance. His leg from the knee down was almost separated from the upper part of the limb, but the portions were placed together and strapped to a piece of rawhide. No special attention was given him, and in a short time he was hobbling about and he continued to mend until completely recovered. While a little crippled, he was otherwise as good as ever.

But one disease troubled the Lakotas seriously and that was a skin disease similar to scrofula. It seldom attacked the body, but came around the neck. This disease we thought came from the gopher and we were taught as children to shun them. Whenever we saw a gopher moving up through the earth, we covered our heads with our arms and fled. The little pockets at the side of the gopher's neck we called quivers, and in them the animal often carried pieces of dry grass an inch or so in length and sharply pointed at one end. These arrows the gopher shot at anyone coming near, and if the person chanced to be hit he was sure to become afflicted with *wahinheya-o,* which means 'wounded by the gopher.'

Bloodletting was practiced occasionally and considered a cure for spring fever and for headache. A slight cut was made in the temple and a little blood allowed to run for headache. For lassitude in the spring the veins in the crook of the arm opposite the elbow were cut, from which a small amount of blood was allowed to flow. Sometimes those who took part in the Sun Dance lost a quantity of blood, but the injured always recovered their normal health without treatment of any sort. Recovery was quick, without shock to the nerves and without blood-poisoning. It is quite likely that the present hysteria for dance 'marathons' warrants more condemnation for senseless cruelty than ever did the Sun Dance.

Neither was the fast an injurious practice, and I have never known of a man being injured by going without food in either the vision fast or the Sun Dance. A three or four days' fast could not possibly injure a strong man and if the Sun Dancers and the vision fasters would have allowed themselves water they probably could have endured the fast much longer than they did. The only precaution the fasting one took was to partake sparingly of food for a day or two preceding the performance.

The three cardinal principles of health with the Lakota

were pure food, air and water, the fast, and the sweat bath. It was a usual custom for the men to go into the sweat-bath with the medicine-man, and when the body was saturated with perspiration to rub it briskly with wild sage. Women had their sweat-houses and did the same thing. But not only in steam and water did the Lakota bathe — he literally bathed in air. The pores of his skin were daily bathed in pure air and sunshine — nature's greatest cleansers. The scrupulous observance of health principles undoubtedly kept the blood stream pure, and helped in the miraculous cures of wounds, bruises, and other injuries.

In speaking of cleanliness, I feel it almost a duty to make a refutation concerning the Lakotas. I have read, much to my disgust, in supposedly correct histories by the white writers that they have witnessed the people of various tribes enjoying themselves eating offal of animals. I wish to say that such statements printed about the Lakotas amount to pure libel. The Lakotas were extremely choice about the selection of their food, and especially meat. They not only demanded fresh food, but fresh water and air. Purity in every sense of the word was observed by them as a people and that, I believe, accounts for the purity of their blood. The air that swept the Lakota plains was pure, and a breath of it went to the bottom of the lungs, filling them with energy, and never was this purity contaminated until thousands of rotting carcasses of buffalo filled it with stench. The habit of eating a small piece of raw liver or kidney occasionally aided digestion and was based upon scientific observation.

Teeth, strong and white, were a natural possession, many old people having the perfect teeth of youth. But hard portions of meat were not thrown away, leaving only soft portions easy to chew; neither was meat boiled to a mushy consistency. It was cooked through, but not well done. It was a custom for the woman of the household who had been breaking up the bones for marrow to place a pile of bone chips on a clean rawhide mat near the tipi door. Around this heap of bones, groups of children often sat chewing on the broken bits. This habit kept their teeth and gums in a healthy condition — it also whitened the teeth and kept us from needing a dentist to do for us what we should do for ourselves. The food we eat nowadays requires almost no chewing at all, and as a race we are becoming too indolent to chew.

The Lakotas were lean and thin, due to their outdoor and vigorous lives. Only the old people sat about much. Life was an active one and there was little time to sit around and grow fat and selfish from overeating.

The surroundings of a Lakota village were kept agreeably clean. Before the days of the plow we lived upon a carpet of green turf, and frequently a move was made so that the tipis could be placed on fresh green grass with clean surroundings. In truth, moving day with the Lakota women was largely a matter of house cleaning and welcomed by them as such.

The women took pride in making beautiful garments and in wearing them on ceremonial occasions. A white earth that not only bleached the skins, but acted as a disinfectant, destroying odors, was used to clean and whiten the skins. Garments, rugs, bags, and other articles of buckskin were sprinkled with the earth and rolled up and laid away for a while, or even buried in it for a time, then taken out and shaken in the wind. The Lakotas were very proud of feather-trimmed garments and ornaments, and these were kept clean and fluffy in the same manner. If white people had followed this custom, they would not have been bothered so much with vermin, of which nearly every white writer complains. The buckskins tanned by the Lakota women were easily washed in water and soap, the root of the yucca plant, made a white suds in which clothes, body, and hair were washed. All better garments and finery were carefully kept in rawhide boxes and bags of various sizes and shapes that were decorated in painted designs. Sweet grass or a few delicately scented leaves were put in with the garments to impart a pleasant odor.

The pride of both Lakota men and women was a splendid head of hair, and especial attention was given to its care as a mark of good breeding. The women were especially proud of long hair and brushed and smoothed their long braids to keep them from breaking. Frequent washings in *hupestola* kept the hair glossy. Every morning a married woman had her hair brushed and her face painted for the day by her husband. This was a mark of respect that every Lakota brave paid his spouse.

The tipi was never infested with rodents, the only species of rat being those that lived in the woods, but they never found shelter in the village. They were strictly woods rats and never purloined food nor chewed up clothing. With no rotting timbers about dwelling places, and no darkened closets and recesses, there was little space to harbor them; then, moving as the people did, taking their villages from one wind-swept place to another, there was scant encouragement for these pests to attach themselves had they been inclined.

Though we used furs continually, we were not beset with insect hordes which the world is now combating so furiously. Moths, bedbugs, fleas, cockroaches, and weevils came simultaneously with the white man, so they must have been co-travelers. Our furs wore until they went to pieces with usage and age, and air and sunshine was the only treatment we gave them. It was customary in summer to raise the sides of the tipi all around, making it look something like an umbrella. This was done every day. In winter the clear bright days looked like general washdays in the village, for everywhere there fluttered feathers and garments on the *hunpes*. Crisp cold air enlivens both furs and feathers and a bedraggled breath plume will come to life in a short time under the magic touch of air. Then again on some days the snow that fell was not damp, but fine and dry, and feathers were put out to 'breathe the snow.' Every woman possessed among her household utensils the *hunpes*, which were long poles forked at one end and sharp at the other, so that they could be thrust easily into the ground. The forked ends supported a cross-pole and upon this line the household garments were hung.

Worms infested the trees at a certain stage of decay and in summertime flies and mosquitos were common. Today the malarial mosquito is a dread foe of the white man, but if such a mosquito existed in the past, it was unknown in the Lakota region. When bathing in pools the boys often tested their nerves in a foolhardy way by allowing mosquitoes to alight on bare bodies and bite, trying to see who could stand the sting of these insects the longest. These contests were without ill effects, but had there been danger, such knowledge would have long before found its way into the lore of the tribe.

Standards of appearance, of course, mark every people, but one custom, to which the white man was addicted, and upon which the Lakota could not look with excuse and toleration, was that of wearing beards and mustaches. Upon this custom the smooth-faced Lakotas looked with abhorrence, considering it all that was slothful and untidy, not to say utterly unclean. The careless use of tobacco, which was sacred to the Lakotas, only added to their mystification and disgust.

VIRTUES

That most history concerning the Indian attributes to him few of the virtues, inspires me to mention some of them for him; for the Indian, like every other man, was possessed of both faults and virtues.

The Lakota was industrious, his whole life's necessity tending to make him so; and in the natural, unhampered state of living he was, from his very needs, active. With his body development, inactivity and slothfulness were inconsistent. The sweeping statement, 'the Indian is lazy,' is in itself an indictment against writer and believer of laziness and carelessness in the inability honestly and correctly to compare the social arrangements of the Indian and the European. It is true that the Indian found it all too easy to adopt the vices of the white man, thereby bringing on himself the contempt of his victor, and at the same time he has never been able to adopt the course of economic action which the white man chooses to call 'enterprise.'

Within the last few months a man of public affairs stated before a considerable congregation that the native American would now rule the continent if he were only possessed of European 'enterprise,' with an inference of a mental inequality because of this difference. Of course, no matter what might be the Indian's ethical attainment; no matter what his spiritual conception of his humane consideration of life or animal life, never could he arrive at that superior and elevated status of the white man's world called 'enterprising' until he had changed his whole idea of human evaluation. To the Lakota every other individual in the tribe was as important as himself and it was his duty to preserve the identity of the tribe. In opposition was the European concept of 'glory to the conqueror — every man for himself and the devil take the hindmost.' The natural environment of the Indian having been destroyed, his natural reactions have ceased to function, and the industrious régime of an open, free, and hardy life has disappeared under influences that are alien to all his traditions.

Maybe they are kind and altruistic motives that prompt the white brother to seek to remake the red man in his own likeness, and even some red men themselves hope they are 'progressive,' having donned the white collar for breechclout and outrageous boots for the comfortable and beautiful moccasins; nevertheless, Mother Nature and Wakan Tanka rule, and the last drop of Indian blood will disappear in white veins before man can remake his brother man.

The Lakota was brave. Over and over again father said to son, 'You must be brave,' or, 'You must grow into a brave man,' or further reminded his son that 'A coward is to be despised and my son must be honored for his bravery.' Such teachings as these were drilled into the minds of young children until they became an inseparable part of their consciousness. Lakota warriors thought that eating the heart of a turtle would make them brave and help them to stave off death when ill or wounded, so that they could go on struggling and fighting. The parts of a dismembered turtle moved and quivered after death, and the Lakota thought that by eating the heart he would die slowly like the turtle.

When I had reached young manhood the warpath for the Lakota was a thing of the past. The hunter had disappeared with the buffalo, the war scout had lost his calling, and the warrior had taken his shield to the mountain-top and given it back to the elements. The victory songs were sung only in the memory of the braves, and even they soon went unsung under a cruel and senseless ban of our overseers. So I could not prove that I was a brave and would fight to protect my home and land. I could only meet the challenge as life's events came to me. When I went East to Carlisle School, I thought I was going there to die; nevertheless, when father confronted me with the question, 'Son, do you want to go far away with these white people?,' I unhesitatingly said, 'Yes.' I could think of white people wanting little Lakota children for no other possible reason than to kill them, but I thought here is my chance to prove that I can die bravely. So I went east to show my father and my people that I was

brave and willing to die for them. I was destined, however, to return to my people, though half of my companions remained in the east in their graves. The changes
in environment, food, and clothing were too sudden and
drastic for even staunch bravery to overcome.

Strength is evidenced not only in action, but in restraint
as well, and in restraint the Lakota was schooled. Not
only was he a man of brawn, but a man of will. In the
distribution of food, this quality was uppermost. When
food was brought into the village, the sharing must be
equal for old, young, sick, disabled, and for those who
did not or could not hunt as well as those who hunted.
There must be no hungry individuals; so long as one had
food, all would have food. There was never the hungry
on one hand and the overfed on the other. All shared food
as long as there was any to share. If a hunter disobeyed
the custom of sharing and was caught making away with
game, he was severely punished by the Fox Lodge.

Killing for sport was unknown to the Lakota. His attitude toward living creatures would not permit him to
slaughter a species until it was exterminated. All had a
right to live and to increase.

SENSES

The conditions and surroundings of Lakota life were
such that much depended upon the senses of hearing, seeing, and smelling. This keenness not only protected and
aided in procuring food, but added much to the enjoyment
of life. The senses of the Lakota were, I believe, developed to a degree that almost matched those of the animals that he caught for food. On the other hand, with
senses alive and alert to the myriad forms of life about
him, his own life was full and interesting. Half-dormant
senses mean half living.

Training began with children, who were taught to sit
still and enjoy it. They were taught to use their organs

of smell, to look when apparently there was nothing to see, and to listen intently when all seemingly was quiet. A child who cannot sit still is a half-developed child.

Eyes that looked daily over great plains became able to distinguish objects either in the sky or on the earth for such distances as would afford protection to a large extent, providing fight or flight were necessary for safety. Reliance on eyesight for objects close at hand, or minute in size, came from training also. My mother, who was an excellent maker of moccasins, did not need to measure a foot for size. A glance was sufficient to cut and sew a perfect pair of moccasins.

The young boy was taught not to be afraid of the darkness, but to listen to sounds just as if he were on a scouting or hunting trip. All children were taught not to fear darkness, but to be cautious. Father used to tell me that whatever I feared in the dark was also afraid of me.

'A-ah!' spoken quickly and sharply was a word that brought everyone to attention at any time or place, night or day. Whenever this word was given by anyone, it meant that all, no matter with what they might be occupied, must stop and listen; and everyone did, even to children and dogs. There were so many things to listen for — the howling of wolves whose cries always portended a snowstorm, and the quack of geese flocks flying by night before coming wind and rain; then there was the scout to be on the lookout for, who usually gave his call when a mile or so from the village, and the return of the hunters whom the entire village willingly busied itself to receive. The hunter relied as much upon ears as upon eyes for the detection of both enemies and game, and by lying upon the ground and putting an ear close to earth could tell whether the herds he pursued were walking or running. Nothing was aimless or without purpose to these alert people — the rattle of a rolling pebble or stone, the whirr of bird wings disturbed at their rest, or the warning snort of a horse.

The nose was a feature by which a man was judged for strength, bravery, and fighting ability by the Lakotas. The ideal nose was rather large, not broad but a little turned down at the tip; while the possessor of a snub nose turned up at the tip, was not to be trusted much for strength, either physical or mental. It was said of the latter that he could not walk against the wind.

Most animals have a distinctive odor — the deer, wolf, badger and mountain-sheep all betraying their presence to the experienced hunter. For the Lakota the buffalo had only a slight smell, while the horse had a strong odor, carrying it in the small vestigial toe on the ankle. For this reason the Lakota sometimes scaled off a small bit of this portion of the horse and put it into his medicine-bag.

Human beings are not exempt from this characteristic, and there is history among the Lakota that one who has been lost or for some reason been away from his people for a long time, upon regaining contact with them finds them as strong and distinct in odor as any of the animal species. And, for that matter, sharing with us in this manner is all life — tree, plant, vegetable, and bird. Not only was the white man's cattle most obnoxious in smell at first contact, but the people themselves were quite distinctly and decidedly unpleasant in odor. To the actuality of things, however, there was doubtlessly added the suggestion of uncleanness in the European custom of wearing thick matted hair on face, chest, and arms. Adverse emotions were thereby excited in the minds of the clean-limbed, smooth-skinned Lakotas. It is a theory of mine, and perhaps quite worthless, that food has something to do with hair appearing upon the face. I can remember grandfather, noting that the young man and especially the returned students all plucked hair in order to be smooth-faced like the old men, saying that there had been a day when no man found it necessary to give attention to this toiletry. He himself was as smooth-faced as a young boy.

In speaking of the sense of feeling, I do not mean only the sense developed in finger-tips, which women used when testing the texture and thickness of the skins they tanned, but the inner feeling which is called judgment. The women seldom took a skin in their hands to test it for quality, but, as it was spread upon the ground, ran the tips of their fingers over the surface. Light as was their touch, any thick spot was found. The scouts who traveled largely by night felt the trail with their hands on the darkest of nights; they felt the proximity of water by the currents of air and in the same way discovered themselves close to a high bank by air currents upon their sensitive skin. But just as important were inner feelings that I believe came from natural experiences, but so fine that sources are hard to define and place. These senses were protective senses also and they served well until the general disruption of our society took place. Then it was that we lost much of our inner power, which vanished at the same time with our physical attainments.

There were some who had the power of *wakinyan* — the power of great intuition and the ability to foretell events. Walk Ahead, a friend of mine, came to me to warn me not to take the trip to England with Buffalo Bill for the second time. Walk Ahead had another name, Wakan Hunska, or Tall Holy, the name he had earned as all men of his time did. Wakan Hunska was a tall, handsome, middle-aged man, thoughtful of face. One would know him for a man of strength. I was loading my wagon and making all preparation to go to Rushville, there to take charge of the band of Sioux for the Buffalo Bill Wild West Show. Wakan Hunska came to me, and solemnly shaking hands, said: 'Nephew, I don't see why you are going with the others, and I ask you not to go. *You may know* why I say this to you.' That was all he said, and made no explanation. Though I had much respect for him, I continued on my journey to Rushville, where all was a bustle of excitement, boys and men packing their belongings, and families engaged in parting. While making ready, two young men, who had been with me on the previous trip to England, came and asked if I would consent to let them off and get two other men in their places. I inquired why the change of mind, since most young men were keen about the trip, and they explained that one night just before reaching Rushville they had made camp and gone to sleep in the tipi. About midnight, both had been suddenly awakened by a deafening crash and screams of terrified people. Rushing outside, they found the night was perfectly calm and still, and they then and there understood what was bound to happen to those who took the journey. I excused them both and took in their places two other young braves who were eager and delighted for the opportunity to go. For his eagerness one of these young fellows lost his life.

Just before we reached Chicago the disaster occurred. Our train, while stopped for a few moments, was crashed into by a swift-traveling one, and a passenger car filled with Lakota braves was torn to splinters, and human bodies crushed in among the wrecked steel and timbers. When I returned home, recovering from what seemed fatal injuries, Wakan Hunska came to see me. 'Nephew,' he said, 'what I saw came to pass!' But where are our prophets and wonder workers today? Where are those with the magic song of Last Horse?

I was in camp once with a band of Lakotas getting ready for a *woemahaha*, a time of fun and gayety. Feathers were flying, horses were being groomed, and everywhere an air of joyous expectancy for the Lakotas entered into their festivities. The sun shone brightly, but suddenly became clouded over and soon large drops of rain began to fall, accompanied with gusts of wind which threatened to put a stop to the merrymaking. Anxiety took the place of joy. But not for long, for Last Horse, the Thunder

Dreamer, came from his tipi, hair streaming down his back and wearing only breechclout and moccasins. He carried only his Thunder Dreamer rattle in his hand. Walking to the center of the circled village, he raised his face to the clouds. Instantly everyone stopped in utter and reverential silence, watching him intently. He raised his voice in the Thunder Dreamer's song. Last Horse sang, his spirit soared above earth among the clouds, and he talked to his brothers the Thunder warriors of the sky. Soon the clouds began to part, as with his hands Thunder Dreamer Last Horse motioned them to drift in opposite directions. The sun shone once more and the festivities went on.

Today the potency of song and ceremony are gone; our youth are scornful; our medicine-men can no longer cure. There is no solidarity of faith to work its magic wonders.

While the Lakota matched wits with his food-animals he also matched physical strength with them. Until the horse arrived, and even after, two strong muscular legs were for him weapons of defense, a means of locomotion and a mainstay when forced to flee from dangers too formidable for battle. Though he became a most expert horseman he was primarily a footman, preferring to hunt, travel, and fight on foot. He hunted the moose, buffalo, elk and bear with success, standing long marches with scant food and water. Running was an everyday accomplishment, and a rocky path yielded to him as the pavement to a city dweller.

In my time I remember when deep snow made horse-travel impossible. Important government messages were to be carried, and Sorrel Horse volunteered to deliver word that otherwise would have to wait, for he traveled paths inaccessible to a horse.

The warrior, too, relied upon his own strength to reach places a horse could not reach. He climbed mountain peaks to get the lay of the land, and climbing hilltops and

crags was easier on foot than urging a horse over steep
and rocky trails. Hiding from the enemy was also easier
on mountain-side or plain if not encumbered with a horse.
The Lakota trained himself to hide by trying to become
as artful as his wise mentors and guides — the animals,
birds, and insects. There were tricks and wiles employed
in trying to become a part of the landscape. Disguise,
stalking, and detouring were all a part of the skill to both
hunter and scout. To remain motionless for long hours at
a time was as much a part of this skill as was well-directed
activity. Aiding control of muscle and motion was mental
control, or fortitude, as in the case of the eagle-catchers
who were forced to remain silent and immovable in a
sitting posture for perhaps a half day or longer.

Around the life of the warrior there seems to linger the
glow of most romantic thought and feeling. To him is at-
tributed bravery, skill, power, fortitude, and last of all
there is bestowed upon him unstinted glory and praise —
and this is well. But one of the most important and in-
dispensable members of Lakota society, and so considered
by that society, was one not so often seen nor so much
talked about — the scout. He was the man who preferred,
usually, to work alone, either by night or day, and whose
outstanding quality was scrupulous honesty. He ran
terrible risks, was not a fighting man, yet knew how to
fight when he had to, and was withal the most relied-upon
man in the tribe. In him was reposed the utter dependence and faith of a people for their livelihood-food
and safety from danger. His training was rigorous, his
word was inviolable, and in calling he was bound to serve
his tribe. The dangers to which he was exposed demanded
of him the keenest development and alertness of senses,
particularly observation.

Every natural object was watched for any significance
attached to its motion or appearance. No movement was
too slight for the scout to ignore, and no sound too mean-

ingless to go unheeded. The soaring maneuvers of buzzard or eagle were to be looked into; the calls of the sand or prairie cranes were announcers of the always important weather changes; a croaking frog proclaimed a tiny marsh or a hidden spring, and at once more caution intuitively arose; while a distant smoke column might reveal the advance of an enemy party.

Even the black, horned ground-beetle commonly called tumble-bug, once common on the plain, the scout stopped and attentively watched, providing the scout were looking for buffalo. The two horns on the top of the insect's head were movable in all directions, but were invariably pointed and held toward the buffalo herd, probably attracted in that direction by stamping hoofs too distant for even sensitive human ears to detect. Sometimes we called these beetles ball-players for their habit of rolling up balls,[1] round and perfect as marbles, out of manure of horse or buffalo. A beetle, sometimes two of them, rolled these balls about here and there as if enjoying a game.

It was this ability to discern and observe small things that made the scout's work valuable. Minute details in appearance of objects, and changes in actions and manners of animals were noted; also the condition of man or animal trails he followed — bent twigs, trampled grass, sky and landmarks — things that would fade from a mind equipped with compass and stakes. Not wishing to leave a trail of his own to betray his travels, he built no monuments, however small; but his keen eye registered all, placing them in his memory, there to stay until needed, whether it be a week, a month, or a year.

All the while the scout traveled, he realized that while he watched he was being just as intently watched. Numerous eyes of the animal world were upon him, and human eyes, too. Often he turned quickly to scan the land-

[1] Professor Gilmore says these balls contained the eggs of the beetle until hatched.

scape back of him, and if he had reason to suspect the close presence of an enemy scout, he lay in wait for a long while until the enemy watcher was located.

In the village the scout was ever waited for. Even at night when the village slept, there was for him a welcoming fire and watcher. Placed conveniently in the village was the scout's tipi, in which fire burned at all times and some-one constantly kept watch.

When perhaps a mile or so away, the returning scout gave his call, and if it were night, the watcher, usually an old man, went about the village awakening the people, and at once the council members, and those who wished to join them, gathered at the scout's tipi. News was im-portant, and the scout or scouts came in running and panting. Straight into the tipi, where council members with the pipe were waiting, ran the scout, dropping upon one knee before the fire. One of the head councilmen lit the pipe and smoked, handing it to the other councilmen, and lastly to the scout, after which some of the older folks might choose to smoke. However, the pipe was not re-filled, but as soon as it had burned out it was handed back to the man who lit it. All the time the pipe was going round, there was no talking, only silent waiting, and not until the pipe had been laid aside did the scout speak. Still in a kneeling position, the scout told where the buf-falo were, how far away, their number, and whether they were moving fast or slow. The head councilors decided when the hunt should start, and as buffalo did not ordinarily travel at night, most hunts were begun in early morning. In case of war or the approach of an enemy, a start might be made at once, and all preparations were strictly for arming and departure. The idea that a 'war dance' must be held is erroneous, the fact being that there was no such thing as a war dance either before or after a battle, nor at any other time.

All the while the scout talked, he pointed only with the

thumb, a traditional custom of the scouts only. Doubly certain must the people be of the word of the man upon whom depended so much and in whom rested so much of their faith. 'By the thumb' the scout spoke even after he had smoked the sacred pipe. If a people were in need of food or in need of protection from enemy or calamity, a careless word might mean their destruction. For ages the index finger has been used, until its use has become automatic and without conscious thought, but to use the thumb one would first direct or concentrate his thought to his action.

In the Lakota society, service was its own reward without thought of promotion, more pay or added gewgaws for personal decoration — the thing that puts a price upon and stultifies true service. Many a true scout has remained one to his last day on earth. His reward was the utter faith of his people and their songs and dances of praise. Never was he humiliated, for cross-questioning, forced corroboration, and verification are undignified and the children of mistrust. So the scout has honored his name for all time and even today remains the symbol and criterion of truth and honesty.

LANGUAGE

In language and means of communication the Lakotas were not limited to the use of words, there being employed several other means of conducting human conversation. However, if the richness of a language is based upon the number of words in it then perhaps the Lakota language would not be considered a rich one, particularly so since it did not possess the great number of adjectives and descriptive words that are embodied in the English language. For instance, for the words pretty, fair, beautiful, attractive, handsome, exquisite, lovely, bewitching, and so on, the Lakota language has but one word, *hopa*. *Owotanla* means straight; *zunta* means honest; *waste* means good, and *wowicake* means truthful. There are no words for loyalty, fidelity, integrity, allegiance, and fealty, but the phrase, *owanyeke waste*, which means everything is good for the eye, covers all the words enumerated.

Lakota conversation was effectively carried on by the language of symbol and design, language of the blanket, the hand-sign language, smoke, and mime.

The language of symbol and design was employed in the decoration of the tipi, clothing, skin and rawhide articles, in flags, banners, tomtoms, shields, and in ceremonial and medicine articles. This symbolism was rich and was combined and interrelated with legends, stories, songs, and ceremonies. Some symbols, for instance, the sunflower and buffalo, carried the long story of the coming, by vision, of the Sun Dance to the Lakota people so long ago that the time is no longer known.

Among the Plains Indians the blanket was in almost daily use as a means of conversation, especially distant conversation, as across the village or from a hilltop. But in other innumerable ways was it used. The brave wore his gaily painted and decorated robe carelessly and gracefully as a part of his regalia; the housewife put her blanket on, fastened it at the neck, capelike, with two large rawhide buttons so that her arms would be left free for work, then belted it around the waist, making pockets in which to carry various things; the old men wrapped their blankets about their knees as they sat on the ground, so that they comfortably rocked back and forth, while the lover could scarcely go wooing without his robe. It was the custom for young men to wrap the blanket about the body and head, leaving only one eye visible, and many times the young woman could only guess who her bashful lover was. If the wooing progressed, it was etiquette for the young woman to allow the blanket to be thrown over her shoulders as they walked together.

When the scout came in sight of the village and had given his signal call, he announced the nearness of the enemy or the rapid coming of the buffalo herd by rolling up his blanket and throwing it up in the air several times quickly, catching it like a ball. This signal meant 'Hurry up.' The hunters and warriors got their weapons and prepared for either a hunt or a battle.

If the scout waved his blanket up and down slowly a number of times, then spread it on the ground and jumped over it, that notified the watchers that plenty of buffalo were near. The hunters then waited for the scout to tell them how many buffalo were near. If he walked, say, a quarter of a mile one way, then returned to the blanket and walked a similar distance in the opposite way and back to the blanket, that meant a very large herd was near. But if he walked just a few yards each way and back to his starting point, it meant that not so large a herd had been sighted. In either case preparations were made — the hunters filled quivers with arrows, knives were sharpened, wood was brought for fires, and general activity began.

The blanket was also used for summoning. It was waved in an outward motion from the body and back again. The man used the right arm and the woman the left arm.

Smoke was used for distant communication and was always watched for by those in the village if the hunters, warriors, or scouts were expected. This sort of signaling was usually begun when within a couple of days' travel from home. Smoke meant victory, and if a war-party returned without making smoke there would be no victory to relate.

Of the various modes of communication, perhaps the most dramatic were the mime dances of the braves — hunters, scouts, or warriors, and sometimes, the dances of the women in full male regalia. The Lakota was an

actor, in some cases exhibiting splendid ability in the performance of tribal presentation. A close observer of animal life, his imitations of walk, manner and behavior of
animals were most artful. Characteristics, through body
motion, facial expression, intricate steps, symbolical dress,
and even muscle contortion, were brought out with faithful portrayal. Animals like the turtle were imitated and
this would call, naturally, for muscle control and subtle
suggestion.

When the braves got together for their dances, it was a
time for much feasting and social intercourse. The warrior
danced his exploits; the scout his adventures; the hunter
his fortunes, and the medicine-man his experiences. Story-
telling, no matter how conducted, will always delight a
people. Furthermore, history was repeated and kept alive.

The Plains people have always been distinguished from
other native people by the beautiful and expressive use
of the hands in what is known as the 'sign language' — it
being the communicating gesture most often seen and
noted by the European. Other modes freely used by the
Lakota, being more confined to his close social life, would
naturally not come so readily to outside notice.

The hand language had its source in necessity. In a
large village, a half-mile or more across the circle, the
shouting of many people would be confusing. The de-
meanor of the Lakota was quiet and dignified, and he
indulged in no foolish mannerisms. If one man was watching another for an important message, he could not be
bothered with useless and senseless motions. The natural
use of this language is graceful and beautiful, and but a
part of the Indian's method of acting. Books have been put
on the market purporting to teach the hand language,
but it is as impossible to learn it in this manner as to learn
stage acting from photographs, or piano playing by
watching someone play. Most hand-language books are
useless except that they convey a fair knowledge of the

importance and scope of this method of speech. According to Professor Melvin Gilmore, Father Buechel at Pine Ridge has collected nearly thirty thousand Teton-Dakota words, and thinks that is not so poor.

CHAPTER IV

HOME AND FAMILY

THOUGH the leaders of the tribe selected the site for the village, the woman of the household selected the place and particular spot for her tipi. If she chose to place her tipi close to the banks of a stream, she did so; or if she preferred the protection of a wide outspreading tree, the choice was hers. The woman of the household had no 'lord and master' when it came to deciding where she and her children were to live. When a likely place had been found, the first things to be considered were whether the ground could be easily drained in case of rain and whether under the grass and leaves there were gopher and small animal holes, for such holes might be the homes of snakes as well as rodents.

The woman of the family, or mother, not only selected the site of her tipi, but she put it up herself. If the tipi were very large she might need assistance, but the help of a man would not be welcomed. There were always plenty of other women about — perhaps a grandmother or some other relative, and they were always willing helpers.

As soon as the tipi was put up, a fire was built. Clean grass was gathered and spread on the floor and over this rugs of rawhide were thrown. These rugs were stiff and kept their place on the floor, and with the hair side up were pleasant to live on. They were easily lifted up and not infrequently taken outside to be dusted and cleaned.

The furnishings of the tipi home were all the handiwork of the women. They tanned and sewed together the skins in the tipi, made floor rugs suitable in size, filled soft buckskin pillows with cottonwood floss and finished the blankets spread over the tripod bed. Painted bags and clothes containers decorated with brightly hued quillwork hung against the brown walls of the Indian woman's home. Everything was from her industrious hand and there were no overseers of the arrangement. No home, whatever the material used in construction, is cleaner, more sanitary or livable-in than a freshly erected tipi. And no home, dimly lit with shaded lamps, is more cheerful than a tipi home lit by the flickering glow of a cedar fire.

The home was the center of Lakota society — the place where good social members were formed and the place whence flowed the strength of the tribe. Here it was that offspring learned duty to parents, to lodge, to band, to tribe, and to self.

In the home there came into being the faith and simplicity that marked the native people. There took root their virtues and cultural attributes. Forces, sensed but not seen, called good, went into the deep consciousness of these young minds, planted there by the Indian mother who taught her boy honesty, fearlessness, and duty, and her girl industry, loyalty, and fideity. Into the character of babes and children mother-strength left the essence of strong manhood and womanhood. Every son was taught to be generous to the point of sacrifice, truthful no matter what the cost, and brave to the point of death. These impulses — generosity, truthfulness, and bravery — may be dressed and polished in schools and universities, but their fundamental nature is never touched.

After childhood days, mothers still could not forsake the part of guide and teacher — for youth, as well as childhood, must be directed, and there was no substitute. So Lakota mothers taught youth how to worship and pray, how to know mercy and kindness, and how to seek right and justice.

In the social life of the Lakota woman, neglect of children was unknown and there was no such thing as an 'orphan.' If a child unfortunately lost its own mother, and father too, perhaps, it was still assured care, and received, in some cases, more than it would ordinarily have had. Special attention was given to children because they were parentless and I have seen braves give them fine horses just to show that they were willing to share the responsibilities of the children's care. When bands were visiting, it was the courteous custom of the visiting band to make presents to the *wablenica* (parentless child) and the Sun Dances were always occasions to give generously to them. Kindness and ceremony marked much of the attention showered upon little children. There was no institution of charity, the word charity not even existing in the Lakota language. 'Cold charity' was displaced by *wablenica*, which is simple kindness and warm humanness.

Woman's work, generally, was to cook for the family, keep the tipi in order, and sew the clothing of the household members. The good wife never allowed one of the family to run low in clothing. There were garments to be made, and moccasins, robes and blankets, and sometimes gloves, caps and scarfs. Buttonholes were never made, probably never thought of, but very pretty buttons were fashioned of rawhide and either painted or covered with porcupine quills. Sinew was split for thread, coarse strands for heavy work and medium fine or very fine strands for decorative work, then folded into little bundles and placed in a sewing kit. When the men came home from the hunt there were skins to be cleaned and tanned. New tipis were made and old ones, for the sake of frugality, made into clothing for children. From rawhide were made moccasin soles, bags and trunks for holding ceremonial garments, headdresses, and other articles to be kept in neatness and order.

Then there were washdays and house-cleaning days for which there were supplies of *haipajaja* or soap and suds made from *hupestula*, the root of the yucca plant; wood ashes for bleaching and removing hair from skins; and, for an extra touch of cleanness and whiteness, *makasan,* a creamy white earth that had been pounded into a fine powder. Sometimes this powder was stirred up with water, making a mixture like starch, in which a white buckskin garment was immersed, then hung up to dry, after which the powder was shaken out. All of these supplies the women got for themselves, as well as supplying the family needs for fruits and vegetables. The demands on the housewife were numerous, for she dug in the earth for her paints, made paint-brushes from the inner spongy portion of a socket bone, fashioned and decorated cradles for her children, made the *travois,* and, in days before the horse, broke the dogs that drew them. In addition, Lakota courtesy demanded that the housewife look after the needs of visitors who arrived with torn and rent clothing and worn moccasins.

The good wife always kept plenty of food stored and cooked so that it could be served at any moment. The thought was to not only meet the food requirements of the family, but to be able to serve any one who came to the tipi, strangers or relatives, children who came in from other tipis, or any old people whom the children might bring in. If the husband brought home friends unexpectedly, he could be sure that his wife would receive them hospitably without any request from him.

Many of the courtesies of Indian social life included the preparation and serving of food, and among the Lakota it was a custom of good will just as it is with the white man. When a white friend wishes to extend a courtesy it is usually by asking one to dine. A feast in honor of my father was sometimes given in this way: Some of my mother's relations would invite her over to their tipi. At once the women would begin preparing food for a number of people. When all was ready, they would tell mother to ask father to come to the feast and bring with him some of his friends. Father would gladly accept the invitation and would bring with him, as a rule, some of the old men of the village and there would be singing, eating, story-telling, and a general good time. The meal which the relations offered to father was their good will expressed in their most generous way. All his relations wished him to remain on good terms with his people, so if father could ask a number of old men to share good food with him, his chances for remaining popular would be better. The feast tended to strengthen the ties between father and the head-men of his band and also between him and his wife's relations.

Visiting bands were often received with a feast of welcome. As soon as the visitors stopped and began putting up their tipis, our women and girls built fires and cooked great quantities of food. They then carried the food over and spread the feast for the visitors, waiting upon them with every attention. The visitors ate and enjoyed themselves, but were never allowed to help in clearing away the remains of the feast. This was done by the women after the visitors had departed.

Sometimes a lone stranger came to our village for a visit. He was usually taken from tipi to tipi for a round of feasting and gossip, for the visitor was sure to have news to tell and he was encouraged to tell of his travels and of the people of his band. When the round of visits began, the stranger was given a long stick, pointed at one end, which he carried with him from tipi to tipi, each family putting on his stick some dried meat until it was full and sometimes more. This meat was to supply the visitor with food on his return or continued journey.

I well remember how much we all liked the brown lump sugar that was first brought to us by white traders. It was not so plentiful and anyone having a bag of it was considered fortunate. Scarce as it was, I went to mother's buckskin bag in which she kept it stored and gave a lump of this precious stuff to everyone who came to our tipi. Mother never once forbade me to take her sugar.

The serving of a family meal was a quiet and orderly affair. Mother placed the food in front of her while we children all sat quietly about, neither commenting on the food nor asking for any favors. Father, if at home, sat in his accustomed place at the side of the tipi. He, too, remained perfectly quiet and respectful, accepting the food that mother offered to him without comment. The serving was done on wooden plates, the soup being passed in horn spoons of different sizes, some of them holding as much as a large bowl. The food was portioned to each one of us as mother saw fit, her judgment being unquestioned, for we never asked for more. Before serving us, however, mother put a small portion of the food in the fire as a blessing for the meal.

Grandmother, next to mother, was the most important person in the home. Her place, in fact, could be filled by no one else. It has been told and written that old people among the Indians were sacrificed when they became useless. If this is the case with other tribes, I do not know of it, but I do know that it was never done among the Lakotas. Most old people were revered for their knowledge, and were never considered worthless members to be got rid of. Parental devotion was very strong and the old were objects of care and devotion to the last. They were never given cause to feel useless and unwanted, for there were duties performed only by the old and because it was a rigidly-kept custom for the young to treat their elders with respect. Grandmother filled a place that mother did not fill, and the older she got the more, it seemed, we children depended upon her for attention. I can never forget one of my grandmothers, mother's mother, and what wonderful care she took of me. As a story-teller, she was a delight not only to me but to other little folks of the village. Her sense of humor was keen and she laughed as readily as we.

Another undisputed place which grandmother occupied was that of medicine-woman in the family. She prepared all food for the sick and looked after them; she kept the bags of herbs and made the teas which she gave us to drink, and when we children got hurt she bound our wounds or bruises and dried our childish tears.

Then grandmother, with the help of grandfather, was our teacher. When grandfather sang his songs, she encouraged us to dance to them. She beat time with him and showed us how to step with his tunes. Seldom did she go walking in the woods or on the plains without taking us with her, and these hours were profitable ones in knowledge, for scarcely a word or an act but was filled with the wisdom of life.

Mother's and grandmother's tipis were quite close together and they saw a good deal of each other, working together and visiting back and forth. The men folks of the family were, for the most part, away from home during the day on hunting or scouting parties. But whenever father was at home and he chanced to walk out of the tipi, he covered his face with his blanket until he was sure that he would not see his mother-in-law. In this way he showed his respect for her, and had he not observed this courtesy she would have had every right to be affronted. She, too, avoided him, and if by chance they met, she hid her face. Had she allowed him to look upon her, it would have been an unforgivable breach of manners. In order to show her great respect for my father, grandmother often cooked some meat in her tipi, and calling my mother over would give her the meat saying, 'Take this to my son-in-law.' In this way she let him know that she thought highly of him.

The men, when at home, were shown a good deal of attention by the women. This was but natural, as it was the hunters, scouts and warriors who bore the greatest dangers, and consequently were the recipients of much care and consideration. Young warriors bearing for the first time the hardships of life were specially considered by the women. I remember one winter a party of young hunters returned home exhausted and near starvation, having seen no game. On reaching the village, they entered the first tipi they came to, which happened to be that of an old woman. Without a word, these young men began putting the meat, which was strung on a pole inside the tipi, on the fire to cook, and feeding themselves until it was gone. All the while the old woman ran about crying, not with anger or sorrow, but with joy for the return of the young men, and with gladness for the supply of meat that she was able to furnish. Had a white man witnessed this occurrence, it would probably have been interpreted in a manner far from correct.

Women and children were the objects of care among the Lakotas and as far as their environment permitted they lived sheltered lives. Life was softened by a great equality. All the tasks of women — cooking, caring for children, tanning and sewing — were considered dignified and worth while. No work was looked upon as menial, consequently there were no menial workers. Industry filled the life of every Lakota woman.

Whether, from the Caucasian point of view, the position of the Indian woman in the tribe was a hard one is not the question. People are fitted for life as are trees, plants, birds and animals. If a Lakota woman were given the choice to continue living the free hardy life of her ancestors or to become transported into the toil of mill, factory, or laundry, it would be only good sense on her part to prefer the still pure air of the plains and the cheery fire of a comfortable brown tipi beside a rippling stream.

Busy as Lakota women were with things of service, they still had time for *wokanpan owa*, or painting. The word 'painting' covered all the decorative work done by women of whatever sort. Every woman was a decorator, some of them becoming *wayupika* or skilled. Geometric designs were especially liked by the Lakota woman, and it is this characteristic that stamps the art work of her tribe, there being a class of design now known as Sioux design. Many books have been written telling of the significance back of these designs, but I have seen grandmother sitting on the ground, and, while laughing and talking, draw designs upon the earth with merely the idea of making something pretty. Bags, purses, trunks, warbonnet and awl cases, garments and robes were decorated in beautiful designs and colors. The women, however, never decorated the outside of the tipi nor the shields and war implements of the men. This was left to the men, who seldom used geometric designs, but drew figures of men and animals and objects of nature by which they told of historic events such as travels, battles, captures, and various other exploits.

Today the only means whereby native designs might be kept alive is through the use of the white man's beads. The Lakota woman no longer pounds out earth paints, porcupine quills are scarcer, and the process of dyeing and sewing them seems tedious to the younger generation, and the plants from which once were brewed lovely colors grow no more.

In home-building, man had his share with woman. Though the only things he provided for the tipi were the poles and the fresh skins, yet a man's family was his first thought. He had no word in the arrangement of his wife's tipi nor its management, yet there were his strongest ties. Every man's faithfulness to his band was strong, but of all human ties that of family was the strongest.

The headmen who led the *ikalaka aya*, or moving village, selected the site for the new settlement and decided whether it should be arranged in a circle, as it usually was if on the plain, or whether the tipis should be scattered through the woods or lined up along the banks of a stream. If the village was a large one, or if several bands had come together for ceremonial purposes, the laying-out was

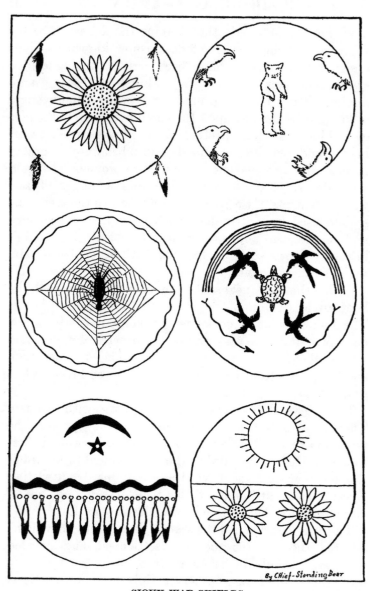

SIOUX WAR SHIELDS

turned over to the Fox Lodge. These lodge men arranged
the placing of the tipis and marked the site of each one
with a stick. No matter how great the number of people
to be thus provided for, there was never any confusion.
All was quiet order, without show of authority or loud-
given commands. If it chanced to be winter time, each
man cleared the ground of snow before his wife set up the
tipi, but he had nothing to do with the packing and un-
packing of household goods. Work in the Lakota home
was quite clearly defined for man and woman, and with
justice to both.

A good husband was first of all a good provider and
that is one reason why he was much away from home.
The haunts of animals had to be learned, herds located, and
sometimes followed. Oftentimes prairie fires took hunters
far from home in search of new grass areas, and again
drying streams or springs shifted the location of animals.
Rainfall, changing seasons, and many other circumstances
kept the hunter on the march for food. A man who would
hang around the village trying to do the work of women
was not considered manly.

There was a class, however, that associated with both
men and women. They were the *winktes*, the hermaphro-
dites. These people, it seems, would prefer to be classed
as entirely men or women, but were unable to do so.
Usually they were betrayed by their actions, the voice, or
the way in which they wore their blankets. Everyone accepted the *winktes* with kindness and allowed them to
choose their own work, be it either man's or woman's,
and one of the bravest men I ever knew was a *winkte*. They
were scarce, however, and in my life I have not known
more than half a dozen.

No one was ridiculed by the Lakotas for being unfortunate, but they did not hesitate to laugh at and scorn a
lazy man — a man who was able-bodied in every way,
yet who tried to lie around the village and have the women

wait upon him. Few Lakotas can bear to be ridiculed, and when the villagers began to call such a man a *winkte* he usually left the village and got to work.

The making of garments, even to moccasins, was woman's work, but moccasin-making was also part of the warrior's training. Men away from home for a length of time might find themselves in need of footwear, so every well-trained boy knew how to cut and sew moccasins. The only other sewing done by the men was the making of war-bonnets, though all decoration was left for the women.

The first thing a dutiful husband did in the morning, after breakfasting, was to arrange his wife's hair and to paint her face. The brush was the tail of the porcupine attached to a decorated handle, and in place of a comb a hair parter was used — a slender pointed stick, also with a decorated handle. The husband parted his wife's hair, then carefully brushed and plaited it into two braids which were tied at the ends with strings of painted buckskin. These hair-strings were sometimes works of art, being wrapped with brightly colored porcupine quills and either tipped with ball tassels of porcupine quills or fluffs of eagle feathers. Bead hair-strings were later made, and they, too, are very pretty. When the hairdressing was finished, the part in the hair was sometimes marked with a stripe of red or yellow paint. Next, the husband applied red paint to his wife's face, sometimes just to the cheeks, sometimes covering the entire face. If the woman was to be exposed to the wind and sun all day, she usually had her face covered with a protective coat of paint mixed with grease. It was 'style' for the Lakota woman to use much red paint, but the custom was very likely a necessary and comfortable one before it became a mere matter of style. Many Lakota women had skins quite fine in texture and in childhood were light in color. Such skins, of course, burned easily in the hot wind and sun, consequently children were often painted with the red paint and grease, both boys and girls, the mother performing this duty and not the father. The native custom of painting and the choice of color probably led the white man to name him *redskin* or *redman*, which description has become actual truth in the minds of some people.

If the man of the family was to be home for several days, he busied himself in many ways, lightening the work of the woman. He cut down trees for the ponies and for wood, made and repaired her saddles, cut up meat conveniently for drying, and, when there was nothing else to be done, gladly amused the baby of the family. A man who unduly scolded his wife or who beat her or his children was not considered a good man. A man who would inflict punishment upon the women and children was considered a weakling and a coward. Whenever it was said about a man, 'He ought not to have a wife,' that was expressing strong disapproval of him.

Many times a couple went strolling and then it was his duty to precede her. For a couple to walk about arm in arm was looked upon as silly and ill-bred, and the man who walked about with his wife in front of him was jeered at. In walking ahead, the man took the brunt of danger and assumed the position of protector for the woman and children who came behind. The young men walked ahead of the old people for the same reason. The Indian man has been much and unjustly derided for his seeming attitude of unkindness toward his womenfolk. Everyone reads that the Indian 'lazily rides his horse while his wife trudges behind carrying the burdens,' or that 'the buck rides ahead of the squaw.' Aside from the fact that both 'buck' and 'squaw' are inappropriate and inelegant terms, the idea of injustice and laziness is expressed with all the contempt that so naturally springs from ignorance. All customs of people are decided by necessity, which is not only the 'mother of invention,' but the mother of behavior as well. Now, in the days of the Lakota the people did not travel broad roads, kept and patrolled, but trails over steep hills, through winding canyons and deep woods. Many times these trails followed by the Lakotas had been made by the feet of countless animals which might at any time take a notion to dispute the way with the traveler. There was danger of surprising a feeding mountain lion or bear that would resent being intruded upon, or of meeting elk, wolves, buffalo, and even smaller animals like the badger, which might refuse to allow man to go peacefully on his way. But there are no better trail-makers than these animals, and all of them, large and small, travel the best way up and down hills and moun-tains steeps, finding the easiest grades and the smoothest, surest ground. If the enemy proved to be a human one, the man in the lead would be the first exposed to danger. After white men came among the Lakotas, their fear for a time was increased and they considered the dangers to life multiplied until certain adjustments took place. But the custom of Indian men walking or riding ahead of wo-men, children and the aged, unhampered with household goods, is clearly prompted by the best motive in the world.

Father was in the habit of hunting occasionally just to give a feast for the wise men. These wise men were the elders who had come close to the Great Mystery and who had much knowledge. Most of these wise men had sacri-ficed the body to the Great Mystery and bore the marks on their arms. A friend helped in the ceremony of sacri-fice by picking small holes close together on the arm, usually from shoulder to elbow, or a little below, with an awl or other sharp implement. Blood flowed freely, and when the arm had healed it was scarred for life. But through this sacrifice and through meditation and prayer, wisdom was gained for which the wise man was greatly venerated. The wise men were always a part of every council, but, unlike the braves and the chiefs, seldom spoke at length. Their powers were felt in prayer, and blessings they gave were always effective. They blessed the generous and the feast-givers by saying, 'Some day, grandson, you will wear this white cap of mine' (meaning his head of white hair), and, 'You will wear this buckskin shirt of mine' (meaning the wrinkled skin of his body). This blessing was also a prophecy that long life and wisdom would come to the prudent and thoughtful young man. A Lakota proverb says, 'The man who gives much will live a long life, while the selfish man will live a short one.'

Many times the braves came to see father for just a social time, but whatever the occasion it was mother's duty to pass food about. No good wife would wait to be told by her husband to prepare food, but as soon as guests arrived she would at once begin to serve. If the company were many, the wife might call in some of her women relations to help. As soon as the food was served, the women left the tipi and there was no conversation between the visitors and the women of the household. Also when councilors gathered in a tipi, the women either left or sat very quietly.

In family visiting, which was common, conversation was more free, though the men always avoided talking to sisters or to female cousins. Customs of this sort are so old that we know nothing of their origin, but one explanation is that they were adopted long ago when the family arrangement was different from what it is now. These manners are disappearing except among the very old people, the young assuming the free and easy manners of the white people.

But men of olden times were brave and the plan of Lakota society was to fit them to be protectors of the home. All about the Indian, fidelity and loyalty were expressed by lesser creatures and he was a true student of nature. Inspiration came to him from the source of all things.

COURTSHIP

The romance of courtship seems to touch the interest of all people, and Indian courtship has been told in song, story, and picture. But Lakota courtship according to old tribal customs was not done under the prying eyes of strangers.

The rules of courtship were definite ones, just as were all rules regarding Lakota conduct; but before the time for courting arrived both young men and young women learned from their parents that they must have certain knowledge and must observe certain conventions. When the playtime of childhood was over, young men and women began to be more thoughtful and dignified in their manners. There were no meetings at any and all times of the day in the village, the young woman staying close to her tipi and the young man busying himself with the hunters or warriors. Whenever a young woman went out she was accompanied by an older woman — a sister, aunt, or mother — for it would have seemed very improper for her to wander about alone. No young woman in doing so would have been unsafe, but she would have felt awkward and conspicuous in breaking a rule of conduct.

Good courting manners in Lakota youth forbade his calling at a young woman's tipi, whistling for her, or winking at her; and no presents were given until an engagement took place. The engagement, however, was a secret between lovers and no public announcement was ever made of a betrothal. If a young man should present himself at the tipi of a young woman he would get no welcome and would not be invited in. If his visit was intended for her brother or father it would be so understood and he would not speak to the young woman.

Dignity and reticence in speech and manner were most admired in Lakota women and one who talked and laughed loudly was considered extremely rude. Boldness in either sex was a rare and disliked thing, but now and then a young person would not be curbed and 'went bad,' as it is commonly expressed. It was not an educational principle to teach the young to 'Speak up,' 'Hold your head up and talk,' or, 'Make yourself heard,' but rather, 'Be quiet,' and, 'Be slow of speech.' Restraint was taught and practiced, and compared with the assertive youth of today — the 'bright' and the 'smart' — Indian youth would be considered backward. But there was a time when Indian youth was taught to go forward and that was in the time of danger.

Most young men in their first attempt to talk socially with a young woman were so shy they could scarcely speak, but a low, subdued voice being mannerly, the shy young man would not find it hard to speak quietly. At times the young man was not able to speak at all and then the meeting would be a silent one; and, besides being silent, some of these meetings were amusing. It is courting history that when a young man dresses up, paints his face, and wraps his best blanket about him, covering all but his eyes, and starts out to 'put his best foot forward,' as the white man says, something is almost sure to happen. When the young beau comes face to face with the charming girl he has been longing to see, he often forgets his lines. It is not the part of the girl to start the conversation but to listen — and sometimes there is nothing to listen to.

Once a young man caused us much laughter by forgetting everything he would have liked to say to his lady love. Meeting the young woman, he stood beside her for a long time in a panic of restlessness, scraping his feet, fumbling with his neck, adjusting his vocal cords and tearing his blanket. The girl stood quietly and poised, waiting for her suitor to regain his composure and begin the conversation, but this seeming hopeless, she finally said, 'Well, why don't you say something?' Quickly, without thought, he answered, 'If you will only stand still a moment I have something to say.' At this the girl laughed and the young man was so overcome with embarrassment that he walked away without another word.

It takes more than a laugh, however, to discourage a hardy young man, and he is sure to go courting again. Sometimes the bashful one goes to a sympathetic friend or relative for coaching, and sometimes he rehearses his speech like an actor. But who cares after he has won!

It was the custom for Lakota girls to visit from tipi to tipi or stroll about the village in the evening with a companion — either another girl or an older woman. Each young brave then awaited his chance to speak to the chosen one by placing himself conveniently in her path. When it came time for him to address the girl of his choice for a few moments, the companion stepped aside. The girl listened sometimes without reply, and she might do this several times without discourtesy to the young man. As long as she listened, the suitor could be satisfied. If the young woman happened to be popular, there might be a number of young men all wrapped in their blankets waiting to speak with her also. So long conversations were naturally not favored by the waiting ones, and the young man speaking showed both taste and wisdom by not tarrying too long at the side of the young lady. Six, eight, or even a dozen young men might be in the waiting group, each taking his place in line upon arrival and all watching to see that no one overstayed his time. If a young man became so interested that he forgot the courtesy due the others, he would receive a gentle warning, a clod or a pebble thrown at his back, but the second warning would not be so polite.

One evening I stood talking to Grace Spotted Tail, the daughter of Chief Spotted Tail and a very popular young woman. I had walked home from church with Grace and her mother, who walked a few steps behind us. When we reached the tipi door, the mother went inside while Grace and I stood conversing. There were seven or eight other young men waiting to speak to Grace, so after a few moments I turned to go. But I had been away to Carlisle School for a long time, and Grace had much to say to me, so we continued our talk. Soon I felt a brush against the back of my blanket and I knew it was time to depart. But Grace doubtless wanted to have some fun with me, so she wrapped her hand tightly in my watch-chain, as I was wearing civilian clothes under my blanket. Thus I was detained longer. But in a few moments I was forcibly reminded of Lakota courtesy by a decided kick on the back part of my blanket that caused me to sway slightly forward. Here was a case where only the young lady could keep the others from piling on me, which she did.

Of course, when a girl has once and for all decided upon her sweetheart, there is nothing for the other suitors to do but to seek other fields. Then it happens occasionally that a girl does not wish to be courted, but desires to be let alone. If so, she refuses to stop, and walks into some friend's tipi or back to her own where she is safe from intrusion. But most young women are proud of their popularity and maybe out of those who wait for her hidden in their blankets she hopes there will be a certain one.

Every morning the young women accompany the older women to the spring or stream to carry water to the tipi. As they walk the paths back and forth the young lover may meet the girl of his choice for a few moments' conversation. Just a few words he spoke while she silently listened, then the lover passed on.

Most courtships had their beginning at the big social and ceremonial gatherings when the various bands were together. Each band's village was decorated for the celebration and there was much display of finery and parading in regalia. Braves with flying feathers dashed here and there on horses groomed and shiny, and with woven wreathes of sweetgrass about their necks. Groups of singers from each band marched about, entertaining and singing praise songs. Every band had braves they wished to honor and tell other bands about, so the older men sang songs of praise for them, and the braves danced their adventures or mimed them. At night the fire burned in the dance circle and around were grouped the old and wise in the dignity, and the brave and the beautiful in the glory of fine robing. There was feasting and preparations for feasting. The scene was a gay and lively one, and the braves and maidens saw one another at their best.

The young women, who came accompanied by their mothers or other women companions, were dressed in white buckskin dresses, moccasins and leggins which were sometimes decorated in designs embroidered with dyed porcupine quills. The well-dressed women were much admired generally, and felt pride in displaying pretty clothing and tasty finery. From the style standards of my youthful days the elk-teeth-trimmed dress was the most splendid and expensive and the woman who possessed one was considered fortunate, but the quill-worked and painted dresses were far more artistic. The intricate patterns of design, the color arrangement, and the sewing with sinew of these tiny, pin-pointed quills called for genuine skill and handcraft. Tied to long, black braids, which were the pride of Lakota girls, were worn lovely hair ornaments of dyed buckskin and dyed fluffy feathers of the eagle. On the arm, perhaps, was carried a robe or wrap of softly tanned buckskin banded with quill work or painted designs.

The manner of the women as they sat at these ceremonials was dignified and reserved, though there was a great deal of friendliness in the meetings between friends and relatives. There was little talking between men and women, for the women and the girls sat on one side of the dancing space and the men and boys on the other. Young people did not come together for conversation or for bantering and joking, but there was plenty of appraisal and as soon as the ceremony was over there were numerous meetings.

On the inner side of the circle the people sat while at the outer edge were those on horses — the braves and maidens. All the young men were splendid horsemen, but not alone, for the young women enjoyed the sport of displaying fine horsemanship, too, and it was a dignified means of permitting the young people to parade before one another. The Lakotans had a great fondness for *sunke wakan*, or 'holy dog,' as the horse was called, and a lively, fine-stepping animal was a brave's delight. Upon their horses the men lavished much care, grooming and decorating them with fine blankets, bridles trimmed with quill work, eagle feathers, and sweetgrass wreaths. The trappings of the young women's mounts were especially gorgeous and examples of fine skill in workmanship. The blankets of soft tanned skins were fringed and hung to the horse's knees; belly-bands were wide belts braided in design and porcupine-quill work in lovely colors bordered both sides. The tail of the horse was braided or looped up and tied with red or yellow buckskin ribbons, and eagle plumes fluttered with every movement. The wreaths of sweetgrass perfumed the air. So whenever a girl rode into the firelight of the ceremonial, dressed all in white and riding a splendidly decorated horse, she was an attractive sight worthy of anyone's glance. She would sit on her horse with dignity, her eyes not roving about, and never by the slightest token showing her feeling of preference if she had any.

When the ceremonial came to a close for the afternoon or evening, the girls started home with their mothers or guardians. A young man who had made choice of a girl to whom he wished to pay court followed, and rode or walked close to her, so that she would know he wished to speak. The girl would leave her mother's side for a short distance and listen respectfully to his words. She very seldom made reply, and he expected none, so when the short conversation was over the girl returned to her mother and the man went his way.

In the courting conversation the young man would not speak of his wealth or discuss himself in any way, no matter what might be his claim to prominence. Neither did he make promises. Bragging was a social sin, and if a Lakota man began to tell a young woman what he was going to do and what he could do, she would mistrust him at once. Instead, he told the young woman how much he admired her family, and he might tell her that he would like to become a member of it; also, that he was able and would be willing to help them in time of need. The young man knew that most of all he must prove himself a good provider and hunter to the girl and her family, so he would go hunting and bring a buffalo to her father or brother. This was a more satisfactory, delicate way of showing that he was a capable hunter than talking about it. Works would count with the father or brother, but mere talk would not go far. Also the young man knew that his qualities would be discussed in the presence of the girl and of course he wished to be regarded in a favorable light. The more he showed his industry and worth, the higher he stood in the estimation of the family of which he sought to be a member.

Sometimes a man, when courting, feels that the young woman would like a more material demonstration of his sincerity before consenting to marriage with him. That being the case, the man arranges to present the girl's family with a number of horses. If he does not himself possess many, his relatives will gladly provide them, and the animals, five or six in number, or more, if the band can afford them, are driven to the girl's home. An old man, member of the suitor's band, performs the courtesy of driving and presenting the horses to the girl's family, and then retires. The family in council, including the girl, will accept the gift, providing the young man is also acceptable, that is, not acceptable only from the standpoint of wealth in his band, but regarded as a creditable addition to the family and looked upon by the girl with sufficient favor. If the young man is considered favorably, presents are at once dispatched to his band — things of value, such as beautiful robes, headdresses, or horses. This is not obligatory, and not demanded by the suitor's band, but it is an expression of hospitality on the part of the girl's band to send a messenger to the young man carrying tokens of good will. If, however, he is not accepted, the horses are turned loose to wander home. But usually this demonstration of sincerity on the part of the young man wins the girl.

While it was expected that a young man be a good provider before he asked a young lady to marry him, it was also expected that she be a capable housewife before she accepted the duties of marriagehood. The girl's training in duties that relate to domestic life began while still a child and continued until she knew how to tan skins, cook, and make sinew thread, garments, tipis, and moccasins. She was then entitled to carry about with her a pretty decorated bag which contained awls, sinew, and other implements of sewing. Some of these bags were highly decorated and were a sort of diploma showing certain accomplishment, and no young woman who had not rightfully earned it was allowed to possess one. The Lakota girl who did possess one proudly exhibited it as a guarantee of her eligibility to marriage.

During the courting of young people, the elders stood passively respectful. Not that there was no concern, but the principle of allowing the young individual self-expression was active in courtship as elsewhere. Few mothers made any attempt to interfere with a daughter's choice, but tried by the nicety of her own manners to enhance the girl's chance for a desirable marriage. If a mother wished to observe the greatest courtesy toward her daughter's admirers, she would pass food to all the young men who stood or sat outside the tipi door waiting to speak to the girl. Usually the mother was glad to do this, for she was proud to see her daughter sought after.

The young men, too, appreciated this show of hospitality and after accepting the food would go quietly away. Sometimes they left gifts on the plate in which they were served as a mark of regard for the mother. These were of varying worth according to the warmth of generosity which prompted them, since the young men were in no way obligated to make presents.

I remember one young man's warm enthusiasm cost me my best blanket. One night a friend of mine borrowed my dress blanket to go calling on a young woman friend. He became so pleased over his visit and the reception he got that he gave away the blanket he had borrowed from me, and since he was a friend of mine I, of course, said nothing about it, though I did miss my blanket.

When two young people felt enough interest in each other to become engaged, each might make the other a personal gift. The girl usually gave the man an ornamental hair-string from her braid, and he might give her in return a bracelet or a ring. Since the engagement was a secret affair these gifts were called secret gifts.

Engagements as a rule did not last long, but now and then one of long duration came to light through some incident that portrayed the faithfulness of lovers. An aunt of mine had been courted for many years, but whether or not she had become engaged was not known, for sometimes a woman was courted because the brave would have no other, in consequence of which he would continue the suit as long as the woman remained single and there was a glimmer of hope. Finally one day word came to my aunt that her lover had been left dead on the battlefield, slain by an enemy tribe. The young woman in her grief immediately cut her hair and went into mourning. The family of the slain lover took the heart-broken girl to their home and dressed her up in their best garments, treating her as a daughter-in-law. The father of the young man painted himself black in honor of his son and called together the Fox Lodge of which the young man had been a member. The members of the Lodge came marching in line single-file and singing the death-song. Each warrior knelt on one knee while the father passed along the line, placing his hand on each man's head and touching each man's lips with the pipe of peace. The warriors all sensed the father's grief in his touch, and tears came to their eyes, filling them with the desire to avenge the death of their friend and comrade. The band was in sorrow. But to the joy and surprise of everyone the young warrior came into camp a few days later. An enemy arrow had only stunned him, and, though he had lost the sight of one eye, he had been able to make his way home. At once he and the young woman, who had so mourned him, were married, and to my last knowledge were still living on the reservation in South Dakota.

But young hearts, as ever, are apt to suffer a change of emotion. All promises are not kept, with the consequences that some engagements are broken. Then, strange to say, Lakota love songs are sung, or what the white man has chosen to call love songs of the Indian. In reality among the Lakota the songs that are called love-songs are songs of revenge or derision. If the young woman is the jilted party she bears his displeasure in silence, but if the rejected lover is the man he vents his chagrin in singing songs of the young woman who ceased to admire his charms. To do this he makes up a song, using some of the words of love the young lady has at some time said to him. He sings the song to his friends and it is understood that he is deriding the girl who jilted him.

The words of one song that I recall are:

> *In kpata na wajin na sina ci coze*
> *Ma yan ma yan leci kuwa na*
>
> At the head of the creek I stand and my blanket wave,
> Over here, come over here.

When the young couple were engaged, she called to him to come to see her, but now she did this no more and the disgruntled lover tells his friends about it. Sometimes the young woman becomes angry, but sometimes she sees the humor of it and laughs.

When marriage has been definitely settled between lovers, the young woman sets the date. She may say to him, 'I shall be ready when the leaves turn yellow,' which means in the fall of the year. Or she may say, 'I shall come to you when the chokeberries are black,' and that means midsummer. The young woman may say *wetu*, which means in the spring, or *wanitu*, which means the time when snow flies. The young people make no announcement of the time they have chosen for marriage, this being considered a personal affair about which no one thinks it proper to inquire. The day is set for the meeting at a trysting place. The girl slips away, taking with her only the little bag or case containing her sinew and awls. The young people go at once to the mother of the young man. Marriage has begun.

MARRIAGE

Once the young people left the girl's band, they were considered married. Their mutual consent to this state was considered sufficient and definite. No vows were taken in public and the couple neither planned nor staged for themselves ceremonies as public declarations of their pledges and intentions. Their private pledges to one another to live together as man and wife were binding, and there was no existent authority to add to the strength of their own words. Since no man furnished the emotions which prompted their vows of faithfulness, then no man could supply the lack when faithfulness failed. This was a fundamental fact and the Lakota acknowledged it.

The assumption was that the young people would live together for the rest of their lives, and they usually did.

Oftentimes their engagement had been one of several years' waiting and preparation and not a thing of haste. Furthermore both parties to the marriage had been taught that it was honorable to become homemakers and it was with this end in view that the young man had become a good hunter; why he tried to possess good horses, strong bows, well-made arrows and had gone on one war-party, at least. The girl's training, too, had been to prepare her fitly for the place of homemaker.

Though mutual consent formed a binding marriage, there were ceremonies connected strictly with this event. These ceremonies, which sometimes lasted four or five days, were initiated by the mothers of the couple. Mother-authority sanctioned the marriage, and rightfully so, being the nearest interested person. Had an utter stranger — one who had never seen them and had for them no interest — been asked to receive the vows of the young people and sanction their marriage, it would have been an act without meaning to them. In marriage, as in birth, mother influence prevailed. Mother authority had not yet been willed away and practically annulled as it has since become under the influence of the white man's social order. Today mother-power is weak, scattered to many places — taken over by the teacher, preacher, nurse, lawyer, and others who superimpose their will. This loss applies also to the white mother, for she, too, is blinded and confused by the intricacies of the society in which she lives. And the incongruity of it all is that the child has not become individualized, but has become stamped with the ideas of others. Few today are the youthful individual thinkers and doers who dare step out of the ranks, for the ranks close about them and try to force them to conform. This process was not possible in Lakota society in tribal times. The Indian mother pointed the way, but she followed in her son's and daughter's path. She did not take from, but rather, added to their strength by urging it to express itself.

When the young couple arrived at the home of the man's mother the courtesies of receiving the bride began. The couple walked into the mother's tipi, the girl taking a seat on the man's bed with her face to the wall. She spoke to no one, but sat with her face and head wrapped in her blanket. It was custom to sit thus for a few moments but sometimes the bride was timid, for perhaps she may never before have seen her husband's family, so she refused to uncover her face until somewhat recovered from her timidity. By way of signifying pleasure and extending good wishes, the mother-in-law prepared some food and offered it to the bride who ate in appreciation of the proffered good wishes. I never knew a woman to refuse to accept a daughter-in-law, for she granted to her son the right to choose whomsoever he pleased for a wife. The bride, of course, had brought her workbag with sinew and awl. So, after she had eaten and had begun to sense her welcome, she produced the bag which she carried under her blanket. The mother-in-law handed her a piece of buckskin and a piece of rawhide — materials for a pair of moccasins. The bride considered this a further offering of courtesy and gladly went to work. The girl remembered that her mother had often told her to learn to make moccasins well, 'for some day your mother-in-law will ask you to make a pair.' The bride was eager to show that she was capable of being a good housewife, and that the better and finer her work, the more pleasure she derived from it. When the moccasins were finished, the girl handed them to her mother-in-law. They were accepted, and thereby the young woman became a working member of her husband's family.

Now there took place the *sayapi*, a custom conducted by the sisters of the young man, his female cousins and other relatives. They wanted to do their part in honoring the groom and his wife, so they brought to the bride gifts of adornment such as face-paints and pretty garments. The first thing the women attendants did was to comb the bride's hair and tie to her hair ornamental hair-ribbons. Next they painted her face, using red or orange principally, for *sayapi* means to paint red. In this ceremony the women had a great deal of fun, and so, of course, the bride, too, was made very happy in receiving such attention. Lastly, the bride was dressed in a beautiful costume complete with moccasins and leggins. When the bride was all dressed in the finery she was much admired by her new friends. A great deal of the Lakota woman's pride in bestowing gifts is in knowing that much time and labor have been put into the gift article. Like the Lakota man, the Lakota woman was a splendid giver, and the more lavish her gift, the more pride in the giving.

Now the father of the groom, not to be outdone by the womenfolk of the family in honoring his son, conducted his part of the ceremony. He brought to the village some of his horses or procured other articles of value to give away in honor of his son and his wife. Songs of praise were sung and the gifts were given to old or needy people in the village. If the father-in-law was able to afford it, he had the corn dance and feast given for his daughter-in-law. With the corn-dance ceremony the bride was given the white-eagle fluff for her hair, and this denoted that she occupied the most honorable circle in the band.

These marriage customs and ceremonies performed by the Lakota family members were all prompted from very deep sources of regard and kindness. They were full of the meaning and value of lessons learned from past experiments in the relationships of human beings. What had been learned to be good was done; that which had proven wrong or hurtful was not done. As an instance, though it was rare, the young man's family might have disliked the woman that he brought to live in the village with them. They would not, however, for this dislike, have foregone the pleasure of giving the son and brother honor and happiness. Their love for him would have outweighed their dislike, and out of self-respect they would have observed the marriage courtesies.

The ceremonies of marriage performed by the groom's family were not the final ones, but were followed by the ceremonies of the bride's parents. Only if it happened that the daughter had married a man whom the mother and father did not care to recognize was the daughter's marriage uncelebrated.

The girl's mother, upon discovering the departure of her daughter and noticing the absence of her workbag, knew that the couple were on the way to the home of the man's mother. Announcement of the marriage was made at once, the father selecting the crier of the news and giving away a number of horses. The mother of the bride prepared a feast to be carried to the band of the groom if it were not too far distant, or to be held when the couple came back to the home of the girl. At these meetings of the two bands there occurred the *omawahintun*, or relationship pact between the parents of the couple, which was supposed to last as long as the marriage of their offspring lasted. However, with some of these pledges of friendship expressed in the *omawahintun*, permanent friendships were made, and it has been known for young people to part, although the ties between the respective parents lasted until the end.

Now came the decision of the young couple as to which band they would live with. The industrious man elected to live with his wife's band and help with its upkeep, her family, the old, and the orphans. The first necessity in order to live near the mother-in-law was a new tipi. Early on an appointed morning, the hunters were astir for a buffalo hunt and all the buffalo killed that day furnished the hides for the new tipi. The women all joined in tanning and sewing the skins and it was not long before the new home was established.

Though married, the woman retained her identity and continued to do so throughout life. She never took the

name of her husband, assumed no marriage title such as
Mrs., and never entirely left her own band. No matter how
many times she might marry, a woman used but one name
during life, and that was the name with which she had been
christened in babyhood. About the tipi, woman-personal-
ity was dominant, and always the young wife, like her mother before, was mistress of her realm — the home.

Sometimes the brothers or uncles of the girls offered the
groom a test of his skill and bravery. For much the same
reason that the bride showed her ability to make moccasins
to her mother-in-law, so the groom was allowed to show
his skill as a hunter. The relatives of the bride selected one
of their best horses and lent it to the groom for a buffalo
hunt. At the same time they gave him a bow with only
two arrows. This, of course, amounted to a challenge, but
the young man of mettle gladly accepted and went on the
chase with but two arrows. If he got a buffalo, he presented it to the wife's family, proud of the chance to prove
his worth. A good mate was a man's first prize, and of the
four great tragedies recited by the Lakotas as the hardest
in life to bear, the first one was the loss of a wife and mate;
the second was the babe's loss of its mother before it was
weaned; the third greatest calamity was a famine, and the
fourth was for a warrior to meet defeat in battle. Women
and children were thus placed above all things in importance.

But it was the simplicity and directness of Lakota views
on marriage that gave rise to the opinion in the Caucasian
mind that the Indian regarded marriage ties lightly and
loosely. I have in mind at this moment a history that has
for many years been considered a standard work on the
customs of the American Indian and recommended as
such to the young people of this country. There are, in
this book, statements such as this, 'For a wife, a certain
number of ponies, saddles, buffalo robes, etc., are paid,'
and, 'There is no marriage ceremony, nor formality of any

kind.' While not mentioning the tribe specifically, the chapter deals with the Plains Indians and, so far as the Lakota tribe is concerned, is erroneous. Oftentimes an incomplete history tends to give an incorrect and unfair impression to the reader, and since the native people are more or less obscured by clouds of ignorance and prejudice on the part of his subjectors, the reasons are strong why he should be prepared and encouraged to write his own history.

Many of the rules and regulations concerning ethical and religious conduct that were imposed upon the Lakota after subjection by the Caucasian were incomprehensible to them. Many of them tried earnestly to adjust themselves to the ways of the dominant white man — clothing, food, school, and church all having part in the general readjustment. But the ways of the white man were bewildering — especially his religious ways — and the differences and the rancors that existed between the denominations that had come to lead him into the ways of peace were baffling. When I became, for the time, an Episcopal missionary assistant upon the Rosebud Reservation, I saw many incidents full of poignant bewilderment of the people, yet at the same time amusing.

One of the first enforcements of the Church was to marry all Indian couples by the Church ritual, no matter how long they had lived married under their tribal form of ceremony. One old couple, who had only a vague idea of its meaning, finally consented to remarriage by the Church. An audience filled the church building and the aged couple stood in front of the minister. When the august personage in black questioned, 'Will you take this woman to be your wife?' the old fellow looked incredulously at the minister, then at the interpreter, hesitatingly waiting for some light on the confusing question. After a moment or so he said, 'Why, she is my wife.' At the minister's next question, 'Will you care for this woman through health and through sickness?' a puzzled expression, mingled with exasperation, came upon the old man's face, but he quickly explained, 'I have always cared for her. Every time she gets sick I send for the medicine-man.' But when the minister exhorted them to let no man put them asunder, the old fellow quite feelingly let it be known that 'We have been married these many years and no man has ever come between us, so do you think anyone can now?'

But that was just one more marriage ceremony to go on the ministerial records.

Another minister who came to our reservation was quite determined, by any ways or means, to hold a revival of baptism. Could he only get the Indians to come to church and listen to his eloquence, he was sure they would be won for the church — but, to get them there! So one of the Indian converts was asked if he could assist in a plan to get the Indians to come to church. The assistant agreed to see what could be done. It was soon announced that a feast would be served at the church on a certain Sunday and that all who came would be welcome to partake of the food. Everyone who heard the news came, the Indians and their families thronging the church. But before the feast all had consented to take part in the white man's 'water ceremony.' After a Sunday or two all Indians in the vicinity had been baptized and the feasts were discontinued; so was the attendance at church. But let us hope that this holy man's record for baptizing Lakota Indians placed him in good favor with his superiors.

It was but to be expected that in time both the white man's word and his papers would be mistrusted by the Indians, and the marriage license was one of these documents. Red Stone's mistrust in the efficacy of the white man's license was indicative of the beeling of most of the Indians at that time. Red Stone was a half-witted fellow who had conceived the notion of marrying the finest and most desirable young Indian woman of the community.

Red Stone had said nothing to the young woman of his intentions, but being the most unobtainable of persons, she would naturally be Red Stone's choice. One day while the missionary and myself were making our regular bi-monthly trip through the district, Red Stone told us to bring a marriage license the next time we came to see him, as he wanted to marry Iron Shield's daughter. The minister promised to bring the necessary papers on his nest trip. Red Stone said nothing, but was evidently questioning in his mind the strength of the paper. After we had started away, Red Stone waved to us to stop, and called out: 'When you come bring two of those papers. One is not going to be strong enough.'

Divorce in Lakota society was as incident rather than an occasion. It was the simplest thing to be had and most seldom sought for. If young people, in immature judgment, did not choose the most agreeable mate and if time did not bring adjustment between them, then a parting took place. Seldom, however, did a man grow tired of a mate, and seldom did a wife return to her own parents to live.

If a wife was disposed to quarrel with her husband's relatives, or was lazy, he felt himself justified in leaving her or in asking her to return to her own band. Valid reasons for a wife to leave her husband were if he proved cowardly, if his fancy strayed to other women causing neglect to the wife, or if he beat and abused her. Lakota women often lived in friendship with other wives, but the objector was free to leave at any time. And few wives felt obliged to take abuse or beatings from an ill-tempered husband. The one unforgivable sin in a Lakota husband was cowardice, and no woman would bear the humiliation of possessing a cowardly mate.

Few Lakota men bore the reputation of being lazy, though I have known a number of young men who were not considered industrious and therefore were held out to the young women as men to avoid as husbands. These men were, if the fact has any bearing on the matter, extremely handsome fellows, but in spite of these handicaps sometimes made successful and happy marriages.

When a divorce did occur, it was done quietly and without fuss or disturbance. A couple finding themselves no longer able to endure each other's company separated, and it was not long before the tribe recognized them as single people. No scandal followed and no reputations were destroyed.

In this important matter of marriage and divorce the Lakota custom of ignoring the wrongdoer as punishment was most successful. A man who became known as hopelessly unfitted to be a good husband was called *canniyasa*, which means a failure over and over. A man with this reputation, however much he might dislike it, was forced to live alone.

PARENTHOOD

The day came when the young couple expected a new member in their family. At this time the wife usually went back to live with her own family if she happened to be living in her husband's band. The choice was solely hers, and in either case the women relatives would join her in the necessary preparations. Birth was a happy event in the Lakota home, though the interest and rejoicing extended throughout the band, for the child was not only a family addition but a band addition as well. This was the case whether the arrival be a boy or girl, the same attention being given to each irrespective of sex. Regarding body and health welfare the care was the same, for the boys were to be future warriors and the girls were to be future mothers.

As soon as the wife realized that she was to become a mother, she withdrew from the society of her husband, though at all times he had her in his care. But the husband immediately found duties that occupied his time — the hunt, the war-party, or ceremonies. With the knowledge that a child was about to be born the thought of the couple was for its welfare, and both father and mother were willing to sacrifice for the sake of the health of the child and mother. Not till a child was five or six years of age did the parents allow themselves another offspring. As a consequence Lakota families were not large, four or five children being the rule. But disabled mothers were a rarity and many a grandmother was as strong as her granddaughter. And with all the demands placed by parenthood, seldom was the relationship between husband and wife weakened. Children were influential beings with parents also. I remember my stepmother's uncle, Horse Looking, who fell a victim to the habit of drinking. It made of him a terrible man when under its influence, though in his right mind he was the kindest of men. When he was in a drunken frenzy, the only way to curb him was to get his youngest child and present it to him. He would at once forget his temper and begin to pet and fondle the child.

With the nearing event much preparation took place. Sisters, aunts, and other relatives made clothes of the finest and softest doeskin. A cradle was decorated and paints and powders prepared. But to grandmother fell the honor of officiating as supervisor and adviser on all matters pertaining to the occasion. She had, in fact, started her preparations and arrangements for the event of birth from the day of the wedding. During the waiting period grandmother had baked a red earth clay and pounded it to a fine powder to mix with the buffalo fat which she had rendered into a creamy paste. This mixture served as a cleanser and also as a protector to the tender skin of the child. Then grandmother had gathered the driest of buffalo chips and ground them between stones to a powder as fine and soft as talcum. This powder was a purifier, and soothing to an irritated skin.

Perhaps the hardest duty in the performance of parenthood was not so much to watch the conduct of their children as to be ever watchful of their own — a duty placed upon parents through the method used in instructing their young — example. Children, possessors of extreme vigor of health, with faculties sensitized by close contact with nature, made full use of eyes and ears; and Lakota parents and elders were under scrutiny for conduct and conversation. They were consequently bound to act in as kind and dignified a manner as possible.

So in their sphere, over which no despot ruled, children were a power in the home. No need for a Dickens to espouse their cause against the ogres of tyranny and oppression.

CHAPTER V

CIVIL ARRANGEMENTS: BANDS, CHIEFS, LODGES

THE *Lakota Oyate*, or Lakota Nation, was made up of *Tiyospaye*, or bands. These two words, *Oyate* and *Tiyospaye*, were the only two terms in the Lakota language that pertained to the civil or governmental structure of Lakota society, there being but two bodies or departments making up the organization. Each band was a social unit, under separate chieftainship, yet each band was an integral part of the nation. Other native peoples, not connected with us in a tribal or civil way, were called *Oyate*. For instance, the Crow people were called *Kangi Wicase Oyate*, or the Crow Nation.

In size, bands might be small, medium or large, say from thirty or forty families to one hundred or more families, a band of one hundred tipis or so being considered a large band. However, size was not the factor that gave a band its importance; it was the number of braves and chiefs that could be counted among the band members, for some bands might be half or more composed of women, youths, and children.

It was the rule for several bands to erect their villages close together. This allowed for social activities of which the Lakotas were very fond and, in early days, it added protection and strength to the bands.

The common arrangement, in olden times, was the *dopa* village, or the village of four circles or bands. These four circles of tipis were set in a square, in the center of which was the *hocoka*, meaning middle or center. This inner or middle space was the social meeting ground for the four villages, where games, ceremonies, and festivities of all sorts were held. The *hocoka* was used much like the squares and plazas in the Pueblo villages.

By Chief Standing Bear

THE HOCOKA, OR FOUR VILLAGES

Four was a sacred number and was significantly used in the Lakota scheme of symbology. There were four corners to the sacred earth altar; four major losses or tragedies in life, as mentioned in another chapter; four directions or four winds; and four eagles from each of the four directions — the golden eagle of the east, symbol of the sun from whence comes life; the spotted eagle of the south which carried the souls of the dead to the land of happiness; the black eagle of the west, denoting sunset or darkness; and the bald eagle of the north, which brought the winds and snows of winter. In the ceremony of the pipe it was pointed to the four directions and in many of the ceremonial dances the performers danced to the four directions. The Stone Dreamer sings the Song of the Moon, the words calling attention to the four circles of the *dopa* village over which the Moon is guardian. The sun also sings a song through the Stone Dreamer, calling attention to the four activities or four ceremonies in honor of the sun.

Bands were usually called by the name of some leading chief, such as Little Wound's Band, or Red Leaf's Band, which was quite a large band that existed before my time under the popular leader, Chief Red Leaf. Sometimes a band got its name through some incident of a peculiar character, such as the Brulé Sioux whom the Lakotas called *Sicangu*, or the Burned Thigh People. At some time in the past history of the band, the name was suggested by an accident that happened to one of its members. Within my memory a band of Lakotas began to be called the *Pesla*, or Baldhead Band. Bald-headedness had been unknown among the Lakotas, but with the adoption of the hat they began to lose their hair and this made them conspicuous. Hats were issued with the first annuities, and members of some of the bands began to wear them at once, while others refused, which accounts for the fact that this band was afflicted before the others. My father married into the *Mini Skuya Kicun*, or the Salt Painted Band, which received its name from the incident of the blind grandmother who by mistake painted the children's faces with salt instead of paint.

The way in which the Oglalas got their name is also based on a prank of some young folk. The word Oglala conveys the idea of being covered over with dust or ashes and this is how the word came to be applied to a band. A long time ago, according to grandfather's story, the band was a large one and in it quite a number of boys and young fellows. One day some of them playing in a tipi began to throw the dust and ashes of the floor at one another. They found it fun and boisterously kept it up until all were covered. One of the old men who kept watch over things in the village looked in the tipi door and saw there the boys all covered with dust and ashes playfully scuffling. The old man did not scold, but told the boys to stop, for people would hear about it and name their band, and this is precisely what happened.

After the agency was established, many different bands came together to be all known as Oglalas. The agent probably found it inconvenient to have so many bands in his six districts, so those on the Pine Ridge Reservation were called Oglalas. When the Government finally arranged for allotment, the Indians were told to select the land they favored for a home and the bands became more or less disorganized. In making individual choices of land the bands became separated, the members scattering over the reservation territory. This did not mean, however, that band ties were broken, and even today every individual keeps trace of his band connection.

The bands were governed, as were individuals, families, and the nation, by ancient and traditional customs. And these customs which had, through many years of time, become established in the minds of the people, were based upon human and individual needs. The central aim of the Lakota code was to bring ease and comfort in equal measure to all. There were no weak and no strong individuals from the standpoint of possessing human rights. It was every person's duty to see that the right of every other person to eat and be clothed was respected and there was no more question about it than there was about the free and ungoverned use of sunshine, pure air, and the rains with which they bathed their bodies. There were no groups of strength allied against groups of those weak in power.

The Lakotas were self-governors, and the rules and regulations that governed the conduct of people and established their duties as individuals, families, and bands came from a great tribal consciousness. Deep within the people, mingling with their emotions, was an inherent sense of solidarity — a tie between one and all others that the nation might be expressed.

Though each person became individualized — could be as truthful, as honest, as generous, as industrious, or as brave as he wished — could even go to battle upon his own initiative, he could not consider himself as separate from the band or nation. Tribal consciousness was the sole guide and dictator, there being no human agency to compel the individual to accept guidance or obey dictates, yet for one to cut himself off from the whole meant to lose identity or to die.

The Lakota word for this governing power of custom or tradition was *wouncage*, literally, 'our way of doing.' *Wouncage* constituted, for the Lakota people, the only authority. The manners of neighbor people might be similar, just alike in some respects or totally different, but, for the Lakota there could only be the ways of his people — could only be 'our way of doing.' Therefore it was hard for a person to get away from *wouncage*. In other words, it was harder to break laws than to keep them. Consequently, there were few law-breakers.

Written laws were not a part of the tribal consciousness.

Such laws are written to be, in time, rewritten or unwritten, and that means to be kept and broken. It is a mistake, therefore, to believe that a people without written laws are a lawless people. The Lakotas were, in fact, bound by the only codes that endure — those written into the essence of living. Not even since the coming of the white man have the Lakotas written any of their tribal codes, for they are in the minds of the people from times of remoteness. And they still have memories of that golden day when a man's word was as it should always have remained — potent with the reverence of truth.

Each and every individual regarded himself as the receiver and not the dispenser of ease and comforts. The source from which came all things beneficent was unlimited, and this made hoarding inconsistent. Strength was gained but from one source — nature — and until influenced, the Lakota mind was never blighted with the idea that strength was to be gained through the domination of other individuals. There was domination, but it was self-domination, the mother, father, sister, brother, and all, voluntarily placing their person in secondary importance to the needs of the band and nation. And by thus placing their interest the law worked that they themselves were never neglected. The result was that in the society of the Lakota there were no hungry and no overfed; no groveling and no arrogant; no jails, no judges, no poor houses, no brothels, and no orphan asylums.

Until the coming of the white man there was no word in the Lakota language for law, or law enforcement, in the sense in which the word is used today. The nearest approach to organized authority was vested in the Fox Lodge, the duties of members being mainly supervisory and protective in nature, and whose actual authority was limited principally to the big hunts and marches of the moving caravans.

The word for custom and habit, *wouncage*, had its tradi-

tional meaning of simply following tribal usage without
enforcement of any sort; so with the coming of the white
man and his treaties and written declarations of various
sorts, the word *woope* was coined to meet the situation.
Woope conveyed the meaning of armed soldiery, guns, cannon, policemen, ball and chain, jails and guards, and all
the cruel equipment of war that has come out of the night
of life. The apparent thing to the Lakota was that the
written word was in itself ineffective and without power;
and *woope*, or what the white man called law, designated
not order but force and disorder. Force, no matter how
concealed, begets resistance.

Regulations in the main pertained to the ownership of
property, the division of labor, and the social conduct of
men and women. The woman owned the tipi and all its
furnishings, such as household articles and bedding. Both
women and children owned their ponies, just as in olden
days they had owned their dogs; also the *travois*. Meat
that was in the tipi, either dried or fresh, and food that
had been gathered and stored, belonged to the woman
who was head of the household. The man owned nothing
in the tipi except his war equipment and ceremonial regalia. Songs were owned by the composer, and medicine
articles and secrets were owned by the medicine-man.

In the division of labor the best experience of the people
prevailed. The women built the tipis and furnished them,
cared for the young and ill, made all clothing, and prepared and stored food. The men took care of the horses,
kept lookout for enemies, relayed news between villages,
kept the people in fresh meat and hides, watched water
and grass supplies, decided when to move camp, and held
all councils.

All took part in the social affairs, though the men did
most of the dancing and the singing, since most songs and
dances were recitals of hunting, adventures of travel, and
exploits of war. The men arranged for the sports and
games and the various ceremonies.

All matters that concerned the welfare of the band were taken care of in frequent council meetings where the chiefs and their aids met for discussion. These meetings and all sorts of band gatherings, both serious and otherwise, were held in the Tipi Iyokihe. It was once the custom, when holding a large council, to put several tipis together in order to make room for a large number of people and Tipi Iyokihe means 'putting together or joining many tipis into one.' But in time the words came to have a slightly different meaning, that of a general meeting place, a council or community hall for men. Women only came at times to serve food, or attended the social gatherings with their children upon invitation; but women never attended a council of tribal affairs.

At all times this council hall was open and at nearly all times it was occupied. In leisure time the young men and warriors lounged about, listening to the conversation of the older men, and in the evening the men of the village, young and old, gathered for social purposes. A warrior or scout, when asked, would oblige by telling of his journeys and adventures. When he had finished a story, a tally-stick taken from a bundle kept in the Tipi Iyokihe for that purpose, was stuck in the ground upright, the narrator being entitled to a stick for every adventure which he could truthfully relate. When one story-teller had finished, another would begin. Sometimes a question would arise as to which man in the village had the greatest number of exploits to his credit. Someone might suggest a man who was not present, while someone else proposed that the man be brought in. When the absent one had arrived, he related his stories and more than likely the night was spent in this manner. In this way the listeners lived over the thrills of the adventurous ones and indelible records were printed in the minds of the youths.

Whenever a council of serious import was to be held, it was announced to the village, an old man stopping in front of each tipi and calling, '*Omniciye kte lo!*' This apprised the men of each tipi that a council was to be held. At these councils some formality was observed as to the seating of chiefs and headmen. The chiefs sat at the far side of the Tipi Iyokihe, opposite the door, while the headmen sat on either side of the chiefs, the younger braves filling the rest of the space to the door. At the left of the door stood the old man announcer, whose duty it was, after the meeting, to march around the village and make such announcements as the councilors saw fit. At the right of the door stood a young man, or perhaps two or three young fellows, whose duty it was to wait upon the comforts of the older men. They brought food or water if the council lasted long, replenished the fire if the weather was cold, and burned sweetgrass for ceremonial purposes. These men were in no sense servants, for the reason that there were no menial positions in Lakota society. Young men called upon to perform such duties felt honored and recognized. Many matters might come up at a council meeting, some to be decided on without delay, others to be left for later decision. The records of young men who were being considered for future chiefs were gone into, the migration of the entire band to the Black Hills might be set in motion, or matters of minor importance, such as preparing for a hunt or moving the band closer to the buffalo herds. In fact, tribal needs of all sorts came up before the council.

Occasionally a large number of bands would meet together for the *Oyate Okiju*, or Council of the Nation. When many widely scattered bands wished a council, it was arranged by the *Icimani*, or 'news-walkers,' who traveled constantly between bands, relaying news. The *Oyate Okiju* was seldom held, except for matters of unusual importance, such as the annual prayer ceremony of the Sun Dance or, in later years, for the discussion of treaties.

The manners of those in council were most dignified.

All meetings were opened with the Pipe ceremony, and the feeling for truth became almost reverential. The speech-makers arose quietly, without deference or mannerism, and talked simply and directly. When finished, they sat down and the assembly gave voice to assent or pleasure by saying, 'Ha-a-u!'

It was not etiquette to display arrogance, and the boaster was ridiculed. Falsehood was easily detected and there was no bribing of tongues.

The usual salutation of a speaker was, 'Friends and Relatives!' And the speaker, especially if he were a chief, carefully avoided any words or tones of authority. The will of the assembly was implied in the opening words of the address which were customarily something like this: 'I think it wise that we do so and so,' or, 'If you agree, I (or we) shall do so and so.' There was no such word as democracy in the Lakota language, but the spirit prevailed in the phrase, *Oyate ta woecun*, which meant, 'Done by the people,' or, 'The decision of the Nation.'

The council was the gathering place for the wise, the brave, and the just, and no doubt, there were men who would have graced any conclave. There were men who could not be swerved from right and whom no price could buy. Dress and rank were not exhibited, for no fine regalia and few head-ornaments and plumes were worn. In appearance there was a certain uniformity, the men, in winter, wrapping themselves in their robes, and in summer, folding these garments and using them for seat cushions. Chiefs, headmen, and braves were known only by the places they occupied opposite the door of the hall, and sometimes the greatest among them had the least to say and remained the most inconspicuous.

Last of all, the council made no laws that were enforceable upon individuals. Were it decided to move camp, the decision was compulsory upon no one. A family, or two or three of them, might elect to remain in the old village.

However, in most matters a decision that was favorable for one was favorable for all.

But it must not be thought that there was no distinction among Lakotas as individuals. There were no social strata so definite that some were unattainable by reason of class or birth, but there were individuals and groups who were recognized by virtue of superior intelligence and capacity. As among every people, there were those who were better able to get along in the world than others. There were men so skilled in hunting that they never wanted for food, and there were warriors whose fearlessness not every man could equal. In many and various ways there were individuals who stood out from the rest.

So there were the high — those who were honored and distinguished for superior achievement. There were others who, though not excelling, were good members of society. There were still others who, for no fault of their own, found themselves a little weaker, less capacitated, than the majority members of society. These were not the old and the children, but adults, able-bodied, but unable to achieve. This being the case, nevertheless, weaklings were never the objects of pity, charity, or contempt. When the camp moved, they were taken, and when food was dispensed they were never forgotten. They were never allowed to want, nor to grow sick and die from neglect. But in spite of the careful equality in treatment, these three distinctions were kept in mind.

The Lakotas of high class, if such they may be called, were proud, to be sure, but it was this pride that would not permit them to overlook want and suffering in their kind. The people of this class did not believe in waiting to be called upon to give aid, but took pride in seeing that they were never asked. By anticipating the needs of certain ones in the band the condition of want never came to exist.

I have seen a warrior who had decided to care for an orphan, go to the village crier and say, 'Give this horse of mine to the boy who lives with his grandmother.' The old man would cry the news around the village that such and such a boy would receive a horse. This would be glad news for the boy, and the warrior would receive as gratitude for dispensing good-will and good cheer, songs of praise from a band of singers, these songs being all the warrior would wish or expect by way of recompense.

This outpouring of kindness was, in part, due to the bond of relationship that was recognized between everyone in the band. Outside of family membership every person was an aunt, uncle, cousin, or 'brother's keeper' to someone else. Relationships that white people never recognize, because of their distance, were recognized by the Lakota.

Children were members of both the father's and the mother's band. My father was a member of the One Horse band and my mother was a member of the Swift Bear band, while I was claimed by both bands. I could not, therefore, have married within either one of these bands.

Adoption was another means of forming relationship. For instance, two young men from different bands, becoming fast friends, would decide to adopt each other and to become as actual brothers. No form of ceremony was attached to the agreement, the young men simply taking up their abode together and dividing their time between the two families. This sort of relationship was as binding as if a blood tie existed, and neither young man could marry the sister of the other. Should either one do so, though belonging to different bands, the offender would lose the respect of all band members. Sometimes two young women formed such an adoption and the same rules applied to them.

CHIEFS

Each band had one, perhaps two, and sometimes a number of chiefs, depending somewhat, of course, on the size of the band; but the greater the number of chiefs in a band the greater its worth and importance, for only the finest of men became chiefs. So the fame of a band rested upon its braves and honored men rather than upon the number of tipis, horses, or other goods it might possess.

The common conception of a chief is that of a man who has great power, even power over life, and that he exerts his cruel might upon any and every pretext. And this idea, though far from the truth, has made of chiefs, bloodthirsty and cruel savages, while as a matter of fact most of them were benefactors of their people and were men who gave their best abilities, even sacrificed, to be of service to their fellows.

No Lakota chief ever dreamed of using the power of a judge in court, or a policeman on a street corner, for it was not a tenet of his society that one individual should account to another for his conduct. No chief could declare warfare and command other braves to follow him. Neither could he declare war and remain at home, for to do so would have been to bring about his own ignominious destruction. I remember once my father, before he was chief, started alone on the warpath. He did not ask anyone to accompany him, but was later joined by some friends in his course of running a band of Pawnee off the Lakota's hunting grounds. He brought our ponies to the tipi door, for he intended taking me with him. But some of the warriors did not think it wise to go after the Pawnees at that time, so they protested by turning our ponies loose. Father, however, was determined to go, so he got himself another pony and started out. He was soon joined by others of his band and the Pawnee invaders were run off. Later, after he became chief, father did the same thing, but he had no more power, as chief, to force others to go on the warpath with him than when he was merely a warrior. Even the great Crazy Horse, when presented with the pipe of peace by mediating chiefs who had followed him and his band into Canada, said, 'Ask my people what they wish to do,' and not until they had counciled and consented did Crazy Horse smoke and return to the States.

Boys were trained so that should the honor of being made chief come to them, they would be ready to fill the place. In their minds were stored the history and lore of their tribe, the events of migration and travel, the discoveries of the dreamers, the tales and prophecies of wise men, battles and victories, and secrets the brotherhood of animals shared with the medicine-men. They came to know the names of their great in history and to learn of the exploits of such braves as High Stander, who, seeing himself and companions greatly outnumbered, shouted courage to them, and drawing a cavalry sword which he carried, charged the enemy. With one sweep of his arm, three Crow enemies fell from their horses, and High Stander and his men effected an escape. Then, there was Spotted Bear, who was so brave that even the enemy praised him and kept his name alive. Spotted Bear left his warrior friends one day to go hunting. On his return, and while still some distance away, Spotted Bear saw that his friends were completely surrounded by enemies without hope of escape. Instead of running away as he might have done, he rushed through the enemy line, killing as many as he could on the way and reached his friends, only to die with them.

Finally, every boy got the chance he longed for — the chance to go with some of these men on hunts, scouting trips, or on the warpath. Some of the young men made preparation to get their own 'medicine' by taking the vigil and seeking the vision. If not fortunate enough to become medicine-men, they might, at least, get some assistance, as did Sorrel Horse and Big Turkey.

Sorrel Horse was one of the greatest of Lakota scouts. He could slip up to an enemy camp and remain invisible; so whenever the Lakotas wanted some enemy horses or wished to recover some that had been taken from them,

Sorrel Horse could be relied upon to get them. His medicine was slough grass, which he gathered and put at the back of his head like a feather. Big Turkey did not have the power to make his person invisible, but he obscured his movements by causing a fog to settle down close about him.

Though these two scouts possessed remarkable powers of magic and skill which they used in a similar manner, yet in appearance they were very dissimilar. Sorrel Horse was neither a large man nor exceptionally strong in physique, but was handsome and likable, jovial and carefree in manner, with a ready smile which utterly belied his power and calling. But how different was Big Turkey! He was large and muscular — the personification of strength. His head looked unusually large because of a mass of unruly hair which he seemed unable to confine. Even when he tied it, his hair stood out around his head, remindful somewhat of the fashion of matting and roaching the hair affected by white women some years ago. There was power in every aspect of Big Turkey, but it was when we met the glance of his eyes, though he was harmless, that we quavered. His being was charged with power and a strange, subtle force, while that of Sorrel Horse was hidden. It was the habit of these two men, when taking part in the dances with the other braves, to wrap yards of rope about their bodies, indicative of their power with horses.

Many of the young men were taken for the *Canounye kicicupi*, one of the most crucial periods in a young man's life and the one that tested him as a man. This ceremony was one in which young men were selected to be sent out to get war honors, *Canounye kicicupi* meaning, 'to give war equipment.' White writers refer to this test and ordeal as 'counting coup.' The whole ceremony was conducted with all the solemnity significant of the occasion for with a young, untried warrior, it was a matter of life and death.

In the Tipi Iyokihe were made the rattles, whips, lances, drums, and all paraphernalia used in the ceremony, or given to the young man with which to touch the enemy. When everything was in readiness the ceremony was held in the open so that all could attend. Groups of singers, slowly and gravely, began the brave songs. The young men, simply dressed and not even by the display of a single feather giving token of a desire to be selected, marched in and seated themselves in a circle, with heads bowed over folded hands. The sight was an impressive one and there was a good deal of anxiety, not only for the young fellows, who might fear the ordeal, but for the parents, who were filled with concern. After some time two chiefs came to the center of the circle and there conferred, then carefully looked around and perhaps conferred again. When they had made their decision, the two chiefs walked side by side to a young man and pulled him up. The young man might be one who all the while had been earnestly hoping that he be selected, or he might be a young and timid youth who would pull back in fright; but eventually, only the coward would refuse to stand, for the brave songs were now sung with spirit and defiance. The parents of the young men brought in horses to give away, and relatives and friends sang songs of praise for them. Great braves picked up lances and banners and joined in the dance, imbuing all with courage. Not long after the ceremony, the young men started out to prove their bravery and earn for themselves a new name.

Thus gradually the young absorbed the ideals of the tribe, learning to conduct themselves, and to judge, according to tribal standards. Studying and watching others was training, and they grew keen in appraisal, placing worth not in wealth and power, but in human values. There being much interdependence in the band there was little reason for scheming one against the other, less need for strife in order to gain favors, and no necessity to depose one leader in order to install another.

In the Tipi Iyokihe all discussion by leaders concerning the qualifications for chiefs, the needs of the band and plans to meet them, were discussed in the presence of the young men. Consequently they began to feel the importance or weight of being under observation and appraisal, while at the same time they were being tactfully taken into council.

Another qualification for a 'brave' was kindness or justice in dealing with the offenders of the tribal codes, for there was no stronger test of bravery and character strength than in the attitude taken toward the wrongdoer. Only the brave and fearless can be just.

There was no official punisher or sentence-body in the band or tribe. The fate of the wrongdoer lay in the hands of the people of the band, and no chief, nor headman, in himself, had the power to impose sentence of any sort. There was only the idea which reposed in tribal consciousness that wrong must not be allowed to flourish and right must prevail.

The way of the tribe in dealing with an offender was simple and dignified. There was no violence such as whipping, no taking away of personal effects nor personal liberties, no hounding, no persecuting, and no pompous show of authority.

When it became necessary for the band to protect itself it did so by merely ignoring and ostracizing the violator. Conversation, games, councils, and ceremonies were carried on as if the disfavored one were not about. This sort of punishment was usually sufficient to make the offender change his habits. If the offense were a minor one, such as bragging or strutting, then ridicule and laughter sufficed to put a stop to it, but the boaster was usually quickly detected and his glory short-lived, for he was as quickly resented as he was detected.

On the other hand, if a man's offense were serious, say if he were a murderer, his exclusion from the band would be permanent. He would suffer neither for food nor clothing, but he would not be welcome at the tipis of others and no one would visit his tipi. In time of sickness he would be cared for by near relatives, but he was never again accepted as a creditable member of his band.

But cases of this kind among the Lakotas were very rare, and in all my life I have known only two or three. There is no word in the Lakota language which can be translated literally into the word 'justice'; nevertheless, there was the certain practice of it as evidenced in the phrase, *Wowa un sila,* 'A heart full of pity for all.'

As far back as Lakota memory reaches, the chiefs have been chosen in council. The selection of the new leader was made by the chiefs of one or more bands coming together for the consideration of young men who have become notable and outstanding. A selection might be made in the first council, or several might be held before decision was reached, for proof of the young man's fitness had to be evident to the whole council. Sometimes the matter was deferred from year to year until worth was fully proven, for the place of chief was one to be gained in no way except by merit.

The young chief must know the hard life of the hunter and the perils of the scout and warrior; must be slow in speech and decision; must be honest in council, and have the confidence of the people. While not forgetting the rights of his people, he must not forget the rights of other chiefs. All matters, such as electing new leaders and moving, were done in conference with other chiefs and leaders. And lastly, the young chief must be a giver and not a receiver — a man of self-denial.

When the council had arrived at a choice, the election ceremony was set for a time when many bands were together for some festivity. The election was public, so that anyone having objections might voice them. The man chosen might or might not have been appraised, but in any case it was an honor and also a test of bravery second only to the *canounye kicicupi*. The ceremony began by two chiefs bringing the young brave into the circle and seating him in front of the other chiefs. The pipe ceremony was performed, then handed to the brave, who accepted it with a puff. After speeches by the chiefs, and song of praise, the brave was declared a chief and he took his seat in the circle with the others.

Lakota history has many great names, and perhaps the greatest of these is Crazy Horse, though the old people remember Afraid of His Horse, Bad Wound, Conquering Bear, Little Thunder, and White Hawk. Crazy Horse was revered by his people and wielded a great influence, yet he regarded their wishes as a solemn duty. Crazy Horse had every requisite of a great chief. He was unassuming in manner, quiet in speech, plain in dress, and meek in appearance. But he was a man of sorrow. He felt keenly the injustice dealt his people and consequently had no wish to mingle with their oppressors nor recognize them. The white man knows very little of this great man, and photographs purporting to be his are not authentic. It is a consolation to the Lakota to remember that Crazy Horse was defeated only by superior force and trickery of those whom he considered brigands and not worthy to associate with men of quality. He fell before the false promises of army officers who were no match for him in bravery, and chiefs who were envious of his power. Crazy Horse was an example of the fulfillment of Lakota ideals. The fact that he was produced in Lakota society is proof that it was based on elements that produced men and not savages.

Other than chiefs and braves there were in Lakota society — people of usefulness to their fellows. There were individuals whose duties were similar to those of statesmen, doctors, news purveyors, philosophers, and even sportsmen. Statesmen, known only as 'good men,' studied the rights of people and the duties of one to the other; philosophers gave people faith in the works of nature, gave meaning to the seasons of the year, set the weeks to moons, and observed the virtues of animals; healers used mud, water, earth, air, sunlight, and plants to cure human ills, and in addition cured by faith, for some of them were prophets with spiritual as well as material power; the wise, or holy men, carried the sacred fire and performed the religious duties of prayer and meditation. A body of men skilled in story-telling, pantomime, and jesting, carried news from band to band; and there was the sportsman whose skill in riding, throwing the arrow, and in chance games was so superb that he became the standard for all other men, and that in a society where all men were trained and skilled physically.

In every band was an *icimani* or 'news-walker.' These walking scouts traveled night and day and served the people, as do the newspapers and current magazines now, by purveying and disseminating all sorts of interesting and timely news. It was the business of the *icimani* to go from band to band telling the news he had gathered on the way, and gathering more. Births, deaths, marriages, feasts, battles — everything, in fact, that was news was related and collected. When the *icimani* reached a village he was welcomed as was the stage coach in frontier days or as the postman is today. The people listened eagerly to him, and until his departure for the next band he was the center of interest. The news-walker was a hardy, experienced traveler and kept on his walk in winter as well as in summer. Always a foot traveler, snows never obscured his path, but his life was one of adventure and thrill. Much of his travel was at night so he had, of course, to know his paths well and be ready at all times to encounter sudden storms and swollen streams or an enemy.

Some bands had a *wawahokun kiye wicasa*, an adviser — an old man who was wise and good. In early morning, as the smoke began to arise from the tipis, he sta-

tioned himself in the center of the village, or preferably on
a small near-by hill, and from there talked to the people,
filling their minds with good resolves for the day. His advice to the people was to be careful and good. He reminded
husbands to be kind to wives and children, and to the
weak. He told them that jealousy was a destroyer, and
stealing a sin, sometimes repeating the proverb on sin and
warning little children not to take things that belonged to
others. He asked them to remember that they were here on
earth but a short time, so it did not pay to be greedy but
that it was more noble to be ever mindful of the poor. He
talked to the boys and young men who were apt to grow
careless, telling them to bring back straying animals; if
some were hobbled he told them to change their pasture;
and oftentimes he asked the young boys not to ride their
ponies too much, but to spare them and treat them if they
got sore feet or backs. And this old man practiced what
he preached, else he would have been laughed at.

In many bands there were individuals whom the people
more than honored — individuals of special powers for
which they were reverenced. One of these was the *Wiyan
Wakan*, the 'Holy Woman.' The Holy Woman was considered a great benefactor of her tribe and though in appearance was not different from other women yet her powers set
her apart somewhat. I remember when I was a child, that
if I met a Holy Woman, I was filled with wonder and awe.

The great powers possessed by the Holy Woman had
been received in a vision, and when she went to cure she
carried with her a *hanpospu hoksicala*, a doll made of
buffalo hide and filled with the wool of the buffalo; also she
had her own medicine songs. *Wiyan Wakan* could ward
away evil, cure the sick, prophesy events both good and
bad, knew medicinal plants from harmful ones, knew the
edible from poisonous fruits, could bring the rain, and was
the only woman allowed to make and decorate war shields
for the warriors. It was she who in a dream was given the

game *Tahuka cankle ska*, and the knowledge of dyeing porcupine quills and sewing them into designs.

With her magic power she could hurt us if she willed, and we had no defense, for her power was invisible. This was called *hmunha*. I have seen a medicine-woman play with a medicine-man, each throwing invisible missiles at the other and each trying to ward off the blows. While we could not see what went through the air, I have seen the injured one evidence great pain, and suffer until relieved by his or her own powers of magic.

Whenever a number of bands went on a long march for a big hunt or a change in locality, they were led by the *Waki cunza*, the Twelve Wise Men. These men had sacrified their blood to the Great Mystery, their bodies bearing the scars of this sacrifice, and by virtue of this ceremony their lives were consecrated to the good and welfare of their fellow beings. They had taken vows and always traveled on foot, no matter who in the band rode. Through deep meditation these men had come close to the Great Mystery, so they gave blessings at feasts, advised the people that it was better to give than to receive, prayed that Wakan Tanka never forsake the people of earth, and carried with them the sacred fire, never permitting it to die.

It was the duty of the twelve wise men to keep watch over the people and animals, halting the march now and then for a few days' rest if the way were long. They received the reports of the scouts who came in from time to time, and decided on the next village site.

BUFFALO LODGE

Many of the lodges or societies of the Lakotas were social in character, while others arose for very serious purposes, particularly those brought into existence by dreams or visions.

The Buffalo Lodge was a social order which held no secret meetings. Its members, who joined only upon invitation, were braves, mostly old or middle-aged men, who met for the purpose of keeping alive their war records, telling stories, singing the lodge songs, dancing and playing games. Their gatherings were very popular, the exploits of the braves — scouts, warriors, and *icimanis* — always holding much interest for the people.

A favorite sport was enacting the Buffalo Dance, in which all members danced, but only those who had performed some outstanding act of bravery took the part of buffaloes. The warriors danced about the circle, those impersonating the buffalo bumping and butting the others. Those with lesser records of bravery endeavored to keep beyond the reach of the buffalo dancers, but if out-numbered would have to step pretty lively. This dance called for much activity, and sometimes there was much leaping back and forth over the fire, providing a great deal of fun for the onlookers.

BRAVE LODGE

The Lakotas held very few secret ceremonies, and the so-called secret lodges were only partially so. The Brave Lodge was one of these made up of warriors who had established a record for bravery. New members were selected by the old members, but a young man, on invitation, could refuse membership if he wished or felt that he was not equal to the exactions of a brave. However, few young men refused membership, for it was considered an honor to belong to the order. Before going on the warpath two rattles were made by this lodge and given to two young men to carry to war with them with which to touch the enemy if possible.

The public ceremonies of this lodge were very fine, with braves in full regalia, and were given for the purpose of inspiring young men with bravery.

WHITE HORSE LODGE

The White Horse Lodge was organized by my father, Chief Standing Bear the First. After the United States Cavalry came among us, father noticed that their various groups of horsemen rode beautiful animals all of one color. One body of soldiers rode only black horses, another rode only gray, and so on. Father so greatly admired the white horse regiment that he organized the White Horse Lodge, the qualifications for membership being a record for bravery and the ownership of a white horse. This lodge usually turned out in full force for the Sun Dance, all members dressed in their wonderful regalia and with their war records strikingly painted in red symbols on the white horses. One warrior, I remember, always painted two hands on the breast of his horse, meaning that he had touched the enemy and that his horse had passed over him. Others painted stripes on the sides and flanks of their animals, claiming for every stripe some brave feat. This lodge became quite popular, and I suspect that it was partly on account of the horses lending themselves so well to decoration. At any rate, they made a fine sight and were greatly admired. There was no secrecy about their rituals, nearly everyone knowing the songs of the White Horse Lodge.

FOX LODGE

The Fox Lodge was organized by the Fox Dreamer. This lodge is one of the most important as well as one of the oldest among the Lakotas and was founded in times so remote that its history is now kept only in legend. Order and harmony are the basis of the Fox Lodge and the ritual shows that even in the early and formative days of their social organization the people strove to conduct their human associations with a minimum of force.

This lodge, formed so long ago for the purpose of assisting large numbers of people to work and play together in

peace, is the only body in Lakota society that bears semblance to the complicated law institution of today's society.
The group of men known as Fox men have been, for time
unknown, the peace keepers for all Lakota gatherings —
hunts, migrations, or ceremonies — and, at my last resi-
dence on the reservation, they were functioning in the same
way.

To the Dreamer, being in solitude and contemplation,
the Fox came and taught the songs and dances of the fox.
Also he made a willing sacrifice of his body so that the Fox
men could wear his skin, thereby partaking of fox swiftness
and nimbleness of feet. For this kindness and because the
fox was one of the first animals to aid the people with his
wisdom when they were young, the Dreamer loved the fox.
So when all the songs and dances had been learned, the
Dreamer went back to his people and taught the young men
what he had learned. Thereupon the young men formed a
lodge in honor of the people's friend, the fox.

The members of the Fox Lodge were mostly young men,
reliable, and, like the fox, active and alert, whom the older
men served as instructors and leaders. The lodge was a
popular one and membership in it was looked forward to by
most young men; nevertheless, no young aspirant would apply for admittance — he could only wait for an invitation.
Quite young boys, from trustworthy families, were sometimes taken into the lodge, since considerable training was
required to fit a man thoroughly for active duty as a Fox
man. I became a member when but ten years of age. Three
members of the lodge called upon father and asked his permission to make me a member. He consented, so I accompanied my friends to my first Fox dance. I watched the
proceeding with great interest and when the men got up to
dance I stood behind them and imitated their steps.

Parents, too, were very proud when their sons became
members of this lodge and usually gave away a horse or
some presents. An invitation betokened the high standing

of the family, for it was extended upon the theory that 'blood will tell' and that sons of braves became good Fox men.

The old men taught the newcomers the songs, dances, and rituals of the lodge; also the calls to assembly. They teach that in the performance of duty the tribe comes first. The Fox men must perform such duties of correction as fall to their lot and allow neither ties of family nor sentiment to interfere with tribal justice. Furthermore they are doubly bound, for when a young man has once accepted the vows and pledges of the lodge he can never break them. He remains with the lodge for life.

Fox men must ever be in readiness for assembly signals, and whenever the call of the Fox, an imitative cry of the fox or softly called '*Hui-i-i*' is heard, the response must be immediate, no matter how unimportant may seem the occasion. I well remember my first lesson, when a small boy, for not heeding a call. The Fox men were giving a dance and instead of joining I rode up and sat on my horse and watched the others. All at once I was startled by two of the braves walking up and taking my blanket from me. Before my eyes they quickly tore it up into convenient sizes for breechclouts and distributed it among the lodge men. I turned my horse about and rode home sorely hurt in pride and humiliated for having my disobedience announced to the public. Should a Fox man allow a call to go unheeded in time of peril, or when quick action is necessary, some forceful reminder equal to his offense would be administered to him — perhaps his horse killed or his tipi destroyed.

Fox men carried no bows and arrows, their weapon being a club similar to the one carried by city policemen. The insignia of the order was a fox-skin, preferably the yellow fox, tied to the end of the club.

Oftentimes a number of bands aggregating several thousand Lakotas moved with no other supervision than a few members of the Fox Lodge riding along the side of the caravan or a little ahead of it. Their duties were to see that children did not stray too far away from the main line, to watch the actions of returning scouts, and to remind hunters not to make any undue noise, especially if nearing the vicinity of buffalo. Occasionally someone tried to sneak away for a lone hunt, but if seen was brought back by a Fox man. If the hunter were inclined to defy the lodge man then a number gave chase and brought him back. Everything was all right without further ado, providing the law-breaking member remained good-natured, but if he got into a bad humor and showed resentment he probably had his bows and arrows, and perhaps, his horse taken from him. Whatever the punishment, the offender was supposed to take it gracefully, but if he did not and persisted in being a bad member of society, the Fox man used his club. Seldom, however, did an individual run the risk of such drastic disfavor, and, on the other hand, never did a Fox man use his weapon until forced to do so.

Sometimes the Fox Lodge held the *Cano unye kicicupi* and sent out young men for the brave test — something which only the most courageous relished. Also in times when enemy tribes encroached upon the territory of the Lakotas, it was usually the Fox Lodge braves who went out against them. Then in early days of reservation life when the Government apportioned large stores of goods, blankets, and food supplies, the Fox men were called into action. They helped with the distribution and saw that no one drew more than once.

Each Fox Lodge had its *wicaklata*, two or three women singers and assistants who learned the entire ritual of the Fox ceremony and took part in all performances. Appreciating the honor bestowed upon them, the *wicaklata* appeared in their finest regalia at these ceremonies. The public performance of this lodge was very impressive, the leader, in full regalia, prancing and trotting around the circle in imitation of the fox. Following him in single file were the other members, men and women, of the lodge. Members who had performed some signal deed of bravery rode horses which were also decorated. One song in the ritual was sung in praise of the *wicaklata* and, of course, was sung only by the braves.

KATELA, OR WOMAN'S LODGE

A very interesting organization was the *Katela*, the members of which were all women and mostly elderly women. The *Katela*, which means the 'fallen' or the 'slain,' was a sort of patriotic order very similar in purpose, I should say, to the D.A.R. The women members all had some male relative who had made a war record or had lost his life on the battlefield, 'in performance of duty,' as the white people put it. So the *Katela* was organized in honor of the warriors and braves, and their ceremonies kept alive the glorious deeds of valor.

Public dances were held, the women having full charge, and dispensing plenty of food. Two or three women seated around a big drum furnished the music while the others danced. Those too old to dance assisted with the singing.

The costume for this order was half red and half blue, and it was customary for a dancer to carry a piece of war equipment — a quiver with bow and arrows, a war-club, lance, or shield. Some even painted wounds on their bodies in remembrance of wounds borne by their loved ones. Later, when the weapons of the white man became known, some of the women carried cavalry swords.

CHAPTER VI

SOCIAL CUSTOMS

MANNERS

THE Lakotas were a social people, loving human companionship and association and admiring the use of manners and deportment that accompanied their social life.

The rules of polite behavior that formed Lakota etiquette were called *woyuonihan,* meaning 'full of respect'; those failing to practice these rules were *waohola sni,* that is, 'without respect,' therefore rude and ill-bred.

A good deal of time was spent in merrymaking, with feasts, songs, dances, and social ceremonies, and anyone coming as a visitor, whether friend or stranger, was welcomed.

Such expressions of greeting as 'How do you do?' or 'How are you?' which imply questions, were never used. Men usually greeted a friend with '*Hohahe,*' which means 'Welcome to my tipi.' Very good friends often used an exclamation of pleasure and surprise, '*Hun-hun-he,* 'and '*Kola,*' the Lakota word for friend. To a relative and to close friends the usual words of greeting were '*Hun-hun-he tahunsa.*' All relations, not of the immediate family, and all close friends were *tahunsa,* or cousins, since it was not customary to call anyone by name. For women a smile, and, if at home, the proffer of food, was the genteel welcome, though two women of close friendship frequently greeted each other with the feminine usage of cousin, or '*Hun-hun-he jepansi.*'

The tipi door was always open for anyone to enter and it was not impolite to walk in without knocking and unannounced, for the phrase 'Come in' was never used to bid one to enter, though when the visitor was in he was at once seated as a mark of hospitality. A stranger, however, coming into the village, especially at night, would call out the fact that he was a stranger and would state his business. The man of the tipi would meet the traveler and on finding him an acceptable visitor would say, 'I'll ask my wife to cook you some food.' The stranger then followed his host into the tipi, knowing that he would be received as a guest.

When the visitor departed, there were no effusive 'Good-byes' and no urgent invitations regarding return visits on either side. The visitor, when ready to leave, would simply say, 'It is now time for me to go,' and having so spoken it would have been poor etiquette to beg him to stay longer.

Praise, flattery, exaggerated manners, and fine, high-sounding words were no part of Lakota politeness. Excessive manners were put down as insincere and the constant talker was considered rude and thoughtless. Conversation was never begun at once, nor in a hurried manner. No one was quick with a question, no matter how important, and no one was pressed for an answer. A pause giving time for thought was the truly courteous way of beginning and conducting a conversation. Silence was meaningful with the Lakota, and his granting a space of silence to the speech-maker and his own moment of silence before talking was done in the practice of true politeness and regardful of the rule that 'thought comes before speech.' Also in the midst of sorrow, sickness, death, or misfortune of any kind, and in the presence of the notable and great, silence was the mark of respect. More powerful than words was silence with the Lakota and his strict observance of this tenet of good behavior was the reason, no doubt, for his being given another fallacious characterization by the white man — that of being a stoic. He has been adjudged dumb, stupid, indifferent, and unfeeling. As a matter of truth, he was the most sympathetic of men, but his emotions of depth and sincerity were tempered with control. Silence meant to the Lakota what it meant to Disraeli when he said, 'Silence is the mother of truth,' for the silent man was ever to be trusted, while the man ever ready with speech was never taken seriously.

Children were taught the rules of *woyuonihan* and that true politeness was to be defined in actions rather than in words. They were never allowed to pass between the fire and an older person or a visitor, to speak while others were speaking, or to make fun of a crippled or disfigured one. If a child thoughtlessly tried to do so, a parent, in a quiet voice, immediately set him right. Expressions such as 'excuse me,' 'do pardon me,' and 'so sorry,' now so often lightly and unnecessarily used, are not in the Lakota language. If one chanced to injure or discommode another, the word *wanunhecun* or 'mistake,' was spoken. This was sufficient to indicate that no discourtesy was intended and that an untoward happening was accidental.

Young Indian folk, raised under the old courtesy rules, never indulged in the present habit of talking incessantly and all at the same time. To do so would have been not only impolite, but foolish; for poise, so much admired as a social grace, could not be accompanied by restlessness. Pauses were acknowledged gracefully and did not cause lack of ease or embarrassment.

A woman of correct social manner was modest, low-voiced, and reserved. She sat quietly on the tipi floor, never flouncing herself about nor talking loudly and harshly. A woman who laughed loudly in order to attract attention was put down as common and immoral and was at once discredited and shunned. According to legend, a woman once had a vision in which she saw the Laughing Woman, or Double Woman, as she was also known. The Laughing Woman gave her laugh with its magic power to the Dreamer so that she might use it in curing the sick and ailing. Thenceforth the Laugh Dreamer became a medicine-woman, curing many people with the magic laugh until some evil-minded women mimicked it for the purpose of luring men who could not resist its charm. Therefore loud-laughing women were considered evil and degraded.

Mothers watched over their boys and girls with equal care, though the girls were subjected to more restraint than the boys. They were given more attention as to personal appearance and never allowed to sit in a careless way. A girl was instructed to sit properly with her feet to one side and her dress neatly arranged. Never must a young woman sit with her feet and legs out in front of her. In arising she must do so lightly and gracefully, as if without effort, and never lift herself up with both hands. Her movements in the tipi must be noiseless and orderly. The well-bred girl, like her mother, was quiet and modest, and very respectful in the presence of elders. Woman's sphere was quite distinctly defined and to obtrude from it was considered bold and improper.

When the girl reached maturity, the father, if he could afford it, held the Corn Dance for his daughter. If this was not possible, then he gave away a horse and the village crier announced that the girl, calling her by name, for a time would *tanke yanke isnati*, that is, live outside and alone for the period of a few days. This ceremony was a very proper one, according to Lakota usage, and ushered the girl from childhood into womanhood.

Women had many social hours at their sewing. If a tipi was needed by a new family, or garments were required for a ceremony, a number of women came together for work and gossip. Sometimes they joined in the play of children who were always about, seeming to enjoy this way of passing the time. Then at times the younger women got together and engaged in games. If the games were public, the women dressed in their best regalia and wore their decorations. Several bands might turn out to watch the play, so the young women made the most of the opportunity to please the eyes of the young men present. One of these games was the *icaslohe*; another was *paslohanpi*. Water games were frequent past times, the women and girls swimming, ducking, and diving. They had a way of belting in a garment at the waist and then tying it about their feet, making a sort of balloon which floated them on the surface of the water. They then played *minika popapi*, exclusively a woman's game. The arms were lifted, then brought down with some force, the hands meeting just below the water. This motion made a booming sound and when many played at once a peculiar roar resulted.

Men, in the presence of women, were very deferent. The freedom and ease of the Tipi Iyokihe was dropped for a more circumspect manner. The taboos of speaking directly to sisters and cousins were strictly observed and one unacquainted with the rules of polite conduct would be led to think the men cold and indifferent toward their women, though actually their attitude and intent were of extreme respect. I remember, though just a small boy, the meeting of my uncle, Brave Eagle, with his love. One night the braves were having a Victory Dance. A beautiful young girl in an elk-tooth-trimmed dress and riding a handsome spotted pony decorated with a quilled and fringed blanket that covered it to the heels, rode up and joined the crowd of onlookers. This young woman soon had the admiring eyes of all the young braves, and Uncle Brave Eagle was among the many who were smitten with her charms. Though already dressed in his regalia, my uncle went home to put on more finery and to repaint his face. He then picked out his best horse and came back to the dance to wait until the people had begun to disperse. Watching his chance he joined the young lady and her woman companion as they rode home. Thus began a courtship that ended in the marriage of Brave Eagle and this beautiful young woman. This young uncle took me about with him quite a good deal when he was learning the art of courtship, letting me ride back of him when he went to visit some girl. If he found a line of other suitors ahead of him waiting to see the girl too, he left me on the horse and joined the line. Feeling the importance of being so entrusted, I obligingly sat on the horse and awaited his return. Uncle, no doubt, learned a good deal about being charming to young women, for when he saw the girl with the elk-tooth-trimmed dress on the spotted horse he made all preparations to meet her without asking for my company. But the point is, he was successful.

There were 'beauties' and 'Beau Brummels,' always conscious of the admiration they got from a crowd, but whatever their conduct in private, they never forgot their bearing in public. Some women gained a wide reputation for their good looks, their fame traveling throughout the tribe, and they became sought after by braves of many bands. The 'beau ideals' were usually handsome men, meeting fully the white man's standard of good looks, and I fancy might have looked well in a tuxedo. Only occasionally did a man or woman elect to remain single throughout life, but if he or she did, it was considered a personal affair, and a woman had to be neither a wife nor a mother in order to maintain a place of respect with her people. Elk Woman, I remember, had many suitors, for she was a woman of beauty and the possessor of many virtues, besides being pleasant in manner. But she caused much wonderment, for she turned all away. Finally, Hawk Man, honored in the tribe, came wooing, and their courtship lasted throughout their lives. Though Hawk Man was ever attentive, the two lived with their respective families and the match considered so ideal by everyone never occurred.

No boy was a full-fledged man until he had been out with a war-party and not until then was he considered eligible for marriage. Whether the enemy was met or not did not matter, for there were other tests for bravery besides meeting the enemy. Neither could he smoke in the Tipi Iyokihe with the other boys and young men who had been out with a war party. If a boy smoked before the proper time, some bodily ailment would befall him, so the older warriors warned him.

There was no tribal charm that worked safety for all the people, nor did every warrior have a medicine. However, before going on the war path, many of the warriors went to a medicine-man and got a *wotahe*, a charm in which he could have faith for his protection. Some of the warriors made their own charms and planted them in the earth as an offering to the Great Mystery. These offerings were little sticks sharpened at one end so they could be stuck in the ground, to the tops of which were fastened little buckskin bags filled with tobacco and an eagle feather or, perhaps, a *wacinhin* or hair-feather. As the warrior planted his offering, he often prayed, 'Grandfather, help me.'

There was one charm, however, known as the *cekpa aknake*, which every boy possessed and which he wore into his first battle with the hopes that it would bring him home safely. When a Lakota boy was born, a small piece of the umbilical cord was placed in a decorated buckskin bag made in the shape of a lizard. The bag was stuffed with buffalo wool in which was wrapped the piece of cord. The bag was sewed up and placed on the boy's back and he wore it until he was six or seven years of age. The mother then kept it and gave it to him as a good-luck talisman when he started with his first war-party. The talisman was made in the shape of a lizard, because it can flatten itself on the ground and appear to be dead, whereas it is very much alive and able to run away speedily from its enemies. So the meaning of the talisman was *telanunwela*, or, 'dead yet alive.' If the boy returned in safety, the mother buried the *cekpa aknake* and it was never seen again.

On the return of a war-party, the *ewakicipi* — Dance of the Victors — was held, that is, if the party returned undefeated. Of course, in case of defeat, there would be only mourning. The *ewakicipi*, or Victory Dance, was the young warrior's first official ceremony and an important event in his life. For the first time he decorated himself as a warrior and joined the braves in the dance, telling the people what he had done to prove his bravery. The boy was bound to learn that the people preferred deeds and actions to words, so he did not talk of his experiences and exploits, no matter how important and thrilling they seemed to him. And for a warrior to sing praise songs for himself would have been the worst form of bragging. But this did not mean that bravery was recognized slowly and reluctantly. At all times honors were generously given. But pretense was not wanted and consequently not an easy thing to get away with. The Lakotas felt it an honor to themselves to decorate their brave men and to sing songs of praise for them. So, when manhood had been reached, either the respect or disrespect of the people was merited and possessed by a young man.

Unfortunate braves left on the battlefield were the only ones for whom speeches were made. Their stories were told and retold to the tribe, for they were entitled to honor even though dead. But for those who had come home alive, the polite and subtle way of relating adventures was through the dance and pantomime. No monuments were raised for the dead, who were cremated, and who were inscribed in the memories and unwritten records of the people. Through songs and dances the fame of the departed remained living in the minds of countless generations who enacted and re-enacted their deeds.

The Lakotas, as a whole, were devoted to their religious ceremonies, those of high class taking upon themselves the duty of observing very closely religious etiquette. *Wakan yan tipi* was a saying, the sense of which was 'The place is holy.' So when one came to a place that had been dedicated to Wakan Tanka it was considered sacred and no one would trespass upon the ground. The Sun Dance poles which were allowed to stand from year to year were never desecrated. Children coming upon a pole would at once become quiet and respectful, while older people often stood in silent reverence for a moment or so. Considerable significance was attached to the circle, it being customary for dancers to define it two or three times in a walk before beginning the dance proper. It was also polite custom to walk around the buffalo skull when one came upon it, since it was a sacred object. Mothers and fathers took little children by the hand and led them around the skull in reverence. Nearly every home kept an ordinary pipe (not the decorated ceremonial pipe) for family prayers. It was customary for the head of the family, either father or grandfather, to light the pipe for a moment each morning, point it to the four directions, and send a few puffs upward to Wakan Tanka. Children, during this short ceremony, stopped their noise and playing, not beginning again until the pipe was laid aside.

There were no special days with the Lakota — no days for worship or rest, no holidays for merrymaking or thanksgiving, no birthdays and no days for commemoration. Every day Wakan Tanka was worshiped and every day was enjoyed as much as possible even if it were moving or hunting day.

Each day, or *anpetu*, was divided into morning, *hunhanni*; noon, *wicokanhiyaye*; evening, *h'tayetu*; and night, *hanhepi*. Days were not designated by names although, since the establishment of the church on the reservation, Sunday has been called *anpetu Wakan* — Holy Day. Time was not divided into units of weeks, months, and years, but days were notched on a stick, a notch larger than the rest being cut every tenth day. Each day's absence of the warriors or scouts was notched either on a stick or a block of wood by an old man who kept the scout tipi open. Every evening the mark was made and when the war-party returned, if victorious, the notch was painted black. A division of time, about thirty days, was kept according to the changes of the moon, and some close observers became very learned in the lore of the moon. Years were kept in mind by some outstanding event such as a hard winter, scarcity of buffalo, or some other important happening.

For figures there were words, but no written signs or marks. Little children learned to count very readily, the system being quite simple:

One,	*wance*	Six,	*sakape*
Two,	*nunpa*	Seven,	*sakowin*
Three,	*yamini*	Eight,	*sakalohan*
Four,	*dopa*	Nine,	*napiciyunka*
Five,	*zaptan*	Ten,	*wikcemna*

In continuing the counting to twenty, the word 'again,' *ake*, was used before each numeral; for instance, eleven was *ake wanci*. Twenty, was 'twice ten' or *wikcemna nunpa*, thirty was 'three times ten' or *wikcemna yamini*, one hundred was *opawinge*, and ten hundred was, *opawinge wikcemna*.

Children were told not to count the stars. Though I never heard of a reason being given, I suppose the impossibility of counting them made of it a foolish pastime. But the reason for other customs of the people were not plain, though they may have been in some past period of time. The Lakota, for instance, would not point his finger at the rainbow for fear that it might become sore and swollen at the tip. The rainbow was called *wikmunke*, or 'trap,' because it held the earth in its embrace. It was supposed to encircle everything, so no matter how far one traveled the end could never be reached. Being a trap it caught the rain and brought it to earth, while its lovely colors were evidence of the greatness and power of the Great Mystery, for only His hand could paint on the sky.

When the swallows, which were called *icapsinpsincela* on account of their swift and bold darting here and there, came in flocks flying audaciously about, we knew a shower was coming our way. While it rained we saw no swallows, but as soon as it had gone, again would come the swallows more hilarious than ever. There is no literal translation for the word *icapsinpsincela*, but it was a war term used by the warriors in describing their quick movements and criss-crossing maneuvers in battle, which were similar to the flying of the swallow.

The swallow was not the only bird-harbinger of rain, however, for the crane foretold wet weather by flying high in the air and coming down whistling all the way. These birds were not water birds but were prairie inhabitants having the common name of sandhill cranes. Their songs or whistled notes were quite soft and melodious and their bills were not the lance-like ones of the water heron. This bill was copied in the construction of the wooden love flutes of the Plains people.

There was a fanciful idea that between the turtle and lightning existed an enmity, so whenever the forks of light seemed to reach earth, the old Lakotas would remark, 'A turtle must be there.'

Twins, for some inexplicable reason, were called by a name meaning navels. Other fanciful ideas were that a worm brought the annoying little whirlwinds and that the 'old woman in the moon' never tired of cooking in her pot. When a three-quarter moon appeared it was said, 'Someone has bitten the moon,' and a stormy or windy day was looked for. Also the first man or woman in a group, whether married or single, to sight the moon arising as a thin rim would have a boy for his first child.

Prairie-dogs were known as 'little farmers,' for they cleared the ground about their dwelling places and soon after there began to grow a plant upon which they lived. Whether they had a system of planting or not we never found out, but it was noticeable that wherever these little animals took up their abode their food plants soon took the place of weeds. Neither did we ever see a prairie-dog 'town' in the process of changing location though it was done quite often. If these animals traveled overland they left no trails, though within their 'towns' the trails were numerous, so it was supposed that they dug tunnels through which they traveled in a body. Yet at that we were mystified when they moved their towns from one side of a stream to the other side. The deserted towns of the prairie-dog seemed to be re-fertilized, no doubt on account of the air and water that got into the soil, for they soon were covered with a grass that afforded an excellent feed for our stock. These grassy places, however, we traveled with care, for when the prairie-dogs moved out, the rattlesnakes moved in.

MORALS

The Lakotas had an adage which was much used in conversation and often repeated for the special benefit of the young. Its words were, 'A Lakota may lie once, but after that no one will believe him.' This saying indicates what the Lakotas thought of lying. They despised it above all things, and for the liar had the least toleration. 'Truth is power,' or, '*Wowicake he iyotan wowa sake*' as the Lakota spoke it, and with him truth was a literal power. For time untold, necessity had compelled its use until it had come to be the cornerstone in the structure of society. Whether or not the homely brevity 'Honest Injun' was originated in jest makes no difference, for, in fact, there was a time when the Lakotas, as a race, were honest and truthful; that is, when truthfulness and honesty were dominant and active tenets of the tribe.

Dishonesty of any sort was bad. For instance, bragging, boasting, swaggering, and even an over-show of authority

were considered dishonest. So if one over vaunted himself
in any way he was immediately ridiculed with the saying,
'His face cover is dead.' This saying was pithy with significance. The gesture of modesty with the Lakota was
hiding the face with a blanket or retiring behind a cover
of reticence, so when the cover became 'dead,' modesty
had passed away. The boaster was a person brazen-faced
and unashamed. But he was, naturally, a rare person and
most always young, so to accuse the Indians, as a people,
of being boasters, as has been done, is an undeserved slur
against the Lakotas. Where truth was so imperative,
boasting could have little place.

Many of the moral and ethical ideas of the Lakotas
were crystalized into mottoes or proverbs that were conveniently expressed in conversation and were indicative
of the practices of the people. From time to time they
were repeated for their influence in directing the thought
of children for, in learning to say them after their elders,
the young became impressed with and heeded the lesson
it was intended they should learn. The motto, 'There is a
hole at end of the thief's path,' plainly indicates what the
Lakotas thought of thievery; while, 'Do not speak of evil
for it creates curiosity in the minds of the young,' suggests
the carefulness with which older people spoke in the presence of children. Knowing the naturally curious bent of
a child's mind, adults tried to direct it toward investigation
of worthwhile and useful things. Other proverbs with
apparent meaning are:

> The life of a greedy person is short.
> No one likes a borrower.
> The industrious woman lives in a good tipi.
> The lazy person gets into mischief.
> Any bow and arrow for a skilled hunter.

One historian, whose book has been a standard history
for young readers for a number of years, remarks that,

though the Plains Indians had words for 'good,' *waste*, and
for 'bad,' *sica*, they had ' ... no code of morals, no conception of right and wrong...' thereby proving amply to his
readers that a people with such a limited vocabulary were
consequently limited in their conceptions of the social
and moral obligations of individuals. In the same paragraph this writer continues, 'The expert thief is held in
high honor...' and, 'The Indian is a great boaster, and
is very fond of "blowing his own trumpet."' Now, in
correction of these statements, righteousness, *woco owan-
tanla*, was an aim and a practice with the Lakota with due
reference to spiritual quality quite distinct from being
just materially good; while wrong, *wicowicasa sni*, with
its significant meaning, 'not like a man,' proves that there
was a standard designated as manly conduct. If words
are allied, as it seems they are, to character and traits,
then the following are suggestive of Lakota thought and
practice:

> *Wokikcanpte*, sympathy
> *Wowasunsila*, pity or kindness
> *Wowicake*, truth
> *Woyuonihan*, respectfulness
> *Wootanla*, honesty
> *Wowima haha*, a joker, one who teases
> *Okola kiciye*, friendship
> *Nakicijin*, loyalty

A Lakota had no idea of 'cultivating superior people.'
Any position gained by an individual in his band was due
solely to his own abilities and efforts. No attachment or
relationship could place individuals or give them power;
no luster could be borrowed and no circle crawled into by
bowing and paying homage. Every honor gained, from
scout to chief, and by those who took the ceremony of
Corn Dance or Sun Dance, was gained on the expressed
willingness to serve the members of the tribe.

Friendship with the Indian was strong, this strength

and endurance being in keeping with his strength and endurance of body. In making friendships or tribal adoptions I have never known the Lakota to use the blood method, so often described by white writers, nevertheless their adoption pacts were most firmly kept. Pledges of brotherhood were regarded as real, and the saying, 'Friendship as close as a brother' was, with them, no high-sounding phrase.

Loyalty was friendship's kin and every Lakota a loyalist; but when the white man came with his disturbing influences, this bond, with others of tribal allegiance, was to be tried and broken. In a few cases Indians betrayed their tribe for white man's gold, but usually they fell first for his flattery and insidious whiskey. The Lakotas were a people without an intoxicating drink, and it was with this terrible destroyer that his loyalty was undermined. There were many Indians of whom we know, who refused, for any price, to be disloyal, and there were probably many more of whom we do not know.

Concerning fidelity, human frailty must be taken into consideration, but the Indian woman was a true wife and the Indian man a true husband. The vows on both sides were taken seriously and both man and woman looked upon their marriage contract as something extremely vital to their position in the tribe. The integrity of the home was revered, and a man known as a good husband and a woman known as a good wife were honored members of society. Polygamy was never extensively practiced among the Lakotas, comparatively few men — chiefs or men of special note — taking more than one wife. But this arrangement was not assigned to divine instruction nor given a religious hue; it was wholly and solely an adjustment with the social plans of the tribe. A chief would have considered it much more dishonorable to have one overworked wife than to have two or three to share the duties of his household, and the women were of the same opinion.

Only once in a while would a man take a fancy to the wife of another man, and *vice versa*, and the few 'triangle' cases that have come to my knowledge were looked upon with disfavor by the rest of the band. But fidelity was another Indian virtue to become weakened by the disruption of his society, for the white man was wont to take the things that pleased him.

'A man (or woman) with many children has many homes.' This was a Lakota proverb showing that generosity was not a salving pretense but a deep permeating spirit of humanity. A society that plans a place for its beings of all ages, from birth to death, proves its spirit of generosity beyond all doubt and makes of it more than the mere limiting business of doling food and tipis. Then there was the spirit of generosity in comradeship — generous even to the giving of life, if necessary, one comrade for the other. The hunter who brought food for the old men and the warrior who with glad songs burdened himself with the care of the orphan were all prompted with hearts full of generosity. Before them, Dame Charity with her false virtues, dare not parade.

Let me tell you a story of early days: Meat was once low in the village and a number of hunters went out to bring in some buffalo which were, at that particular time, scarce. Only three animals were found to be divided among every person in camp. Even the hunters who could have availed themselves of a feast did not do so, and though the portions were small, everyone was served.

Now, hunger is a hard thing to bear, but not so hard when all are sharing the same want in the same degree; but it is doubly hard to bear when all about is plenty which the hungry dare not touch. Sentences imposed upon those who, through hunger, take for their starving bodies, are to me inconceivably cruel, even to my now altered and accustomed viewpoint. For one man with full stomach to heap more misery upon one with an empty stomach

is savage beyond compare. Perhaps I sense the degradation all the more, having tasted the sweetness of the life
of my forefathers.

The Lakota was a man of humility, never forgetting his
insignificance in the sight of Wakan Tanka. He was
humble without cringing, and meek without loss of spirit.
He always faced the Powers in prayer; he never groveled
on the earth, but with face lifted to the sky spoke straight
to his Mystery. There was no holier than himself whom
he might importune to speak for him. The Great Mystery
was here, there, and everywhere, and the Lakota had but
to lift his voice and it would be heard.

Simplicity and directness marked Lakota social manners as it did religious behavior. It was not polite to 'put
on airs' nor to ape another tribe in speech, dress, or
manner. Only on occasion was it proper to display fine
clothing and personal achievement, and even then the
warriors shared honors with their brave and intelligent
horses to whom many a one felt he owed his life. The
animals were paraded in fine regalia bearing the wounds
and scars of battle; but all was done without loud and
flowery speeches.

Our greatest warriors and fighting men were invariably
the quietest of men. Laughers and jokers they were, but
unassuming in manner, some of them, like Crazy Horse,
preferring to wear no regalia whatever. In sharp contrast
were they to most of the army men we first met, who were
always uniformed and stern and authoritative in manner.
Whether natural or not, their formality impressed the
Lakota as bluster. It seemed utterly absurd to them for
men to march, halt, salute, or fight according to order, and
they laughed at the antics of the white, blue-uniformed
akicita. The whole system of army deportment seemed to
deprive a man of individuality in the eyes of Lakota
warriors with whom fighting was not a salaried business
but a chosen calling, usually from sentiment or from love
of sheer excitement.

The Indian was a natural conservationist. He destroyed nothing, great or small. Destruction was not a part of Indian thought and action; if it had been, and had the man been the ruthless savage he has been acredited with being, he would have long ago preceded the European in the labor of destroying the natural life of this continent. The Indian was frugal in the midst of plenty. When the buffalo roamed the plains in multitudes he slaughtered only what he could eat and these he used to the hair and bones. Early one spring the Lakotas were camped on the Missouri river when the ice was beginning to break up. One day a buffalo floated by and it was hauled ashore. The animal proved to have been freshly killed and in good condition, a welcome occurrence at the time since the meat supply was getting low. Soon another came floating downstream, and it was no more than ashore when others came into view. Everybody was busy saving meat and hides, but in a short while the buffalo were so thick on the water that they were allowed to float away. Just why so many buffalo had been drowned was never known, but I relate the instance as a boyhood memory.

I know of no species of plant, bird, or animal that were exterminated until the coming of the white man. For some years after the buffalo disappeared there still remained huge herds of antelope, but the hunter's work was no sooner done in the destruction of the buffalo than his attention was attracted toward the deer. They are plentiful now only where protected. The white man considered natural animal life just as he did the natural man life upon this continent, as 'pests.' Plants which the Indian found beneficial were also 'pests.' There is no word in the Lakota vocabulary with the English meaning of this word.

There was a great difference in the attitude taken by the Indian and the Caucasian toward nature, and this difference made of one a conservationist and of the other a non-conservationist of life. The Indian, as well as all other creatures that were given birth and grew, were sustained by the common mother — earth. He was therefore kin to all living things and he gave to all creatures equal rights with himself. Everything of earth was loved and reverenced. The philosophy of the Caucasian was, 'Things of the earth, earthy' — to be belittled and despised. Bestowing upon himself the position and title of a superior creature, others in the scheme were, in the natural order of things, of inferior position and title; and this attitude dominated his actions toward all things. The worth and right to live were his, thus he heartlessly destroyed. Forests were mowed down, the buffalo exterminated, the beaver driven to extinction and his wonderfully constructed dams dynamited, allowing flood waters to wreak further havoc, and the very birds of the air silenced. Great grassy plains that sweetened the air have been upturned; springs, streams, and lakes that lived no longer ago than my boyhood have dried, and a whole people harassed to degradation and death. The white man has come to be the symbol of extinction for all things natural to this continent. Between him and the animal there is no rapport and they have learned to flee from his approach, for they cannot live on the same ground.

Because the Indian was unable, and in some cases refused, to accept completely the white man's ways which were so contrary to his heritage and tradition, he earned for himself the reputation of being lazy. He preferred his tribal ways all the more on account of his disappointment with the white man whose deceit and weaknesses filled the Indian soul with distrust. He clung to his native customs and religion, which he could scarcely change if he would; and so the Indian, who had lived the most active of lives and who had developed an unusually high physical perfection, was adjudged the most indolent of characters. And this reputation, false as it is, has become fixed in the mind of the public.

The Indian was thrust almost immediately from his age-old mode of living into one that was foreign to him in every respect; religious, tribal, and social life was disrupted and he was placed in the impossible position of trying to remake and remould himself into a European.

Food, which had always been procured through the exercise of great energy and industry, was doled and rationed to him; clothing, which so fitted his imagination and environment, was replaced with garments incongruous and, for him, injurious to health; for the cleanly, well-aired tipi, in which he lived when sheltered at all, he was given the army tent and wooden shacks. Even his spiritual life was disarranged, his religious ceremonies, songs and dances forbidden and in some cases stopped by order, thus filling him with resentment. Everything that was natural and therefore healthful, was displaced with things unsuitable, foreign, and unfitted.

The results of this immediate and drastic change were bewildering mentally and injurious physically. The incentive to lead an industrious life was gone and the general upset so disastrous that the decline of the native American at once set in.

Some of the foodstuffs introduced to the Lakota and rationed out to them when the buffaloes were gone and wild plant food was fast disappearing were liked at first taste. Aside from the question as to whether or not they proved wholesome, they served the purpose of keeping them from growing hungry. They took readily to syrup, molasses, gum, candy, sugar, and all fruits, some for the first time seen or tasted, such as bananas, apples, peaches, and prunes. Coffee, baking powder, cornstarch, cheese, and white flour were not so well liked and proved to be not beneficial, while bacon and cattle meat could, at first, scarcely be endured.

Among the articles readily accepted were woolen blankets, while the gay-colored quilts were thought wonderful things to possess. The large cooking kettles and pots were, of all articles, the most prized by the Indian woman lucky enough to get hold of one. However, sewing machines, furniture, wagons, harness, farm implements, and house-building tools were quite unusable at first.

My father was one of the first of his tribe to learn the use of hammer, saw, and nails, and try to build a house. I recall him now, an amusing sight, sitting on the roof of the building industriously driving nails, his blanket wrapped about him and his long hair hanging from under a derby hat. Father was a man who foresaw coming events clearly and he tried manfully to meet the situation with dignity and composure. But to expect human beings, amenable and plastic as they are, to prosper and advance under conditions as imposed by the European was short-sighted and feeble pretense. Had conditions been reversed and the white man suddenly forced to fit himself to the rigorous Indian mode of life he might now bear the stigma of 'lazy' if, indeed, he were able to survive at all. Even today, in the light of a little just reasoning, it is easily seen why the Indian did not and does not wish to discard his way of living for those of a people whom he neither fully understands nor respects.

An element that created distrust in the Indian was the white man's greed. It was not Indian custom for individuals to lay up stores for revenue, to fence land, to capture and hold animals for sale, to fight kith and kin, or to lay by any goods for the sake of mere possession. Any and all goods were to be used by band members at the call of need. If a man were without a horse it was the chief's place to see that he got another; if a family needed a tipi it was the duty of all in the band to lend hands in getting another, and if a child became orphaned it received the care of everyone in the band. There was no possible excuse for hoarding; on the contrary it stood for selfishness and lack of self-restraint, since all goods or accumulated property were tacitly for the purpose of distribution. The opposite viewpoint of the Caucasian allowed him to destroy and covet Indian possessions, and his greed fathered the cruelty which the Indian suffered. Yet, the amazing thing is that the Indian is the one who bears the charge of being cruel.

Against this charge I take a stand, for that the Indian was cruel has also become a fixity in the minds of many — the Indian and cruelty being synonymous terms in numerous written records of the white man. All things have conspired to keep this falsity alive in the minds of an ignorant people — books, newspapers, magazines, motion pictures, and other institutions. Little school children by the thousands have been taught that the Indian is a cruel savage when they should be taught that never did the Indian meet the white man as a hostile but as a friend; that he never fought except as a patriot for his home and fireside; that but for the friendliness of the Indian the Pilgrim Fathers would never have survived; and that many times the native people delayed retaliation for wrongs until it was too late for safety. Not long ago the cover-sheet of a boys' publication which was distributed by the thousands displayed a lurid picture of the face of an Indian, fiendish in expression, and holding in his hand in a menacing manner the dagger of the white man's invention. Books of untold number relate Indian massacres and atrocities, never finding excuse for these deeds, nor relating massacres and atrocities of the white man which are just as numerous and just as merciless. If the public were a thinking public the very fact that history is so palpably prejudiced — the white man always right, the Indian always wrong — would arouse a doubt; would demand a fair accounting for the sake of history, for true knowledge, and respect for truth.

It was not tribal practice, nor was it a rule of their warfare, for the Lakota to torture their enemies. It is Lakota history, not white man's history, that the Lakota instituted chivalry and were the knights of chivalry upon this continent. At times they took captives just for the fun of showing their eminent skill and prowess, took these captives home, fêted them, treating them as guests and not as prisoners of war. When the game was over the 'guests' were dressed in the finery of the hosts, given the best horses in the band, and allowed to go home in state. Even as late as my boyhood days, after the change had come for the Lakota, this was done. I remember one of these 'guests' whom I met in later years when we had both become students at Carlisle school.

I learned the arts of warfare from my father and he was a great warrior. If there had been a system of cruelty I should have learned it, but there was nothing in the regimen of a hunter scout or warrior to make of a Lakota a cruel torturer. Warfare with the Lakota was almost entirely a matter of keeping his hunting territory free from use by unfriendly tribes. War parties, as a rule, were not large, sometimes but two or three men, and his fighting, like his living, was largely up to the individual. Even these fighting men were much more interested in keeping the buffalo and other game on their preserves than in taking captives whom they would only have to feed. Rather than putting all his ingenuity to work on the refining of warfare, such as is being done today, he was exerting his finer energies toward getting closer to the inner secrets of nature and he did make some fundamental discoveries along this line. In other words he was steadily working toward humaneness instead of away from it.

Slavery in any form did not exist among the Lakotas. Each and every person performed his own duties of labor, and not even the animals were brought under this subjection. One of the saddest sights today is the wild animal caged and tortured for me to idly gaze at. 'Animal study' is sometimes a given excuse, but the Indian learned his lessons from the animals in surroundings that were natural to both and where life and its reactions were natural. Furthermore, the approach of the Indian toward the animal kingdom was not in the manner of a detached study but more the natural process of 'getting acquainted' — an exchange of friendship and the bounties thereof. The Lakota built no fences, cages, pens, corrals, nor prisons. Deer runs were occasionally used, but the strongest part of these were the footsteps of the Deer medicine-man over which no deer could step. No attempt was ever made as far as I know to corral buffalo and keep them as cattle herds were kept. Barriers, or runways, were sometimes erected to assist hunters in herding together the animals or in forcing them over a high bank, but these, of course, were but temporary structures. The dog, it seems, became the helpmate of the Lakota far beyond all memory of the time. When, where, and how it came into the domestic life of the people does not appear to be known now. But wolves and coyotes are called *sunke mani tu*, or 'lost dogs' — that is, animals that have strayed from the fold. The dog was held in reverence by the Lakotas, as shown by the songs of the Thunder Dreamer, and through these songs the eating of the dog was sanctioned at feasts, councils, and ceremonies. The Thunder Dreamer learned his songs when the warriors of the Thunder Nation visited him in a vision. The horse was accepted at once by the Indian. According to the story of the Oglala band of Lakotas, the first horse they saw was already domesticated and appeared among them one early morning contentedly feeding within the circle of their tipis. It was a marvel to them — a beast of beauty and fascination. When the Lakota later captured the wild horse it was to make of him a companion and to decorate and ceremonialize him. Songs and dances were dedicated to the horse and it joined the warriors in the dances about the camp fire. In the hands of the Indian the horse would have remained, no doubt, a beneficent animal, but in the hands of the white man it spelt the Indian's doom. But to the glory of the Lakota it can be said that he never enslaved animal nor fellow being. His freedom was such as is not conceivable today, and because of this the soul of man has become hardened.

The white man's estimate of the Indian is established; but seldom, I dare say, have the thoughts of the white man been troubled with the query of the Indian's estimate of the European. However, the attitude of the Lakota toward the white people whom they first saw has its interest and value. The general feeling of the Indian for the white settler was toleration; but always the great wish was to be left alone and have the homeland remain undisturbed by his presence and for all the kindly feeling that sometimes existed, the Indian had no desire to associate and mingle with the white man. The behavior of some of the white people seemed very fine to us, and these we admired greatly; however, not all white people were fine and upright in their dealings, and the Indians, in my boyhood time, were becoming extremely discriminating and watchful. So foreign and strange were many of these first settlers that we found it hard to understand them. Some were rough, loud-talking and swearing, and not too clean; their habit of wearing whiskers and beards added to their strange and foreign appearance. These people built houses by digging into the earth in the side of a band or hill and covering the roof over with earth also, the smoke from their fires seeming to come from the ground. These people endured great hardships, and all the while they were thinking that our women were slaves we felt that their's were. It may not flatter the white man, but the Lakota did not think him considerate toward his women. Whereas the Indian lived a healthy and cleanly life in the environment of the plains, white men and women could not, and their most obvious unfitness to live in our country did not add to whatever feeling of charity we might have had toward them.

The Lakotas were always proud of their prowess as warriors and it was never their opinion that the white soldiery were their equals as fighters. They do not admit today that they were ever defeated fairly; they consider themselves the victims of treachery. To them, no man who required another man to tell him to pick up his gun, to stand, run, halt, salute, and march into the foe, could possibly be a good warrior. Even bedecked officers, whose men did not quietly follow them, but who loudly commanded and brandished swords over their heads, who sometimes were not to be found in the front line of fighting, all in opposition to age-old Lakota methods, did not receive the respect that our own great leaders received. It was honorable custom for a Lakota warrior to meet and defeat only enemies of equal skill; so, for instance, when a Lakota had met and vanquished a Pawnee, a tribe eminently skillful with the bow and arrow, he was much praised. Then, if he threw all weapons away and 'touched his enemy,' he became noted for bravery. It was for such acts as these that the brave one danced a new dance of victory and received songs of praise. The reticence of Lakota warriors in discussing their battles with the white people, even their victories, has been often commented upon. In particular, there was notable silence on the part of Lakota warriors after the Custer battle, though in this instance, their victory was under most adverse circumstances for, on this occasion, the Lakotas had with them their women and children, and being on a buffalo hunt, with no thought of warfare, had no scouts out to warn them of the approach of the army. But it is Lakota history that many of the men they fought that day were not true fighting men from their standpoint.

The following incident shows how fearless some of the Lakota braves became of white soldiery. The buffalo being gone, our band had been promised cattle meat instead, but, as usual, promises being no guarantee, our band became in need of food. When the need became urgent, father put on his headdress and rode out to some cattle which were grazing in plain sight of the fort and began driving them toward our camp. He told us later that first a trumpet sounded, then an officer commanded the men to mount and line up, and these, after some orders, proceeded toward him. Father paid no attention, but went on herding the cattle and turning them toward our village. Whenever the soldiers came quite close, father would turn his horse quickly and show fight, whereupon the soldiers would stop. He would then go on and they would follow, but stop as soon as he turned and prepared to battle. This kept up for some time until father finally reached home with our meat. The old Oglalas still remember this happening, and when I visited them a few months ago, Chief Flies Above recounted it among his memories and laughingly asked me if I remembered the incident.

Regarding the use of flint arrow-points, the Lakotas never claimed to have made them. Weapons of the Lakota, which were the war-club, tomahawk, bow and arrow, and the lance were the discoveries of native artisans; but, according to legend, the spider made the flint points and left them on the ground for the Lakotas to find. They were, therefore, called spider arrow-heads. The legend says that one day long ago a party of warriors were traveling. They had camped and one of them led his horse to the spring for water. There he heard a tapping noise like someone close to the earth chipping on a stone. He listened, but the tall grass concealed whatever might be there so, as the sound continued, the warrior called his companions to come. They, too, heard the noise, so parted the tall grass and at this the spider jumped up quickly and ran away. Where he had been lay an arrow-point and the warrior picked it up and saw that it fitted on the end of his arrow. Thereafter the Lakotas found plenty of arrow-points and have used them ever since to tip their arrows, finding them more effective than the fire-hardened wood or bone tips.

Instruments of warfare, punishment, and destruction introduced by the European to the people of this continent, and some of them to the Lakota, were swords, bayonets, scaffolds, stocks, ducking stools, gun, cannon, ball and chain, branding irons for both human and animal, spurs, steel traps, dungeons, burning at the stake, scalping, the whip and lash, dynamite, and whiskey.

With a sword, the white leader urged his warriors into conflict; cannon ball mowed down our women and children; the wicked gun brought the last buffalo to its knees; the bayonet pierced the side of our beloved Crazy Horse; dynamite desecrated nature by destroying the marvelous dams of the patient beaver, and in one holocaust two hundred Indian martyrs died at the stake; [1] and whiskey — it is an avalanche still on its way.

With these instruments were the peace and order of the Lakota destroyed, crime coming in their place; for certainly there was little or no crime among the people of the plains until their tribal life was disrupted. Some of the crimes the Lakota did not know were arson, slander, bribery, and persecution. Murder was a rare occurrence, and as for theft, many things which the white man considers theft were not considered so by the Lakota; for instance, taking food for the hungry.

Even the branding iron, though the Lakota used it later upon cattle, was at first strange and inexplicable. It was a hateful thing, but in this, when we later became cattlemen, we followed the path of the white man.

Perhaps the Lakota custom of wearing the *pecokan sunpi*, or so-called scalp-lock, has led unnumbered people to believe that the Indian was an inveterate scalp-hunter and that he invited a scalping by wearing his hair in a convenient lock. The Lakota did not wear a braid of hair for

---

[1] I here refer to the burning of Pueblo Indians by the Spaniards.

this purpose; neither did he always wear this braid at the top center of the head.

The men of the Lakotas, and most plains warriors, wore the *pecokan sunpi*, a small circlet portion of the hair which was braided. The term *pecokan sunpi* means 'a braid' and it never at any time had anything to do with scalping, its purposes being for milder reasons than war. The Lakotas loved feather decorations and used them extensively, not only for their colorful beauty, but for the religious significance and for the further meaning attached to them when worn by scouts and warriors. The men wore their hair long and flowing, and since it was not easy to attach ornaments to loose hair, it was convenient to braid a portion on whatever part of the head the decoration was to be worn. This braid, or so-called scalp-lock, might be at the top of the head, back of the head, at the sides of the forehead, or in the middle of the forehead, depending on the style of the decoration and somewhat on the fancy of the wearer. It was the style with some warriors and braves to wear a braid on each side of the forehead, allowing them to hang to the ears where shell and other ornaments were hung. Then when the Lakotas adopted from the Omahas the wearing of the roach, a small braid was run from the top of the head through the roach to hold it in place. So from time historic the Lakota warrior has worn the *pecokan sunpi* as a token of his love of decoration and vanity.

Now the Lakota did wear human hair as decoration on clothing, and here again the white man has misjudged motives and infringed on truth, for the custom had its source in love and not in war. There was no such thing as a war shirt, most warriors stripping for a conflict. There was, however, the *wicapaha okli*, or hair shirt. Upon death of one in a band it was the custom for friends and relatives to cut their hair in mourning; the greater the grief, the shorter the hair was cut. Many of the women had long, lovely braids of which they were very proud and these they gave to male relatives who made a fringe of them for their shirts. The taking of trophies was not an established custom in Lakota warfare, for just as the word of the scout was unquestioned, so the word of the warrior was undoubted, and it was no more required for one to bring in the fresh scalp of his enemy to prove a conquest than it was for the other to bring in a buffalo chip to prove that he had found buffalo. The proof-demanding white man has never, of course, conceded the truthfulness of the Indian, and so another undeserved and ugly characteristic has become attached to him as a race.

Contact with the white man brought changes in the way of living and then came changes in the manner of the people. The natural food supply gone, the Lakotas were faced with a sure, quick loss of tribal morale and integrity. No matter how strong a people may be, they cannot withstand the shock of having the source of their food-supply destroyed. The fate of the buffalo foretold the fate of the Lakota. Age-old social customs were arrested and the easy flow of life diverted. It was as if a runner suddenly felt the ground beneath his feet disappear, leaving him off balance and plunging over a precipice.

Catering to the white man, and especially to the white agent, began. Then came an unnatural shifting of things. Indians who were amenable to white cajolery found prominence in the eyes of the white people and became known and called chiefs by them. One Indian, now notable in white man's history, was known in Washington as a chief before ever his own people conferred upon him the title. Only by mere chance (the refusal of the one selected to go) and the announcement, made voluntarily, that he would fill the place, had he gone to Washington as an emissary. This man was dealt with by white officials as if he were an actual chief of his people, with the result that he gained certain powers others of his tribe did not have. Eventually he was elected chief according to tribal manner. Undoubtedly, this man was a great fighter and warrior, but he was, nevertheless, lacking in the traditional qualifications for a chief. It is not true that only the names of the great and brave from the Lakota standpoint are found on the treaties made with the white men, the actual truth being that the really strong men of the tribe — those regarded by their tribespeople as patriots — refused ever to mingle freely with the agents or soldiery. Their distrust was unshakable and they held themselves apart. They are therefore unknown except in the hearts and minds of the older Indians of today, and so far as most white men or the younger generation of Indians are concerned, they are lost forever. Such names as Quick Bear, Swift Bear, and Black Crow are not often spoken of. Neither is Crazy Horse. This great chief was tremendously popular among the members of his own tribe, but it was for this very reason that he incurred strong enemies among the Lakotas who had been intrigued by white men's promises. Crazy Horse was worshipped for his ability, amounting almost to magic, and for his superb knowledge of strategy in warfare. More than that, he bore a charmed life with the aid of the dauntless hawk, until evil came into tribe in the for them of envy and treachery; but not until the world became chaotic for the Indian did the power of truth and righteousness fail. Crazy Horse, wise beyond words, sought to stave off destruction by refusing contact with the white man, but he was forced to succumb.

Important as is Crazy Horse in Lakota history, he is, as a figure, rather dim in white man's history. Only now and then he appears upon the written page and then behind veils of mystery. To the white man he was a 'fanatic,' a 'trouble-maker,' an 'agitator,' and to General Miles he was 'savagery personified.' All of which only means that he gave the white man a lot of trouble. But so do all great patriots. George Washington gave England a lot of trouble, too.

Crazy Horse was a man of his word and was furious at the duplicity of the white man. According to the Laramie treaty, the Lakotas were to be left alone and no white man was to pass over or through any part of his reservation and hunting ground without the consent of the Indians. Yet, within three years, white surveyors were on the land and Custer was exploring the Black Hills and every tenet of the treaty was disregarded. Crazy Horse saw Red Cloud and Spotted Tail both betrayed by the white man as well as Sitting Bull. They had all signed treaties with the white man in solemn council and the words of the white men had been broken. Crazy Horse saw nothing, knew nothing but treachery from the white man. He felt himself above dealing with men who knew no honor. As by all such men Crazy Horse was sincerely hated and feared. To get rid of him was the dearest wish of many, both white and Indian. And, of course, the most subtle way was to turn his people against him. It was well known that the promise to make him Chief of Chiefs, freely circulated, would make for Crazy Horse many bitter enemies, even though it was not a promise meant for fulfillment. Preparations had been made to send Crazy Horse as a prisoner for life to the island, Dry Torgugas — a sentence which, if carried out, would have been far worse for him than death itself.

From a military standpoint it was quite necessary to rid the land of Crazy Horse. He represented the last stronghold of a weakened and all but subjected nation, so against him trickery and treachery was concentrated and finally prevailed.

Crazy Horse foresaw the consequence of his surrender. It meant submission to a people whom he did not consider his equal; it meant the doom of his race. Crazy Horse feared no man and when he did surrender, it was not from volition on his part but because his people were tired of warfare. When peacemakers were sent to him to ask if he would smoke the pipe of peace it was with due consideration for the wish of his followers that he consented to smoke, and it is but a white man's myth that he was 'induced' to surrender by Spotted Tail.

But what the white man thinks of Crazy Horse matters little; it is his own people we should ask for our truest estimate.

Iron Horse, who is now old and almost blind, remembers Crazy Horse well. He says, 'Crazy Horse was a small man, dark in complexion, with fine brown hair which he wore gathered in a knot in the center top of his forehead. Through the knot was thrust some slough grass worn for magic purposes. On the occasions that I saw him he wore but one feather of the spotted eagle at the back of his head. Crazy Horse was very modest and retiring in nature, but was beloved for his bravery. Eight horses were shot from under him at various times but he was never even wounded, for the reason that he was a great medicine-man as well as a great warrior. His wife, *Tasina Sapewin*, or 'Her Black Blanket,' was my sister. After the death of Crazy Horse she lived here at Pine Ridge with my wife and me. She never at any time was afflicted with tuberculosis, but lived to be about eighty years of age, dying at the Fourth-of-July celebration at Porcupine Creek. The statements that a white physician took care of my sister are false, for she lived with me to her end.

'Other chiefs were very jealous of my brother-in-law and they brought about his death. His parents and my sister took his body from Ford Robinson and buried him close to Pine Ridge. Later, however, they removed the body secretly and buried it in some white sand cliffs near Porcupine Creek. The parents and widow continued to guard the body, refusing to reveal the burial place, and to this day no one knows where his body lies.

'Whenever my sister was asked to disclose the grave of her husband she always refused, saying, "No, you were all jealous of my husband, and for jealousy you killed him. I shall never tell where he is." Though offered money, she kept her secret.'

White Rabbit, now in the eighties, knew Crazy Horse well also. He told me:

'The mother of Crazy Horse died when he was about two years old. His stepmother, who was also his aunt, raised him as her own child. Crazy Horse died young, being about thirty-seven when he passed away. He had two wives.

'I once tried to tell Crazy Horse to give up the warpath and go to Washington, for he would then be made chief of all the Oglalas, a place he well deserved. His power was recognized and the Oglalas would have preferred him to others who became chiefs. But he replied, "No, I have heard that even some of the Indians now want to kill me."

'Another time I tried to persuade Crazy Horse to go to Washington and establish himself with the Government and occupy the place he should, but still he hesitated, for the talk that he was to be made chief over all was causing intense jealousy. He was most modest, but his superiority over other leaders was unquestioned. Other leaders had become jealous of him and they knew that if he went to Washington and became a head chief that they would not receive the acknowledgment they wished. So his death was plotted, but Crazy Horse was our greatest chief.'

Chief Flies Above recounted the names of Fast Whirlwind, Bull Bear, White Blackbird, Conquering Bear, and Big War Leader as some who are revered in memory's history. But, of all our great, he says 'Crazy Horse was the greatest fighting man and chief the Oglalas ever had.'

The most graphic story I ever heard concerning the death of Crazy Horse was told me by Jennie Fast Thunder, a distant relative of mine, who now lives on the Wounded Knee Creek. Jennie, wife of Louis Fast Thunder who was a cousin of Crazy Horse, is now eighty-two years old and stone blind, but her memory is still good. She said:

'I rode with my husband and Crazy Horse to Fort Robinson in a light wagon the day that Crazy Horse lost his life. We were camped on Beaver Creek when word was brought to Crazy Horse that if he would come into Fort Robinson the officers would council with him concerning the matter of making him chief of all the Oglalas. So we started, Crazy Horse and my husband on the seat and I in the back. When about halfway to the fort the interpreter, a half-breed, Louis Bordeau by name, and the agent, who were riding ahead of us, stopped. The interpreter shouted back to the Indians and told them all not to ride so close to our wagon, but to slow down. They obeyed, and we rode on with the agent and the interpreter.

'As we rode along, my husband kept trying to encourage Crazy Horse, who seemed low-spirited. He would say, "Be brave, they have promised to make you a great chief. No matter if they try to kill you, be brave. You and I have fought together and we are not afraid to die together; but they have promised not to harm you, so be brave!" Crazy Horse made few replies and talked very little on the way.

'When the interpreter warned the Indians to stay back, that was the last I saw of Little Big Man for some time. He rode horseback with the others and had been keeping close to our wagon. We followed the agent and interpreter straight to the guard house instead of the officer's quarters where we supposed we were going. We all got out of the buggy. Everywhere there seemed to be Red Cloud's and Spotted Tail's Indians.

'Crazy Horse was at once taken into the guard house, but he had no sooner disappeared inside the door than he rushed out and I heard him using the brave word — the word a warrior uses when he wishes to keep up his courage — *H'g un*. At that moment Little Big Man appeared. I saw him spring to Crazy Horse and grasp him by the arms to prevent his fighting. Crazy Horse was exclaiming, "Let me alone! Let me alone!" As he rushed out, he drew his knife and Little Big Man was struck in the arm. Then I saw an officer, a man with white hair and white beard with shoulder trimmings on his coat, raise a weapon which I thought was a sword. But whatever it was the man commanded, "Hold on! Hold on!" and ran the weapon through the body of Crazy Horse. He sank to the ground, moaning, "They have killed me!" the blood pouring from his wounded side.

'At once the excitement was great, but I remember my husband stopped and picked him up, and Standing Bear the First, who was related to Crazy Horse, placed his blanket on the ground and helped to put the stricken man on it. By this time the excitement had increased and I was terribly frightened. That evening Crazy Horse passed away, and his parents placed his body on a *travois* and took it away, burying it secretly. Whenever anyone asked his wife about the grave of her husband she always replied, "I shall never tell anyone where he is; it was your jealousy that killed him." His parents never told anyone where they had put the body of their son and no living Sioux knows where it is. And white people who claim to know do not speak the truth.'

Before Crazy Horse was killed, the Sioux occupied the territory where Fort Robinson and Chadron, Nebraska, now are. But after our return from the Missouri River we noticed that the Red Cloud Indians stopped where their present agency is. At the time, not much thought was given the matter, but some time later there was reason for speculation. The white surveyors came in and it was discovered that the land west of Pine Ridge was no longer tribal territory. Then there were wonderment and complaint. No one seemed to know when the change had been made; no one seemed to know of any papers or treaty ceding this land. As the surveying progressed, it was found that one half of the waters of the Niobrara River which the Oglalas supposed they owned, was gone, and that reservation land was far north of the river. This caused more grumbling in councils.

In due time the Government erected for Red Cloud a two-story house, fine for its time, in which he lived until he died.

When Spotted Tail returned from the Missouri River, he stopped at Rosebud, to remain the rest of his life. He, too, was favored by the Government, and for him was built a two-story home, the finest and largest in the vicinity at the time.

No monument has ever been erected in memory of Crazy Horse, but in the hearts of the old people there abides the warmth of devotion for this fine patriot.

Life has been strange since the white man came. Indians who accepted his ways have been called progressive. Those who were weak and traitorous in the eyes of their tribespeople have been lauded and praised by white officialdom. They have found a place in white man's history, while many who lived far above treachery, who lived beyond the contaminating influence of the white man's dollar, and who cherished Lakota ideals until they sank beneath the cruel waves of his disdain, are unknown. Today the young Indian who dons a white collar and assumes the mannerisms of the white man and adopts his ways to the destruction of his morals and physique is called progressive. Thus, still, is the Indian deluded.

DRESS

Many pages have been written describing the clothing of the American Indians, and every boy scout knows how to make what he supposes to be a war-bonnet and a war-shirt. But no Indian of my tribe, nor any Plains tribe Indian, so far as I know, ever wore a special garment for war. Lakota warriors engaging in warfare wore whatever they chose, usually nothing more than breechclout and moccasins. Sometimes, however, a Lakota deliberately chose to make himself conspicuous to the enemy just to show how brave he was, and putting on his regalia and headdress dared them to make of him a mark. Then, occasionally a warrior got a premonition that he would be killed, so he put on his finery so that he might die all dressed up.

The *wicapaha okli*, or hair-shirt, which the Lakota trimmed with long fringes of human hair, was called the war or scalp shirt by the white people, because they thought we used the hair of our enemies. This garment has been copied far and wide, used in wild west shows and in pictures, and exhibited by collectors as a type of Indian war-shirt. The *wicapaha okli* was not a war-shirt, but just the opposite; it was a peace or a judge's shirt and was worn only by the peacemakers in the band. In olden days only two shirts of this character were made to a band, the men who wore them being of known judgment, capable of arbitrating the affairs of the tribe. A ceremony was connected with the making and decorating of these shirts. The women mourners, who had supplied the hair, arranged it in little bunches, fastening the end of each bunch with colored porcupine quills. When the hair was all arranged and the shirts finished, the braves gathered for a ceremony of story-telling. Each brave picked up only as many bunches as he had brave stories to tell, not in the usual way of the dance but in words. To each bunch we told a story, thereafter the hair representing the story. When the story-telling was over and the festivities had ended, the hair was put on the shirts as fringe. The garments were then laid away and worn by the peacemakers only when in session for some tribal affair. It was somewhat similar in meaning to the black robe worn by court judges. The real value of the shirts, however, lay in the history they carried and they could be rightly called 'history shirts.' They were rare relics, commemorating the tears of women and the bravery of men.

Clothes are as much an expression of the inner man as are his songs, dances, and poetry. There is profound meaning in the nature and mode of dress fashioned by a people, and why are not their customs directed by forces as deep and fundamental as are the feathered clothing of the bird and the furred clothing of the animal? There was deep reason for the great variance in dress of the invading white men and the natives whom they found on this continent. The races from Europe arrived — veritable armories of steel with rattling musketry and clanking swords, their appearance denoting the nature of the societies from which they came. As combative as the scaled and clawed monsters that once inhabited this continent, they were clothed in keeping with their nature. The European mind was absorbed in conquest, this spirit superseding the impulses of suavity and kindness, and the iron heel of the intruder was pressed upon his human victims by the hot impulses of a heart of steel. With him might was right.

The native American clothed his naked body in golden sunshine to which he offered adoration each morning. He luxuriated in the rain that kindly powers poured upon him as a blessing. Every phenomenon of nature appeared sublime to his wonder and reverence. Living was glorified, untouched by the stigma of hell. Indian life had not so much to hide; life was more open, doors were not locked and barred, and his brain had not been given for centuries to hiding his thoughts, to deception, lying, and subterfuge. His pathway upward was not so strewn with these stumbling-blocks, and could he have been left free and alone to his own devices for a few more centuries, the native American might now be basking in the warmth of true achievement. His ideas of equity, of the kinship and unity of life, might now be bearing fuller fruit, and the Pipe of Peace might still be the symbol of the sacredness of the word and man's duty to man. Faith and belief were such supreme emotions with the native man that at first sight of his destroyer, he almost believed him half-god.

To share alike was schooled into Lakota thought, even with enemies, and this feeling being extended to the animal world made of him the true sportsman of the continent.

The garments of the Lakotas, for both men and women, were most comfortably and hygienically made, being loose-fitting to allow for free movement. Air circulated to all portions of the body, the pores of the skin being unhampered in their natural function of breathing. The dress of the Lakota woman was simple and fundamental in line, hanging from the shoulders with deep yoke and sleeves in one, a style that has been used and adapted by the fashionable modiste. As for footwear, none was ever constructed that so promoted the comfort and natural growth of the foot. In the winter boots were sometimes made of tanned buffalo hide and worn with the hair on the inside. They were light in weight and warm. The wearer of these boots or moccasins was never troubled with corns, bunions, or callouses.

If it is true that people 'love fine clothes because they love fine manners,' then the description is fittingly applied to the Lakotas, for they had a great fondness for decorated clothing. The long trails of beautiful feathers, the flaring headdress, deep fringe, and feather tassels were indicative of much attention to appearance, and certainly one could not well carry a regal headdress and trail without attention to posture and poise, while the significance given to articles of ceremonial decoration indicates the love of ceremony and dignity.

The Lakota loved color, line, design, form, and rhythm.

Some of the articles used to satisfy his fancy for beauty were shells, elk-teeth, dyed buckskin, quillwork, paint, fur, fringe, designs, colored feathers and, after the coming of the white man, beads, bells, and copper wire for earrings and bracelets. Also he was extremely fond of perfume, which he purloined from nature's factory, the plant.

Feathers were used in many ways, both in their natural colors and dyed, but the beautiful eagle-feather headdress was the crowning piece of Lakota regalia, its splendid appearance adding to the attraction of even the handsomest warrior. It has come to typify not only the tribes of the plains but the Indian race.

The white man brought to the Lakota many things which he instinctively liked, some of which were ribbons, beads, mirrors, calicoes, paint, brooms, combs, bracelets, and soap. The large bright bandanna handkerchiefs were much liked by the young men, who put them around their necks or made bands of them for their heads. Another favorite way of wearing the bandanna was to run one through each armlet.

When my father first saw the white man's comb, he thought it a great improvement over the porcupine-tail brush which the Lakotas used, so he proceeded to make one. But first he had to make a tool with which to make the comb, and this tool proved more useful than the comb. Father got two long wooden-handled knives from a white trader. One knife he placed on a block of wood, using the other to make notches or teeth in the one on the block, and soon he had a saw about seven inches in length with a handle. The saw being finished, he prepared the material for the comb. The horn of a buffalo was boiled until it was quite soft, then split and spread flat on the block of wood. After pounding and pressing it smooth, father took his saw and shaped the comb and cut teeth into it. As I remember it was quite a presentable-looking article when finished, and as I sat and watched father work I was filled with admiration for him. To me father was a man whose qualities were beyond question — almost an idol in my boyish mind. When the comb was finished, it was presented to mother and I still have memories of seeing him comb mother's hair with it; and today, if I could, I would rather possess that comb that touched my mother's hair than my most beautiful headdress. As for the saw, it was a marvel of father's skill and workmanship, for we used it for everything from meat cutter to hide scraper.

The clothing of the white man, adopted by the Lakota, had much to do with the physical welfare of the tribe, and at Carlisle School where the change from tribal to white man's clothing was sudden and direct, the effect on the health and comfort of the children was considerable. Our first resentment was in having our hair cut. It has ever been the custom of Lakota men to wear long hair, and old tribal members still wear the hair in this manner. On first hearing the rule, some of the older boys talked of resisting, but, realizing the uselessness of doing so, submitted. But for days after being shorn we felt strange and uncomfortable. If the argument that has been advanced is true, that the children needed delousing, then why were not girls as well as boys put through the same process? The fact is that we were to be transformed, and short hair being the mark of gentility with the white man, he put upon us the mark, though he still retained his own custom of keeping the hair-covering on his face.

Our second resentment was against trousers, based upon what we considered the best of hygienic reasons. Our bodies were used to constant bathing in the sun, air, and rain, and the function of the pores of our skin, which were in reality a highly developed breathing apparatus, was at once stopped by trousers of heavy, sweat-absorbing material aided by that worst of all torments — red flannel underwear. For the stiff collars, stiff-front shirts, and derby hats no word of praise is due, and the heavy, squeaky, leather boots were positive tormentors which we endured because we thought that when we wore them we were 'dressed up.' Many times we have been laughed at for our native way of dressing, but could anything we ever wore compare in utter foolishness to the steel-ribbed corset and the huge bustle which our girls adopted after a few years in school?

Certain small ways and observances sometimes have connection with larger and more profound ideas, and for reasons of this sort the Lakota disliked the pocket handkerchief and found the white man's use of this toilet article very distasteful. The Indian, essentially an outdoor person, had no use for the handkerchief; he was practically immune to colds, and like the animal, not addicted to spitting. The white man, essentially an indoor person, was subject to colds, catarrh, bronchitis, and kindred diseases. He was a cougher and a spitter, and his constant use of tobacco aggravated the habit. With him the handkerchief was a toilet necessity. So it is easy to see why the Indian considered the carrying of a handkerchief an uncleanly habit.

According to the white man, the Indian, choosing to return to his tribal manners and dress, 'goes back to the blanket.' True, but 'going back to the blanket' is the factor that has saved him from, or at least stayed, his final destruction. Had the Indian been as completely subdued in spirit as he was in body he would have perished within the century of his subjection. But it is the unquenchable spirit that has saved him — his clinging to Indian ways, Indian thought, and tradition, that has kept him and is keeping him today. The white man's ways were not his ways and many of the things that he has tried to adopt have proven disastrous and to his utter shame. Could the Indian have forestalled the flattery and deceit of his European subjector and retained his native truth and honesty; could he have shunned whiskey and disease and remained the paragon of health and strength he was, he might today be a recognized man instead of a hostage on a reservation. But many an Indian has accomplished his own personal salvation by 'going back to the blanket.' The Indian blanket or buffalo robe, a true American garment, and worn with the significance of language, covered beneath it, in the prototype of the American Indian, one of the bravest attempts ever made by man on this continent to rise to heights of true humanity.

To clothe a man falsely is only to distress his spirit and to make him incongruous and ridiculous, and my entreaty to the American Indian is to retain his tribal dress.

CHAPTER VII

INDIAN WISDOM

NATURE

THE Lakota was a true naturist — a lover of Nature. He loved the earth and all things of the earth, the attachment growing with age. The old people came literally to love the soil and they sat or reclined on the ground with a feeling of being close to a mothering power. It was good for the skin to touch the earth and the old people liked to remove their moccasins and walk with bare feet on the sacred earth. Their tipis were built upon the earth and their altars were made of earth. The birds that flew in the air came to rest upon the earth and it was the final abiding place of all things that lived and grew. The soil was soothing, strengthening, cleansing, and healing.

This is why the old Indian still sits upon the earth instead of propping himself up and away from its life-giving forces. For him, to sit or lie upon the ground is to be able to think more deeply and to feel more keenly; he can see more clearly into the mysteries of life and come closer in kinship to other lives about him.

The earth was full of sounds which the old-time Indian could hear, sometimes putting his ear to it so as to hear more clearly. The forefathers of the Lakotas had done this for long ages until there had come to them real understanding of earth ways. It was almost as if the man were still a part of the earth as he was in the beginning, according to the legend of the tribe. This beautiful story of the genesis of the Lakota people furnished the foundation for the love they bore for earth and all things of the earth. Wherever the Lakota went, he was with Mother Earth. No matter where he roamed by day or slept by night, he was safe with her. This thought comforted and sustained the Lakota and he was eternally filled with gratitude.

From Wakan Tanka there came a great unifying life force that flowed in and through all things — the flowers of the plains, blowing winds, rocks, trees, birds, animals — and was the same force that had been breathed into the first man. Thus all things were kindred and brought together by the same Great Mystery.

Kinship with all creatures of the earth, sky, and water was a real and active principle. For the animal and bird world there existed a brotherly feeling that kept the Lakota safe among them. And so close did some of the Lakotas come to their feathered and furred friends that in true brotherhood they spoke a common tongue.

The animal had rights — the right of man's protection, the right to live, the right to multiply, the right to freedom, and the right to man's indebtedness — and in recognition of these rights the Lakota never enslaved the animal, and spared all life that was not needed for food and clothing.

This concept of life and its relations was humanizing and gave to the Lakota an abiding love. It filled his being with the joy and mystery of living; it gave him reverence for all life; it made a place for all things in the scheme of existence with equal importance to all. The Lakota could despise no creature, for all were of one blood, made by the same hand, and filled with the essence of the Great Mystery. In spirit the Lakota was humble and meek. 'Blessed are the meek: for they shall inherit the earth,' was true for the Lakota, and from the earth he inherited secrets long since forgotten. His religion was sane, normal, and human.

Reflection upon life and its meaning, consideration of its wonders, and observation of the world of creatures, began with childhood. The earth, which was called *Maka*, and the sun, called *Anpetuwi*, represented two functions somewhat analogous to those of male and female. The earth brought forth life, but the warming, enticing rays of the sun coaxed it into being. The earth yielded, the sun engendered.

In talking to children, the old Lakota would place a hand on the ground and explain: 'We sit in the lap of our Mother. From her we, and all other living things, come. We shall soon pass, but the place where we now rest will last forever.' So we, too, learned to sit or lie on the ground and become conscious of life about us in its multitude of forms. Sometimes we boys would sit motionless and watch the swallow, the tiny ants, or perhaps some small animal at its work and ponder on its industry and ingenuity; or we lay on our backs and looked long at the sky and when the stars came out made shapes from the various groups. The morning and evening star always attracted attention, and the Milky Way was a path which was traveled by the ghosts. The old people told us to heed *wa maka skan*, which were the 'moving things of earth.' This meant, of course, the animals that lived and moved about, and the stories they told of *wa maka skan* increased our interest and delight. The wolf, duck, eagle, hawk, spider, bear, and other creatures, had marvelous powers, and each one was useful and helpful to us. Then there were the warriors who lived in the sky and dashed about on their spirited horses during a thunder storm, their lances clashing with the thunder and glittering with the lightning. There was *wiwila*, the living spirit of the spring, and the stones that flew like a bird and talked like a man. Everything was possessed of personality, only differing with us in form. Knowledge was inherent in all things. The world was a library and its books were the stones, leaves, grass, brooks, and the birds and animals that shared, alike with us, the storms and blessings of earth. We learned to do what only the student of nature ever learns, and that was to feel beauty. We never railed at the storms, the furious winds, and the biting frosts and snows. To do so intensified human futility, so whatever came we adjusted ourselves, by more effort and energy if necessary, but without complaint. Even the lightning did us no harm, for whenever it came too close, mothers and grandmothers in every tipi put cedar leaves on the coals and their magic kept danger away. Bright days and dark days were both expressions of the Great Mystery, and the Indian reveled in being close to the Big Holy. His worship was unalloyed, free from the fears of civilization.

I have come to know that the white mind does not feel toward nature as does the Indian mind, and it is because, I believe, of the difference in childhood instruction. I have often noticed white boys gathered in a city by-street or alley jostling and pushing one another in a foolish manner. They spend much time in this aimless fashion, their natural faculties neither seeing, hearing, nor feeling the varied life that surrounds them. There is about them no awareness, no acuteness, and it is this dullness that gives ugly mannerisms full play; it takes from them natural poise and stimulation. In contrast, Indian boys, who are naturally reared, are alert to their surroundings; their senses are not narrowed to observing only one another, and they cannot spend hours seeing nothing, hearing nothing, and thinking nothing in particular. Observation was certain in its rewards; interest, wonder, admiration grew, and the fact was appreciated that life was more than mere human manifestation; that it was expressed in a multitude of forms. This appreciation enriched Lakota existence. Life was vivid and pulsing; nothing was casual and commonplace. The Indian lived — lived in every sense of the word — from his first to his last breath.

The character of the Indian's emotion left little room in his heart for antagonism toward his fellow creatures, this attitude giving him what is sometimes referred to as 'the Indian point of view.' Every true student, every lover of nature has 'the Indian point of view,' but there are few such students, for few white men approach nature in the In-

dian manner. The Indian and the white man sense things
differently because the white man has put distance between
himself and nature; and assuming a lofty place in the
scheme of order of things has lost for him both reverence
and understanding. Consequently the white man finds
Indian philosophy obscure — wrapped, as he says, in a
maze of ideas and symbols which he does not understand.
A writer friend, a white man whose knowledge of 'Injuns'
is far more profound and sympathetic than the average,
once said that he had been privileged, on two occasions, to
see the contents of an Indian medicine-man's bag in which
were bits of earth, feathers, stones, and various other articles of symbolic nature; that a 'collector' showed him
one and laughed, but a great and world-famous archeol-
ogist showed him the other with admiration and wonder.
Many times the Indian is embarrassed and baffled by the
white man's allusions to nature in such terms as crude,
primitive, wild, rude, untamed, and savage. For the Lakota, mountains, lakes, rivers, springs, valleys, and woods
were all finished beauty; winds, rain, snow, sunshine, day,
night, and change of seasons brought interest; birds, insects, and animals filled the world with knowledge that
defied the discernment of man.

But nothing the Great Mystery placed in the land of the
Indian pleased the white man, and nothing escaped his
transforming hand. Wherever forests have not been
mowed down; wherever the animal is recessed in their
quiet protection; wherever the earth is not bereft of four-
footed life — that to him is an 'unbroken wilderness.'
But since for the Lakota there was no wilderness; since nature was not dangerous but hospitable; not forbidding but
friendly, Lakota philosophy was healthy — free from fear
and dogmatism. And here I find the great distinction between the faith of the Indian and the white man. Indian
faith sought the harmony of man with his surroundings;
the other sought the dominance of surroundings. In shar-

ing, in loving all and everything, one people naturally found a measure of the thing they sought; while, in fearing, the other found need of conquest. For one man the world was full of beauty; for the other it was a place of sin and ugliness to be endured until he went to another world, there to become a creature of wings, half-man and half-bird. Forever one man directed his Mystery to change the world He had made; forever this man pleaded with Him to chastise His wicked ones; and forever he implored his Wakan Tanka to send His light to earth. Small wonder this man could not understand the other.

But the old Lakota was wise. He knew that man's heart, away from nature, becomes hard; he knew that lack of respect for growing, living things soon led to lack of respect for humans too. So he kept his youth close to its softening influence.

RELIGION

The Lakota loved the sun and earth, but he worshiped only Wakan Tanka, or Big Holy, who was the Maker of all things of earth, sky, and water. Wakan Tanka breathed life and motion into all things, both visible and invisible. He was over all, through all, and in all, and great as was the sun, and good as was the earth, the greatness and goodness of the Big Holy were not surpassed. The Lakota could look at nothing without at the same time looking at Wakan Tanka, and he could not, if he wished, evade His presence, for it pervaded all things and filled all space. All the mysteries of birth, life, and death; all the wonders of lightning, thunder, wind, and rain were but the evidence of His everlasting and encompassing power.

Wakan Tanka prepared the earth and put upon it both man and animal. He dispensed earthly blessings, and when life on earth was finished provided a home, *Wanagi yata*, the place where the souls gather. To this home all souls went after death, for there were no wicked to be excluded.

Wanagi yata was a place of peace and plenty where all met in the peaceful pursuits of life — enmity, hate, and revenge having no place there. Not only did the soul of man repair to this place after leaving the earth, but the souls of all things. *Wanagi yata* was a place of green plains on which roamed the buffalo; where lakes gleamed in the sunshine, and myriads of birds hovered over fields of the sacred sunflower.

The Lakota was not a 'heathen' of many gods, nor was he a fearer of devils. There was no place of eternal punishment ruled by a despotic power; no goblins, evil spirits, or demons to mar the sanity of thought. The physical expression of the Lakota being sane and normal, so was his spiritual expression.

The contemplative and spiritual side of Lakota life was calm and dignified, undisrupted by religious quarrels and wars that turned man against man and even man against animal. Not until a European faith came was it taught that not life on earth but only life after death was to be glorified; and not until the native man forsook the faith of his forefathers did he learn of Satan and Hell. Furthermore, until that time he had no reason to think otherwise than that the directing and protecting guidance of the Great Mystery was as potent on this side of the world as on the other.

For the most part the Lakota was a silent and solitary worshiper, though in many of the religious rituals prayer was offered in speech and song. Prayer, however, was not so much a matter of supplication as it was of thanksgiving, and favorite words for beginning a prayer were, *Tunka sila le iyahpe ya yo*, which translated says, 'Father, receive my offering.'

Sometimes a silent family prayer was held. The father or head of the family smoked a few puffs while the mother and children sat in respectful silence until he had finished. If a number of people had gathered for devotion, they usually seated themselves in a circle while some brave performed the pipe ceremony. The pipe was passed around the circle, each male member of the group taking a puff; or, if a brave did not care to smoke, he touched the tip with his lips or laid his hands gently and respectfully upon the stem. Still another way of conducting devotion was to blow the smoke in the mouth into cupped hands, then rub the hands over head and arms as if pouring water over the body. Again, the sacred or offering pole might inspire one to prayer. A brave, usually a father or head of a family, would get his pipe and stand beside the pole. He would first give the pipe ceremony, then sing his song of prayer, everyone hearing his voice joining him. Even children at play stopped until the prayer song was over.

Sometimes a two or three days' ceremony of *Waunyapi* was held. A sacred pole was placed either inside the tipi, between the fire and the door, or just outside the door, to which anyone in the village wishing to join the ceremony of giving thanks tied a bundle of food or other gift as expression of gratefulness. Sometimes these bundles were so many that they were tied to all the poles, and gifts were taken to some solitary place and there dedicated to Wakan Tanka.

An object of special veneration, for which a shrine was erected in a tipi only for that purpose, was the white buffalo hide. Because of their rarity these hides were never made into garments but were kept for ceremonial purposes only. It was said by hunters that these white or albino buffaloes, which were nearly always female, could far outrun the dark animals. Shrines were also erected in memory and respect of the dead in which a strand of hair, typifying the living spirit of the buried body, was the object of adoration. The hair of the loved one was wrapped in a bundle the covering of which was beautified with paintings, porcupine-quillwork or design, and then hung on a tripod which was painted red. The tripod was very often placed just outside the tipi door where it was easily watched and protected from rain. At other times a tipi was especially erected to house the shrine to which gift offerings were taken and tied to the poles to be distributed to the people on a day set for memorial services. Anyone entering the tipi of the sacred bundle was quiet and respectful, and should the camp move, the tipi and the tripod were the first to be set up.

Our altars were built on the ground and were altars of thankfulness and gratefulness. They were made of sacred earth and placed upon the holiest of all places — the lap of Mother Earth. The altar was built in a square mound, each side being from a foot and a half to three feet in length, according to the size of the ceremonial space. One half of the altar was painted green to symbolize the earth and the other half painted yellow to symbolize the sky. At each corner of the altar was placed an upright stick and to the top of each stick was tied a small buckskin bag holding the sacred tobacco. The buffalo skull was placed in the center of the mound on the heap of earth. Close to the altar and against a rack stood the pipe, without which no altar was complete.

Altars were built whenever circumstances called for them and at no set time nor special place; and any individual prompted by the spirit of devotion could erect one. They were built for all religious ceremonies, such as the Confirmation and Sun Dances and sometimes for the sick. If a sick one was being treated in the sweathouse, then the altar was placed opposite the opening of the sweat-lodge. When the ceremonies were over and the altars were no longer needed, the earth was scattered.

Wild sage, which was a symbol of cleanliness and purity, was a necessary part of every sacred ceremony. It was brought to the Lakotas in a vision, and the Sun Dancers wrapped it around their ankles and wrists. Small sprigs of it were tied to the eagle-bone whistles next to the mouthpiece, and when the dancers began to feel thirst they chewed a bit of it. Those who went into the sweat-lodge either because of illness or for purification rubbed their bodies with this sweet-smelling shrub, and a tea brewed from its leaves relieved headache and indigestion. Every altar was adorned with it and, according to legend, the floor of the holy tipi in which the Sun Woman sat for ten days and nights was carpeted with its boughs.

But of all things held sacred and reverent, the pipe stood supreme in the minds of the Lakota people. It, too, was brought untold years ago in the decalogue of the Sun Woman to be held forever sacred and its mandates to be unquestioningly obeyed. The pipe was a tangible, visible link that joined man to Wakan Tanka and every puff of smoke that ascended in prayer unfailingly reached His presence. With it faith was upheld, ceremony sanctified, and the being consecrated. All the meanings of moral duty, ethics, religious and spiritual conceptions were symbolized in the pipe. It signified brotherhood, peace, and the perfection of Wakan Tanka, and to the Lakota the pipe stood for that which the Bible, Church, State, and Flag, all combined, represented in the mind of the white man. Without the pipe no altar was complete and no ceremony effective. It was used in council, all religious dance ceremonials, in consecrating a life to the labor and service of band members, smoked by the scout to bind his word to truth, in salute and reverence to the rising sun, and by the man who mourned for the death of a loved one that it might dispatch grief and bring peace and solace.

To own a pipe was to own a priceless possession and in many tipis there was one carefully cared for — not the finely decorated pipe, for that was usually cared for by a chief or one of the peacemakers — but a simple pipe whom any reverent one might own. Those who did not have a pipe in their tipi were always welcome to go to a tipi where there was one and there smoke and commune with Wakan Tanka, but it was an article that was never borrowed. Smoking was the Indian Angelus, and whenever its smoke ascended, men, women, and children acknowledged the sacred presence of their Big Holy.

Peace was the pipe's greatest significance — a peace never more deeply and thoughtfully conceived by any man or society of men. Of all symbols that ever inspired men the Pipe of Peace was the strongest. Standards, typifying the ideals of societies, have been worshiped and followed, but none have exerted so great an influence toward peace and brotherhood as this symbol. Its motto was *Wolakota wa yaka cola*, 'Peace without slavery!' Not another standard but has been desecrated by war; not another but has led men into unholy conflict and there *are none to keep them from war except the Pipe of Peace.* If this sacred symbol was taken to Lakota warriors in the thickest of battle, they would at once obey its mandate and retire. To disobey was to suffer personal disaster and it is Lakota history that no warrior ever disobeyed without at last dying an ignominious death.

Peace — that ideal which man may sometime reach — was symbolized in the Pipe of Peace and, under the society of the pipe, or codes symbolized by the pipe, native man made the most effectual effort at arriving at peace ever made on this continent. It was but a start, perhaps, but its strength lay in the fact that under the Great Peace, women had begun the necessary foundational work for the elimination of war by raising sons who could participate only in pursuits of peace. War was excluded from the existence of a certain portion of the male population and in this move the Indian mother pointed the way and the only road to the realization of peace between all men. The acceptance of a kinship with other orders of life was the first step toward humanization and the second step was the dedication of sons to peace, the spiritual value of which is incalculable; and not until the women of the land come back to the forsaken road, emulate the Indian mother, and again raise sons for peace will there be any substantial move toward 'peace on earth and good-will toward men.'

Perhaps more nonsense has been written about the medicine-men than about other persons of the tribe, for their rights and powers, like those of the chiefs, have been overestimated, misunderstood, and misinterpreted. A medicine-man was simply a healer — curing, or trying to cure, such few diseases and ailments as beset his people in the body, having nothing to do with their spiritual suffering. A medicine-man was no holier than other men, no closer to Wakan Tanka and no more honored than a brave or a scout. He lived the same life in the band that other men did, wore the same kind of clothes, ate the same variety of food, lived in the same sort of tipi, and took care of his wife and family, becoming a fair hunter and sometimes a very good one. More often he was an excellent scout, but seldom a great warrior. But as a member of his band he occupied no superior position, and simply filled his calling with as much skill as he could command, just as any physician, lawyer, or baker does today.

The medicine-man was a true benefactor of his people in that his work was founded upon and promoted the Indian ideal of brotherhood, and all service rendered to fellow beings was for the good of the tribe. Such wisdom and 'magic power' as he had achieved must be shared, as were food and clothing, with his fellow man. He made no charge for his helpfulness in ministering to the sick, for the comforting songs he sang, nor the strength he gave them; and when a medicine-man was called, he never was known to refuse the summons.

Now the medicine-man derived his knowledge from the

infinite source — Wakan Tanka. For him knowledge was
not in books, nor in the heads of professors, but in the
works of Wakan Tanka as manifested in the creatures
and beings of nature. This association of knowledge
with all the creatures of earth caused him to look to
them for his knowledge, and assuming their spiritual
fineness to be of the quality of his own, he sought with
them a true rapport. If the man could prove to some
bird or animal that he was a worthy friend, it would
share with him precious secrets and there would be formed
bonds of loyalty never to be broken; the man would protect the rights and life of the animal, and the animal
would share with the man his power, skill, and wisdom.
In this manner was the great brotherhood of mutual helpfulness formed, adding to the reverence for life orders
other than man. The taking of animal life for food and
clothing only became established, and frugality became
regarded as a virtue. Animal life took its place in the
scheme of things, and there was no slavery and no torture
of four-footed and winged things. By acknowledging the
virtues of other beings the Lakota came to possess them
for himself, and for his wonder and reverence and for
his unsurpassed humbleness and meekness Wakan Tanka
revealed himself to the medicine-man.

In order to place himself in communication with the
other earth entities the Lakota submitted to the purification ceremony, the fast and vigil in solitude, for only
in so doing could he experience the vision or dream during
which the dumb creatures could converse with him. But
not every man who tried was fortunate enough to receive
the vision. It was a test which required fortitude and
strength, and though most young men tried, few were
successful. Nevertheless, every boy longed for the vision,
and even as children we tried to hear and see things that
would add to our knowledge and power. We watched
the medicine-men and repeated their acts in our play

until the time came to try to be a dreamer. If the young man in solitude was unable to meet and talk with some spirit entity he could never share its powers, and even though he met every sacrifice the communion might not come about; and if it did not he would never be a medicine-man.

To go into the vision was, of course, to go into the presence of the Great Mystery, and this no Lakota man would attempt to do without first cleansing himself physically and spiritually. Accordingly he began the task of purification; he purged himself of material things, putting aside the thought of food, the chase, fine clothes, the ceremony, and dance. In the solitudes the dream-seeker felt that he would come into the precinct of spiritual power; would speak to beings with whom he could not speak in life's daily existence, and in recognition of his high resolve they might offer to him the gift of their powers and for this exalted contact he wished in every way to be worthy. Earnestly a young man endeavored to cast fear from his mind. The danger from prowling enemies was ever constant and he would be defenseless and, perhaps, weak in body from the fast; so, however devout in his purpose a youth might be, he did not always go through with his self-imposed task. Sometimes a young man stayed his allotted time only to be unrewarded for his vigil, while another's youthful fears brought him home without accomplishing his dream.

A young man having decided to begin purification, asked the assistance of the medicine-man, for only occasionally did a man get a dream without taking the purification ritual, and still less occasionally did a woman receive a dream and become a medicine-woman, for they never took the fast and the lonesome vigil. Upon request, the medicine-man arranged the sweat-lodge, carpeted it with wild-sage, and built an altar in front of its door. He, and perhaps some friends of the dream-seeker, went into the lodge and the purification ceremony began with the smoking of the pipe. All in the group took the sweat while the medicine-man sang, and when the ceremony was over each one rubbed his body with the leaves and branches of sage. This ceremony might be repeated for several days, or until the young man felt that he was thoroughly pure in body, and by that time the songs would have strengthened and fortified him in mind and spirit also.

The youth then started on his journey to the place of his vigil, wrapped only in his robe. The friends who accompanied him, usually two in number, carried for him the four staffs to mark the four corners of his resting place, and when they arrived there, they planted the staffs in the earth and tied to the top of each a flag of red or blue cloth or buckskin. Sometimes ten small sticks, each topped with a small bundle of tobacco, were placed at the foot of each large staff. A buffalo robe was spread in the center of the square marked by the four staffs and on the robe the young brave lay or sat, the pipe clasped in his hands. His friends then left and he was alone. Were he fortunate and received a dream, he was thereafter known as a dreamer or medicine-man.

The Lakotas had some wonderful medicine-men who not only cured the sick, but they looked into the future and prophesied events, located lost or hidden articles, assisted the hunters by coaxing the buffalo near, made themselves invisible when near the enemy, and performed wonderful and magic things. Last Horse was one of our famous medicine-men and was an exception in that he was a splendid warrior as well. When I was a boy I noticed that Last Horse at the ceremonies always came out and performed a dance around the fire by himself before the other dancers came in. When I became older I came to know that Last Horse was a Thunder Dreamer and that it was his place to bless the dog feast, always served for Thunder Dreamers, before the others partook of the food. The powers that helped Last Horse were the Thunder Warriors of the sky, and oftentimes he, and other Thunder Dreamers also, combed their hair in a peculiar way, as they imagined the warriors of the sky did. Their long hair was brought forward and tied in the middle of the forehead, and into the knot a feather, which pointed back, was fastened. This made them look fierce and warlike, as they supposed the thunderous sky warriors must look.

In 1878 I saw Last Horse perform one of his miracles. Some of my band, the Oglalas, went to visit the Brule band and by way of entertainment preparations were made for a dance and feast. The day was bright and beautiful, and everyone was dressed in feathers and painted buckskin. But a storm came up suddenly, threatening to disrupt the gathering, so of course there was much unhappiness as the wind began to blow harder and rain began to fall. Last Horse walked into his tipi and disrobed, coming out wearing only breechclout and moccasins. His hair streamed down his back and in his hand he carried his rattle. Walking slowly to the center of the village he raised his face to the sky and sang his Thunder songs, which commanded the clouds to part. Slowly but surely, under the magic of the song, the clouds parted and the sky was clear once more.

White Crow was a Stone Dreamer and the stones told him many wonderful things. One day when my father was away, my stepmother became ill and lay on her bed in great pain, unable to arise. I sent for White Crow, who brought with him no medicine-bag, rattle, nor the usual drum; neither did he sing or talk to mother, but merely sat and looked at her as she rolled in pain. After a while he took a small piece of root which he had with him and cut it into two smaller pieces, telling mother to chew one of the pieces and swallow it and also to chew the second

piece and rub it on her chest where the pain was. This
mother did as quickly as possible, for she was seriously
ill. Her recovery was almost immediate, for it seemed
no more than five minutes before she was up and preparing food for White Crow. I was so delighted and
curious, that I offered White Crow my best horse if he
would give me the name of the plant. He refused, and
I then offered him fifty dollars for it, but I found that it
was not purchasable at any price.

Chips was another Stone Dreamer and his fame was
wide among his people, for he would go into the sweat-
bath and there locate lost articles or horses and absent
people. While taking the purification ceremony the *tunkes*,
or hot stones, brought great inspiration to Chips, so when
he went to the place of vigil they came to him in spirit
and offered him service. So Chips always carried stones,
some of them painted in colors, in his medicine-bag.
When he was making medicine they would fly to him
and they could be heard striking the tipi and after we
moved into houses I have heard them dropping down
the chimney and have seen them lying about on the floor
where they had fallen.

There were many men, medicine-men and those who
were not, who, in my early youth, did marvelous and
unexplainable things. Sorrel Horse, the wonderful scout,
had a medicine which, I believe, was the wolf, for he
could travel with ease through snow so deep and weather
so cold that it tried even the strongest of Lakota braves.
It was a common saying in my time that Sorrel Horse
'traveled like a wolf.' I never will forget the sorrow of
Sorrel Horse when his grandmother perished one winter
in a deep snow-drift. She had attempted to go home
alone one night from a dance and, being very old, had
stumbled into the snow and had frozen to death. Sorrel
Horse stripped and mounted his horse and rode through
the high snow-drifts, singing his brave songs and lamenting

for the lost one. When he came near my home he was blue with the bitter cold, but still singing, so I induced him to come in and consoled him until he was willing to clothe himself against the storm.

Crazy Horse also had a medicine, though he never claimed to be a medicine-man. The Lakotas believed that the hawk was his protecting power, for he escaped so many dangers, and the father of Crazy Horse always said that had his son had less faith in the white man and made his medicine before going to Fort Robinson on that fateful day his death would have been prevented. The white man laughs at the 'magic' of the Indian, but that is because he does not understand the Indian's touch with nature.

The Thunder Dreamers were the *heyokas*, or clowns. They painted zigzag stripes on their bodies to simulate lightning, and arrows and war horses, and were, unlike most medicine-men, excellent warriors, many times using their powers to bring on a storm that would place their enemies at a disadvantage; also in olden days, before their powers were destroyed, they could stop the rain at the pleasure of their people; but in that day there was no dearth of rain as now, and the land of the Lakota was a paradise of green with an abundance of small streams, lakes, and springs which have since dried up and disappeared. Besides their serious business, which they carried on with the help of the sky powers, the Thunder Dreamers furnished fun and amusement at the various gatherings and festivities. They always made great sport around the kettle of hot dog soup which was served at the ceremonies by plunging their hands and arms into the boiling liquid and flinging it about, making the others run to safety. Many times I have seen a large kettle emptied of its contents in this manner, but so powerful was their medicine that they were never injured and any one but a Thunder Dreamer would have been severely burned.

Much of the fun created by the fun-makers was by doing things opposite to the usual way; for instance, going into the tipi by crawling under instead of walking in by the door, or by coming out feet first. Now and then a Thunder Dreamer carried on his joking all the time, and one of these fellows was Break Shells. This dreamer did so many funny things that he made a sort of Bill Nye reputation for himself. Break Shells' sister once made for him a fine pair of moccasins with a great deal of quillwork on them; finishing them, she threw them to him across the tipi, saying, 'Ohan,' or 'wear them,' as he full well knew; but since the word ohan means 'to cook' as well as 'to wear,' Break Shells promptly threw one of the moccasins into the kettle of boiling soup. The sister was so disgusted that she walked out of the tipi without a word. It was customary with the Lakotas to remove one moccasin and with the bare foot hop across a stream that was too wide to jump across, but one day when Break Shells came to a stream he took off his moccasin, held up his bare foot, and hopped across with his shod foot. Everyone, of course, laughed. Another time Break Shells was driving some beef cattle from the plains to a corral near the village. One of the animals gave him a lot of trouble by running back toward the open country every time it got near the gate. Break Shell's father came out to watch, and seeing that his son's blanket was hanging and flying in the wind, yelled to him, 'Drop the blanket and shoot!' Break Shells threw his blanket to the ground and as quickly as he could turn his horse, which was running, back to where the blanket lay on the ground, he shot it twice. With a gesture of hopelessness, the father turned and went back into his tipi.

That our medicine-men had great powers there was never any doubt among us, and it was only when their hearts became filled with unrest and defiance that their powers waned. They helped to make our lives joyful, to bring the rain so the grass would grow, to bring the buffalo near, and to get in closer touch with the forces of goodness. They were with us all through life, in sickness, and in death.

When death came, only the braves who died on the battlefield were not given burial, but all who passed away in the village were given due respect. The first preparation for burial was to paint the face of the departed as if for a festive occasion and dress the body in the finest of clothing. Then a buffalo robe was wrapped about it, and lastly the body placed in a buffalo rawhide and securely tied with rawhide ropes, after which it was carried by *travois* to the foothills or mountains, preferably where the bundle could be fastened to the branches of a tree. However, if carried to the plains, then a rack of poles was built and the body placed upon it. Should the body be that of a warrior, his favorite horse was sometimes taken to the bier and there killed, so that it might go with its master to the land of souls. Only close relatives and family attended this service, the men and women cutting their hair short in mourning. There is no ceremony performed, and only the weeping and wailing of the sorrowing is heard, oftentimes grief keeping them there until sympathetic friends took them away to smoke for them and comfort them. Though the Indian loved flowers, he never strewed them over his dead. An offering was sometimes made in the form of a prayer-stick painted green at the lower end to symbolize earth and the upper end painted yellow to symbolize the sky, to which was fastened an eagle feather and a breath plume to carry unspoken prayers to Those Above. There was but one chance that the soul of the Indian would not reach the land of the souls and that was if he had not been tattooed with the mark of his band. If he had not this mark to identify him, the guardian of the milky path across the sky would not permit the spotted eagle and the soul he carried to pass, causing the soul thereafter to wander forever homeless. On my arm is the mark of my band, placed there when I was very young. First a spot on my arm was rubbed until the blood was almost ready to flow, then a design was pricked into the skin with a bone needle and pulverized charcoal of false indigo was rubbed in. When the scab from this wound healed and fell off, the design in blue was permanent. With this tattoo the spotted eagle could safely pass the guardian on the milky road and proceed on his journey with his charge to the land of souls where all lasting reunions would sometime take place. This land was in the south and when the body lay cold, the eagle with strong and never-tiring wings lifted to his back the soul and carried it away; he always knew when it was time for the journey and was unfailing in his attendance in the hour of death. In this after life the Lakota came to realize the ideals of his earthly life. *Wanagiyata* was a pleasant place, with green fields, streams, and an abundance of food, its peace undefamed by torture and torment. Nothing so proves a soft and humane spirit as the conception and ideals of life hereafter, and it was the very beneficence of the Indian's attitude that left him unprepared for the harshness of the white man's vindictive religion. He was mystified, baffled, and bewildered by it and its infliction upon him, in some cases, of unspeakable cruelty. The Lakota's religion and philosophical ideas were an inseparable part of him — his as much as the blood that vitalized his being. His very thoughts were drawn from the land he called native, and the winds that blew over its soil, the rivers that ran through it, and the mountain peaks that drew his gaze upward all colored his consciousness with their subtle influence. And no more can the Indian be robbed of this intangible color than he can be robbed of the color of his eyes or skin, for Nature is more powerful than man. Thus the inanity and cruelty of trying to force the separation of man and his religion and, whatever else it does, it brings disarrangement and discomfort and reflects upon the mental and spiritual status of the enforcer. Every man has a right to his Great Mystery, but no man ever explained Mystery. And what man can?

CEREMONY

The Lakota people were very fond of social gatherings and dancing, feasts, games, and display of finery, but for all that their religious ceremonies were of first importance to them. Through ceremony, obedience and allegiance to the Supreme Being were acknowledged and the traditions of the race kept alive; also, teachings, codes by which the manners and morals of the people were guided, custom, commandments, experiences, and events of tribal importance were handed down from generation to generation in this form. Furthermore, the Lakota lived his æsthetic life, through ceremonies, for they embodied his love for song, music, dance, rhythm, grace of motion, prayer, chant, ritualism, color, body decoration, and symbolic design. Tribal culture culminated in ceremony, and to be instructed in ritual and ceremony was to be an historian of the tribe.

Ceremonies were held for all main events of life — for birth, christening, entrance into lodges, consecration to service, in celebration of victory, and for the giving of thanks. Contrary to general thought, less attention was paid to war in these ceremonies than to anything else. Most of them were for the purpose of giving thanks for food, health, and like comforts, and though thankfulness is the most human of qualities, these ceremonies yet remain to the average person 'heathen.' Why more heathen to give thanks under the blue sky than under the roof of a man-made place of worship? We read that May-Day, Easter-Day, Thanksgiving-Day, and other celebrated days had their origin in 'heathen' festivals.

Well, if found good and adopted, are they any less heathen for the adoption? Again, there is a 'veil of mystery' that is supposed to hover over Indian ceremony. This veil is simply the failure of the white mind to comprehend the Indian, but why expect the man who must cloister himself within ornate stone walls and sit on cushioned seats in dim lights, to comprehend the one who stands and faces his sun for four days?

Since song was the usual method of keeping the Lakota in touch with his Wakan Tanka, it formed a large part of all ritual. Many songs were dreamer songs received while in communion with spirits of beings personified as humans. Some of the dreamers who brought songs to the people were the Elk, Duck, Thunder, Hawk, Wolf, Spider, Fox, Crow, and Stone. The wisdom of these beings was given to the dreamer in song and he in turn sang them to help his people. Now the words of the song might not be clear in meaning to any but the dreamer himself, but that did not destroy its potency to cure when sung by the medicine-man.

It is quite hard to translate these songs into the English tongue and when this is accomplished the words are, usually, meaningless. However, an explanation of these translations will show the character of the songs.

When the bears came to the dreamer they taught him the following song:

He iye ki ya mani yo	Recognize everything as you walk
He iye ki ya mani yo	Recognize everything as you walk
He iye ki ya mani yo	Recognize everything as you walk
He he ya pe lo	That is what we say
He he yo	
Maki sitomni yan	All over the world
Wan ni yanqian u he iye	They come to see you
Ki ya mani yo	Recognize everything as you walk
He he ya pe lo	That is what we say
He he yo	

While in the spirit condition the dreamer was in contact with the spirits of all things of the world, though in the case of the Bear Dreamer only the bears spoke to him and gave him bear powers. The bears told him to recognize all things of nature and to observe and learn from them. The animals would thereafter observe and learn from the dreamer, and he should do likewise. The dreamer, like the bear, would always be powerful and fearless and the song would be magic in power. When the dreamer went to cure the sick, he was instructed to carry the claw of the bear with which to probe and cleanse wounds, then put over it some clean earth soil. I have seen this done and the healing of wounds was very rapid.

In the following song it is the fox that speaks to the dreamer and gives him a song which makes of him a Fox Dreamer.

To ke ya inapa nun we	He that goes out first
To ke ya inapa nun we	He that goes out first
Sunge la waste toke ya inapa nun we	The pretty fox goes out first
He wakan yan inapa nun we	He goes out holy
He wakan yan inapa nun we	He goes out holy
Kola he ya ce e-e-e yo	His friends all say he is holy

The fox had knowledge of underground things hidden from human eyes, and this he shared with the dreamer, telling him of roots and herbs that were healing and curing; then he shared his powers of swiftness and cleverness as well as gentleness. The fox would be holy to the dreamer, who would wear in his ceremonies the skin of the animal, and the brotherhood being sworn, the Fox Dreamer never hunted or killed the fox. He obtained the skin from those who did.

The Stone Dreamer sang a song about the night sun, or moon, and also one about the day sun, which was taught to him by stones. The stones were possessed of extraordinary knowledge, for they were on the earth, in the earth, and in the sky visiting the sun and moon, so they taught the following song to the dreamer, that he might derive power from these heavenly bodies.

The moon song:

Wanka tan han he ya u we lo	Coming from above saying
Wanka tan han he ya u we lo	Coming from above saying
Mita hocoka topa wan la ka nun we	You will see my four villages
He ya u we lo han ye wi kin	That is what the moon says
He ya u we lo e ya ye yo	As it comes down

The sun song:

Wanka tan han he ya u we lo	Coming from above saying
Wanka tan han he ya u we lo	Coming from above saying
Mita we cohan topa wan la ka nun we	You will see my four deeds
He ya u we lo anpewi kin he ya	That is what the sun says
He ya u we lo e ye ye yo	As it comes down

Whenever horses or articles were lost, the Stone medicine-man was called, for he could send out his flying stones and they would locate the missing things. The medicine-man was always called with the pipe for the best results.

Of all dreamers the Elk Dreamer was the most picturesque. He was neither singer nor dancer, but an actor, and his greatest power was over women. He had power to protect himself and other men from the wiles of women, or to help them to secure the chosen woman for a wife. He could not, however, assist them in realizing an evil intention, for his powers, like those of all medicine-men, were powers of good. The Elk Dreamer wore a picturesque costume and horned mask to symbolize the elk and was called *Hehaka gaga*, which means 'making up to look like an elk.' He was very much in evidence at festivals, parading around the village with his assistants, giving the amusing and entertaining elk performance.

His assistants were young and active men and boys dressed to represent young deer, with their bodies painted yellow and wearing deer masks. They carried on a pantomime of deer and elk feeding or watering and being surprised and attacked by a hunter. The Elk Dreamer manipulated a magic hoop with which he protected his band from the invisible weapons of the hunter, who was also a medicine-man with magic powers. Finally a battle took place between the two medicine-men which was very exciting and realistic. One of them was sure to be injured, then treated and cured by the uninjured magician, who took the missile from the mouth of the wounded one. These injuries were real, the wounded one actually suffering until he was cured, and it was claimed among the Lakotas that a medicine-man had once killed a white man in this manner.

Lodge members, either men or women, sometimes composed songs that became lodge songs; or sometimes they composed simple melodies without words. These were used in the ceremonies of the lodge, being sung by any of the members who cared to sing them.

Sometimes during the night or stillness of day, a voice would be heard singing the brave song. This meant that sorrow was present — either a brave was going on the warpath and expected to die, or else a family was looking for the death of some member of it. The brave song was to fortify one to meet any ordeal bravely and to keep up faltering spirits. I remember, when we children were on our way to Carlisle School, thinking that we were on our way to meet death at the hands of the white people, the older boys sang brave songs so that we would all meet death according to the code of the Lakota — fearlessly. Then when Buffalo Bill took a number of us to England, the ocean became very rough, and it being our first sea voyage we thought death was staring us in the face. The ship seemed very small and helpless in the middle of that vast expanse of tossing, tumbling waves, so when death seemed imminent we sang our brave songs and had anything happened we would have gone down singing.

Some Lakota songs have been sung for so many generations that no one knows who the composers were nor how long since they were composed. One of these is the Fire song. I learned it from grandfather, who sang it lying on his back on the ground, beating his chest with his fists to keep time. He told me that the first people to sing the song all sang it that way, for it was composed before the day of the tomtom. This gives the Fire song an interesting history, for we know that the tomtom is a very old instrument. The words of this song are:

Wan kata he ya pe	From above someone said
Wan kata he ya pe	From above someone said
Wan kata he ya pe	From above someone said
Makata ile ile ye	That there is fire under the earth
he eyape	
E ye yo	

This song was composed back in the days when Those Above spoke directly to the ones here on earth. Perhaps the fire spoken of alludes to a volcanic eruption, but at any rate it is a song of tradition.

Some Lakota songs had no words, just tunes, and the Lance song is one of this kind. It was sung by the braves, while the lances were being given to the young men who were to go out and try to 'touch the enemy.' The occasion was a trying and solemn one, and the purpose of the song was to make the young men feel the importance of being brave and successful in returning with honors.

Dancing was just as much a part of the Lakota's life and its meaning as song, and with dances he expressed the same emotions as he did with song — sorrow, bravery, ecstasy, valor, love, supplication, and devotion. Still other dances were enactments of past history, such as adventures, travel experiences, and battles. Another class of dances were named after and dedicated to certain animals, showing his love for and dependence upon the animal kingdom, such as the Fox, Horse, and Buffalo dances. In these dances the actions and steps were imitative of the animal impersonated, and required of the performer high development of skill in pantomime and at times utmost strength and control of muscle.

The Fox dance, a quiet, simple, and dignified measure, was dedicated by the Fox Lodge to the Holy Fox for his kind and gentle powers. The skin of this animal, placed about the neck of one who was ill or restless would, in a few moments, induce rest and sleep, a cure which I have myself experienced. Also the qualities of nimbleness and grace of this little animal were the inspiration for the trotting steps of the Fox dance and for the many pretty songs and tunes in the ceremony. There was absolutely nothing objectionable in the dance, yet just after I returned from Carlisle I learned that the agent had forbidden the holding of Fox dance ceremonies. Not knowing this order, I attended a dance, as I was a Fox member, and the next day I was put under arrest. I explained to the agent the nature of the ceremony, a thing he should have acquainted himself with before ever issuing such an order. When the agent realized that he had no grounds for my arrest, he ordered me to have the name of the dance changed, being determined to issue a command, no matter how foolish, but this I refused to do. Of course, my disdain for him did not make me popular with this arbitrary gentleman, but then I have never been popular with most agents.

The Buffalo Dance was a much more vigorous one, requiring plenty of room for the running and charging buffalo and it was up to the audience to keep out of the way if they did not wish to be jostled or knocked over. Women and children usually scattered to places of safety when the Buffalo dancers began their performance.

The Victory Dance was a very dramatic performance given by the braves who took this opportunity to display strength, bravery, war skill, and to decorate themselves a great deal. Some of them used their favorite war horses in order to give a faithful and dramatic picture of what took place on the battlefield. The animals, too, seemed to sense the meaning and glamour of the occasion and I have seen them prance, snort, and act with their masters in a most marvelous way. The acting in these dances was sometimes very fine — the receiving of a wound, the rescue of a friend, an escape with the assistance of a friend, all being enacted with realism. I remember once my father danced on the outside of the group and in the opposite direction to indicate that he alone had once upon a time turned the enemy backward, single-handed. Women sometimes take part in the Victory Dance, donning the war regalia of the men. As they dance, they sing the Victory Song and carry the war shield or lance in honor of some brave left on the battlefield or one too modest to proclaim his own bravery.

The Sun Dance was the greatest of all ceremonies with the Lakotas, for upon its precepts their society was established. Given to them during an earthly visit by the Holy Woman, emissary from Those Above, this ceremony forms the Lakota decalogue.

In ten days and ten nights of speech-making the Holy Woman declared the laws and ethics upon which the Lakota people founded their society; and for about ten days each year the whole people of the tribe were commanded to meet and perform the sacred and detailed ritual of the Sun Dance according to Her instructions.

One account of the coming of the Holy Woman as told by Wayajuju is as follows:

'Over a thousand years ago the Lakotas put up their village near a distant ocean of the west. Two of their young men were one day on a journey and coming to the top of a hill, there stopped to rest. In the distance they noticed an object moving toward them, so they waited and watched. Closer and closer came a figure until a beautiful woman stood in front of them.

'The young man on the left at once began to think evil thoughts, so the woman told him to sit on the ground. To the other young man she said, "Go back to your village and tell the people to place a tipi in the center of it, for I am to come and teach them for ten days and ten nights." As the young man turned to obey the command, he glanced toward his companion, but he was no longer there. Only a cloud that ascended to heaven obscured the place where he had sat.

'When the young man reached his village, he told the people what the beautiful woman had said, so they at once put up a tipi and she came and for ten days and nights talked. The Holy Woman instructed them in the songs, ritual, dances, and meaning of the Sun Dance. She told them that the Great Mystery, seeing that they needed guidance, had sent her to instruct them. She commanded them to build a cross of only certain wood and placed together in a certain way. "Look among your woods," she said, "and there you will fine a gentle tree — the cottonwood. Then get some branches of the cherry tree and tie them into a long bundle for the cross-piece of the pole, this bundle to symbolize womanhood which the Great Mystery has given to man. From the cherry tree branches you must hang the figure of the buffalo and the figure of a man, both made from rawhide. Also you must have something to represent the blue sky."

'Then instruction was given regarding health and rules of clean living; also the use of herbs and roots for healing.

'When the woman came to the four most important moral commandments she shouted them in a loud voice:

'"You shall not kill!"

'"You shall not lie!"

'"You shall not steal!"

'"You shall not commit adultery!"

'Then the Holy Woman presented the people with the Pipe of the Calf to symbolize prayer and a Holy Arrow to symbolize protection. The Pipe shall always be carefully kept by the Lakotas but the Cheyennes are today guarding the Holy Arrow. The last commandment to the people was to hold the sacred ceremony of the Sun Dance once every year, and this they faithfully did until oppressed by another people.'

Much of the preparation for the Sun Dance was ceremonial in character. The first thing built was a large circular wall, opening toward the east, to enclose the dance circle. Men, women, and young people joined in the happy work of going to the woods and getting poles and long willow branches to weave into this wall. This was an offering to the Great Mystery, and the more branches and leaves one brought, the more, they felt, they had done for One.

Next came the cutting and setting of the Sun Dance pole or cross. The cottonwood tree standing in the forest was called *waga can* or fleecy wood or something near that translation, since it was named from the fleece that floated from its pods certain times of the year. But when the tree had been made into a pole and decorated and its cross-piece attached, it was then called *can wakan*, or 'Holy wood.' The cutting and bringing in of the pole was also done with ceremony and consumed two days' time. The first day the famous scouts gathered in full regalia and mounted on their horses. They rode out supposedly in search of the pole, but went in an opposite direction from the woods instead of towards it. The people awaited their return in the dance circle, and when they were sighted on their way back, young braves rode out to meet them, always riding around them. When the scouts reached the circle, they dismounted and sat in a half-circle about the fire. A number of them told their most thrilling war stories, using the thumb to point, and acting as if they had actually just returned from the warpath.

The second day in the early morning everyone went to the woods for a day of festivity to bring in the pole. The various lodges sang their songs and gave their dances, and feasts were served. A number of young boys and girls, sons and daughters of great warriors and chiefs, were selected for the ceremony at the tree. As they were grouped about the tree, each one in turn with an ax in hand struck the tree as if to chop it down. The boy or girl selected for this part of the ceremony felt much honored. Singing and dancing continued until the actual choppers of the tree felled it. The procession then started for the dance enclosure, the tree bearers, perhaps some fifteen or twenty of them, in the lead, the rest of the people following. Three times the company stopped at a long-drawn call of 'Wo-o-e-e-e.' The fourth time the young horsemen dashed forward for the enclosure, where hung a dummy figure made of willow leaves and branches, each horseman trying to be the first to touch it. The successful one would bring home an honor from his next war expedition. When the tree bearers and the rest of the people reached the enclosure, the tree was decorated with the figures of a man and a buffalo and as many rawhide ropes attached as there were to be sacrificial dancers. Then the holy wood was raised.

Usually, the first dance to be held was the *Owanka onatoza wacipi*, or a 'smooth the grass dance,' which was a sort of house-warming affair. Also before the actual sacrificial dance began, many preliminary dances and ceremonies were held such as 'Give away' dances in which presents were exchanged or given to the poor, or ear-piercing and naming ceremonies were held for the children.

Now the sacrifice was made for several purposes. The Sun Dance itself was one great tribute to the Great Holy for life and its blessings; also it was a prayer for all good things — plentiful food, health, and preservation of life — that could come to the tribe. Perhaps the brave intended going on the warpath and promised to give the dance on his safe and sound return, or perhaps he had a loved one who was very ill and he hoped by blood sacrifice to make his prayer for the recovery of the loved one, worthy of recognition by Wakan Tanka. But whatever the reason might be, the participants entered voluntarily, no wise man nor leader influencing them in any way. The sacrificial dancers seldom numbered more than two and usually there was but one. The helpers, those who joined in the fast and the dance, as a rule numbered about fifteen or twenty.

The brave, having decided to do the sacrificial dance, called his medicine-man, who announced to the village that the brave would give sacrifice in the coming Sun Dance. The medicine-man stood a pole in the ground and decorated it with his medicine articles, then standing close to and facing it announced to the Great Mystery the name of the one to make the sacrifice. The brave at once began to prepare himself in body and spirit. Several days before the ceremony, both the sacrificial dancer and all who danced with him placed themselves in the care and guidance of the medicine-man, who helped to strengthen them for the ordeal. In the medicine tipi the dancers take the fast, the sweat-bath and the whole ritual of purification, some of which was secret.

When the day of the ceremony, which the Oglalas called *Wi wanyano wacipi*, 'To dance while looking at the Sun,' arrived, and all was in readiness, the dancer lay flat on the ground on his back. The medicine-man cut a place in the chest, through which he thrust a small stick about four inches in length and no thicker than a lead pencil, to which a rawhide rope was fastened by buckskin strings. The wound was cut scarcely more than skin deep, and though bleeding became quite profuse during the dance, death was never known to ensue. And seldom did a dancer remain attached to the rope past midday, for if he were not successful in freeing himself, his relatives gave away some valuable present to help him pull free. Often, after a short rest, he was able to rejoin the other dancers, the ceremony usually ending the fourth day. But for the duration of the Sun Dance ceremony both the onlookers and the participants gave themselves devotedly to silent prayer.

CHAPTER VIII

LATER DAYS

IN THE foregoing chapters I have given a description of Lakota tribal life — my life, and that of my ancestors, upon the plains of what are now the States of North and South Dakota; of our freedom, our love for nature, and respect for life, animate and inanimate; our trust and faith in the Supreme Power, Wakan Tanka; and our principles of truth, honesty, bravery, and brotherhood peace which guided our social lives. In this chapter I shall draw another picture — one that shows the changed life of my people — as it is and has been since the coming of the white man. I began this book as I began my life, amid scenes of natural harmony where youthful life had happy care and direction from all the tribe, where maturity was gladdened with health, generosity in act and spirit, and strength from the unlimited Source, and where old age looked calmly to a future of security and peace. I close it with a scene to present far different from the one upon which I gazed when held in my mother's arms. Today my people, and all native people of this continent, are changed — degraded by oppression and poverty into but a semblance of their former being; health is undermined by disease, and the moral and spiritual life of the people deadened by the loss of the great sustaining forces of their devotional ceremonies. Our Indian boys and girls are going to segregated schools, are there taught to scorn all tribal institutions, and, to add insult to injury, are discountenanced by the race that brought their decline. There is not a tribe but has been poisoned by oppression and the thwarting of the natural course of life.

From the very first, the white strangers, who came unbidden, yet remained to become usurpers, assumed an attitude of superiority toward us, and because of this attitude there arose many false ideas concerning the Indian race that endure to this day. Though these white people did not observe the same high principles which we observed, and though they violated all of our rights as natives in our own land and as humans, and even the rights of creatures that we had so long protected, they looked upon us with disdain. They did not try to understand us and did not consider the fact that though we were different from them, still we were living our destiny according to the plan of the Supreme Dictator of mankind. Being narrow in both mind and spirit, they could see no possible good in us.

So for nearly four centuries the American Indian has been misinterpreted as to character, customs, practices in marriage, home, family, and religion. He has become imaged in the minds and hearts of a whole public as a whooping, yelling, vicious person without moral conscience and ethical scruples engaged in but one pursuit, that of war.

Irreparable damage has been done by white writers who discredit the Indian. Books have been written of the native American, so distorting his true nature that he scarcely resembles the real man; his faults have been magnified and his virtues minimized; his wars, and his battles, which, if successful, the white man chooses to call 'massacres,' have been told and retold, but little attention has been given to his philosophy and ideals. Books, paintings, and pictures have all joined in glorifying the pioneer — the hunter, trapper, woodsman, cowboy, and soldiery — in their course of conquest across the country, a conquest that could only have been realized by committing untold offenses against the aboriginal people. But who proclaims that every battle by the American Indian was a holy fight for the protection of wives, little children, and homeland; that every 'massacre' was the frenzied expression of the right to exist? Lurid fiction, cheap magazines, motion pictures, and newspapers help to impart the wrong idea that a scalp and a war dance are counterparts of native American life, while the truth is but not recorded, that the white man was always first met with friendliness on the part of the native; that whole tribes of people were sedentary and agricultural in occupation engaging only in defensive warfare; that, according to Caucasian war records, it was the white man who made scalping a part of organized military operations and also turned it into a business for profit, and that the finest warwhoops are produced under the influence of 'firewater.'

So, through the very agencies that reach the mass of people, that purport to instruct, educate, and perpetuate true history — books, schools, and libraries all over the land — three have been graven false ideas in the hearts and minds of the people. Even the boys and girls throughout the country, whose sources of information are inadequate, have the thought that the Indian is a curious creature, something to be amused at, and as not having contributed worth-while things to the culture of this country. This in spite of the fact that history for this continent did not begin with the landing of the Pilgrims, and that many notable cultural events had taken place before the coming of the European; that some of the truest and greatest patriots have been American Indians, and that such names as Red Jacket, Tecumseh, and Crazy Horse would brighten the pages of any history, while the name of Sequoia not only lights the pages of American history, but the history of achievement of all mankind.

The mothers and fathers of this land do their children an injustice by not seeing that their offspring are taught the true history of this continent and its people: that the Indian fed and nourished the weary travelers from over the seas and made it possible for them to remain to enjoy life and freedom; that they were not warlike demons, but that their philosophy was one of kindness; that some of their governmental principles were unequaled for equity; that some of their crafts are even today unsurpassed; and that this country has native contributions in song, stories, music, pageantry, dance, poetry, and oratory worthy of perpetuation. True, some noteworthy scholars have done diligent work along the lines of preservation, but their works have not yet found popular recognition. True, that valuable data have been compiled and can be found in reference libraries, but these statistical works lack the human touch, and the Indian of the cheap magazine and the movie still remain as the best type of the First American. So it is the parents and the grade teachers of this land who may now fulfill the duty of demanding that true histories be placed in the hands of the young.

It is now nearly four hundred years since 'civilization' was brought to us, and this is the situation: All groups of public opinion and action, the schools, universities, men's and women's clubs, churches, and other organizations are apathetic toward the Indian and his situation. If but two organized groups, the schools and the Federated Women's Clubs, to whom Charles Lummis so naïvely left the solution of the question and who have done nothing, were to concentrate action for just one year, something would be done. Even the law has forsaken him, and the Indian today is not only unheard and unheeded, but robbed, pillaged, denied his heritage, and held in bondage. The greatest hoax ever perpetrated upon him was the supposed citizenship of 1924 when President Coolidge signed a bill that freed the Indian. The signing of that bill changed not in the slightest measure the condition of the Indian. Not one agent was removed from office, Indian boys and girls are still segregated in school life, and the reservation and reservation rule still exist.

I grew up leading the traditional life of my people, learning the crafts of hunter, scout, and warrior from fa-

ther, kindness to the old and feeble from mother, respect
for wisdom and council from our wise men, and was trained
by grandfather and older boys in the devotional rites to
the Great Mystery. This was the scheme of existence as
followed by my forefathers for many centuries, and more
centuries might have come and gone in much the same way
had it not been for a strange people who came from a far
land to change and reshape our world.

At the age of eleven years, ancestral life for me and my
people was most abruptly ended without regard for our
wishes, comforts, or rights in the matter. At once I was
thrust into an alien world, into an environment as different
from the one into which I had been born as it is possible to
imagine, to remake myself, if I could, into the likeness of
the invader.

By 1879, my people were no longer free, but were subjects confined on reservations under the rule of agents.
One day there came to the agency a party of white people
from the East. Their presence aroused considerable excitement when it became known that these people were school
teachers who wanted some Indian boys and girls to take
away with them to train as were white boys and girls.

Now, father was a 'blanket Indian,' but he was wise. He
listened to the white strangers, their offers and promises
that if they took his son they would care well for him,
teach him how to read and write, and how to wear white
man's clothes. But to father all this was just 'sweet talk,'
and I know that it was with great misgivings that he left
the decision to me and asked if I cared to go with these
people. I, of course, shared with the rest of my tribe a
distrust of the white people, so I know that for all my dear
father's anxiety he was proud to hear me say 'Yes.' That
meant that I was brave.

I could think of no reason why white people wanted Indian boys and girls except to kill them, and not having the
remotest idea of what a school was, I thought we were go-

ing East to die. But so well had courage and bravery been trained into us that it became a part of our unconscious thinking and acting, and personal life was nothing when it came time to do something for the tribe. Even in our play and games we voluntarily put ourselves to various tests in the effort to grow brave and fearless, for it was most discrediting to be called *can'l wanka*, or a coward. Accordingly there were few cowards, most Lakota men preferring to die in the performance of some act of bravery than to die of old age. Thus, in giving myself up to go East I was proving to my father that he was honored with a brave son. In my decision to go, I gave up many things dear to the heart of a little Indian boy, and one of the things over which my child mind grieved was the thought of saying good-bye to my pony. I rode him as far as I could on the journey, which was to the Missouri River, where we took the boat. There we parted from our parents, and it was a heart-breaking scene, women and children weeping. Some of the children changed their minds and were unable to go on the boat, but for many who did go it was a final parting.

On our way to school we saw many white people, more than we ever dreamed existed, and the manner in which they acted when they saw us quite indicated their opinion of us. It was only about three years after the Custer battle, and the general opinion was that the Plains people merely infested the earth as nuisances, and our being there simply evidenced misjudgment on the part of Wakan Tanka. Whenever our train stopped at the railway stations, it was met by great numbers of white people who came to gaze upon the little Indian 'savages.' The shy little ones sat quietly at the car windows looking at the people who swarmed on the platform. Some of the children wrapped themselves in their blankets, covering all but their eyes. At one place we were taken off the train and marched a distance down the street to a restaurant. We walked down the street between two rows of uniformed men whom we called soldiers, though I suppose they were policemen. This must have been done to protect us, for it was surely known that we boys and girls could do no harm. Back of the rows of uniformed men stood the white people craning their necks, talking, laughing, and making a great noise. They yelled and tried to mimic us by giving what they thought were war-whoops. We did not like this, and some of the children were naturally very much frightened. I remember how I tried to crowd into the protecting midst of the jostling boys and girls. But we were all trying to be brave, yet going to what we thought would end in death at the hands of the white people whom we knew had no love for us. Back on the train the older boys sang brave songs in an effort to keep up their spirits and ours too. In my mind I often recall that scene — eighty-odd blanketed boys and girls marching down the street surrounded by a jeering, unsympathetic people whose only emotions were those of hate and fear; the conquerors looking upon the conquered. And no more understanding us than if we had suddenly been dropped from the moon.

At last at Carlisle the transforming, the 'civilizing' process began. It began with clothes. Never, no matter what our philosophy or spiritual quality, could we be civilized while wearing the moccasin and blanket. The task before us was not only that of accepting new ideas and adopting new manners, but actual physical changes and discomfort has to be borne uncomplainingly until the body adjusted itself to new tastes and habits. Our accustomed dress was taken and replaced with clothing that felt cumbersome and awkward. Against trousers and handkerchiefs we had a distinct feeling — they were unsanitary and the trousers kept us from breathing well. High collars, stiff-bosomed shirts, and suspenders fully three inches in width were uncomfortable, while leather boots caused actual suffering. We longed to go barefoot, but were told that the dew on the grass would give us colds. That was a new warning for us,

for our mothers had never told us to beware of colds, and I
remember as a child coming into the tipi with moccasins
full of snow. Unconcernedly I would take them off my
feet, pour out the snow, and put them on my feet again
without any thought of sickness, for in that time colds, catarrh, bronchitis, and *la grippe* were unknown. But we
were soon to know them. Then, red flannel undergar-
ments were given us for winter wear, and for me, at least,
discomfort grew into actual torture. I used to endure it as
long as possible, then run upstairs and quickly take off the
flannel garments and hide them. When inspection time
came, I ran and put them on again, for I knew that if I
were found disobeying the orders of the school I should be
punished. My niece once asked me what it was that I disliked the most during those first bewildering days, and I
said, 'red flannel.' Not knowing what I meant, she laughed,
but I still remember those horrid, sticky garments which
we had to wear next to the skin, and I still squirm and itch
when I think of them. Of course, our hair was cut, and
then there was much disapproval. But that was part of
the transformation process and in some mysterious way
long hair stood in the path of our development. For all the
grumbling among the bigger boys, we soon had our heads
shaven. How strange I felt! Involuntarily, time and time
again, my hands went to my head, and that night it was a
long time before I went to sleep. If we did not learn much
at first, it will not be wondered at, I think. Everything was
queer, and it took a few months to get adjusted to the new
surroundings.

Almost immediately our names were changed to those in
common use in the English language. Instead of translat-
ing our names into English and calling Zinkcaziwin, Yellow
Bird, and Wanbli K'leska, Spotted Eagle, which in itself
would have been educational, we were just John, Henry, or
Maggie, as the case might be. I was told to take a pointer
and select a name for myself from the list written on the

blackboard. I did, and since one was just as good as another, and as I could not distinguish any difference in them, I placed the pointer on the name Luther. I then learned to call myself by that name and got used to hearing others call me by it, too. By that time we had been forbidden to speak our mother tongue, which is the rule in all boarding-schools. This rule is uncalled for, and today is not only robbing the Indian, but America of a rich heritage. The language of a people is part of their history. Today we should be perpetuating history instead of destroying it, and this can only be effectively done by allowing and encouraging the young to keep it alive. A language, unused, embalmed, and reposing only in a book, is a dead language. Only the people themselves, and never the scholars, can nourish it into life.

Of all the changes we were forced to make, that of diet was doubtless the most injurious, for it was immediate and drastic. White bread we had for the first meal and thereafter, as well as coffee and sugar. Had we been allowed our own simple diet of meat, either boiled with soup or dried, and fruit, with perhaps a few vegetables, we should have thrived. But the change in clothing, housing, food, and confinement combined with lonesomeness was too much, and in three years nearly one half of the children from the Plains were dead and through with all earthly schools. In the graveyard at Carlisle most of the graves are those of little ones.

I am now going to confess that I had been at Carlisle a full year before I decided to learn all I could of the white man's ways, and then the inspiration was furnished by my father, the man who has been the greatest influence in all my life. When I had been in school a year, father made his first trip to see me. After I had received permission to speak to him, he told me that on his journey he had seen that the land was full of 'Long Knives.' 'They greatly outnumber us and are here to stay,' he said, and advised

CHIEF STANDING BEAR THE ELDER VISITING HIS SON AT
CARLISLE

me, 'Son, learn all you can of the white man's ways and try to be like him.' From that day on I tried. Those few words of my father I remember as if we talked but yesterday, and in the maturity of my mind I have thought of what he said. He did not say that he thought the white man's ways better than our own; neither did he say that I could be like a white man. He said, 'Son, try to be like a white man.' So, in two more years I had been 'made over.' I was Luther Standing Bear wearing the blue uniform of the school, shorn of my hair, and trying hard to walk naturally and easily in stiff-soled cowhide boots. I was now 'civilized' enough to go to work in John Wanamaker's fine store in Philadelphia.

I returned from the East at about the age of sixteen, after five years' contact with the white people, to resume life upon the reservation. But I returned, to spend some thirty years before again leaving, just as I had gone — a Lakota.

Outwardly I lived the life of the white man, yet all the while I kept in direct contact with tribal life. While I had learned all that I could of the white man's culture, I never forgot that of my people. I kept the language, tribal manners and usages, sang the songs and danced the dances. I still listened to and respected the advice of the older people of the tribe. I did not come home so 'progressive' that I could not speak the language of my father and mother. I did not learn the vices of chewing tobacco, smoking, drinking, and swearing, and for all this I am grateful. I have never, in fact, 'progressed' that far.

But I soon began to see the sad sight, so common today, of returned students who could not speak their native tongue, or, worse yet, some who pretended they could no longer converse in the mother tongue. They had become ashamed and this led them into deception and trickery. The boys came home wearing stiff paper collars, tight patent-leather boots, and derby hats on heads that were meant to be clothed in the long hair of the Lakota brave.

The girls came home wearing muslin dresses and long ribbon sashes in bright hues which were very pretty. But they were trying to squeeze their feet into heeled shoes of factory make and their waists into binding apparatuses that were not garments — at least they served no purpose of a garment, but bordered on some mechanical device. However, the wearing of them was part of the 'civilization' received from those who were doing the same thing. So we went to school to copy, to imitate; not to exchange languages and ideas, and not to develop the best traits that had come out of uncountable experiences of hundreds and thousands of years living upon this continent. Our annals, all happenings of human import, were stored in our song and dance rituals, our history differing in that it was not stored in books, but in the living memory. So, while the white people had much to teach us, we had much to teach them, and what a school could have been established upon that idea! However, this was not the attitude of the day, though the teachers were sympathetic and kind, and some came to be my lifelong friends. But in the main, Indian qualities were undivined and Indian virtues not conceded. And I can well remember when Indians in those days were stoned upon the streets as were the dogs that roamed them. We were 'savages,' and all who had not come under the influence of the missionary were 'heathen,' and Wakan Tanka, who had since the beginning watched over the Lakota and his land, was denied by these men of God. Should we not have been justified in thinking them heathen? And so the 'civilizing' process went on, killing us as it went.

When I came back to the reservation to resume life there, it was too late to go on the warpath to prove, as I had always hoped to prove to my people, that I was a real brave. However, there came the battle of my life — the battle with agents to retain my individuality and my life as a Lakota. I wanted to take part in the tribal dances, sing the songs I had heard since I was born, and repeat and cherish the tales that had been the delight of my boyhood. It was in these things and through these things that my people lived and could continue to live, so it was up to me to keep them alive in my mind.

Now and then the Lakotas were holding their tribal dances in the old way, and I attended. Though my hair had been cut and I wore civilian clothes, I never forsook the blanket. For convenience, no coat I have ever worn can take the place of the blanket robe; and the same with the moccasins, which are sensible, comfortable, and beautiful. Besides, they were devised by people who danced — not for pastime, excitement, or fashion — but because it was an innate urge. Even when studying under the missionary, I went to the dances of my tribe.

All the while the agent or white rule became harder and stricter. The missionary oftentimes was an ally to the agent in trying to stop everything the Indian naturally did either in the pursuit of living or pleasure. A rule would come out forbidding something to be done, and in a short while another order would be issued forbidding something else to be done, until gradually and slowly rights began to disappear. On the commissary door and in the trader's store there one day appeared a printed notice, by order of the agent, that no returned student would thereafter be permitted to attend any tribal dance. This was done in an effort to make young people turn away from things traditional. In a short while there came another order which allowed the old people to hold but one dance a week, and no more. Soon another rule followed, stating that whenever a horse or present was given away, it must be done silently. Though there was nothing to disturb but the endless ether, there must be no glad announcing and no shouts of joy. The singing of praise songs by old men and the calling of gift-givers to some poor person were not to the liking of the white rulers. Cursing and yelling at football and baseball games were all to their liking and most certainly in order. But ceremonial gift-making was not to the order of their doing.

Senselessness and heartlessness increased with the issuing of orders, and this one came: No one could give away a beef for food unless he possessed more than thirty head of cattle. But even worse was yet to come, for soon the order was issued that no Indian family could kill a beef, whatever the need, unless the agent gave permission. And this order to a people who have ever been the greatest conservators, and who practiced frugality to a point never dreamed of by the white man!

One day I decided to visit my sister, wife of Hollow Horn Bear, who lived not more than eight or ten miles away, but across the line of my reservation. Not being a free man, but a subject and hostage, I was bound by agency regulations to get a permit before I could cross the line of my reserve. Now the agent lived forty miles away and his rule was an intolerable one, so I visited my sister without a permit. For that rations were taken from me and my family for three months. Still I was defiant and I would not ask for my rations back. I was a diligent and industrious farmer, and I hotly resented the indignity of being punished like a slave. Seeing that I was ignoring him, the agent at once ordered me to his office. I quit my work and rode in. When I stood in his presence, he took his time about putting aside his paper and turning in his swivel chair to face me. Then in a pompous manner he said, 'Standing Bear, I understand that you left the reservation,' knowing full well that my sister lived but a short distance from me. Standing straight, I answered firmly, 'I did.' 'Well,' he asked, 'you know it is against the regulations?' 'I do,' I replied, just as firmly as I had before. The agent thought a moment, then he said: 'Standing Bear, you go home and bring your wife and children all in. I want to count them; when this is done you may return home and I will give you back your rations.' The very absurdity of the thing almost made me speechless, and, as I hesitated, he asked, 'Do you understand?' More firmly than ever I answered, 'Yes, sir!' 'Are you going to do it?' the agent still questioned. I was now very disgusted and thoroughly angry, but trying hard to hold my temper; nevertheless, I answered with unmistakable promptness and feeling, 'No, sir!' When he saw that I was leaving him, he called me back and, handing me a piece of paper, told me to take it to my district farmer. I did, and it was an order to resume my rations.

More and more as time went on white influence was felt. The boys and girls coming home from school were dressed as white people and among themselves spoke only the English language. They began having socials and parties, and when the contact with the white people became more or less close, there was some social mingling and inter-marriage.

One of the first games learned by the Indians was pool. The braves would go into a brave hall, most of them dressed half-white and half-Indian. Some wore civilian clothes and hats with long hair and moccasins; others wore blankets, and some their feather headdresses. Two braves took up the game while the rest lined up for bets, and soon things would be pretty exciting. Perhaps over in a corner by himself would be a dignified old warrior looking on and trying to appear not too interested, nevertheless watching every move, unable to keep the gleam of interest from his eyes.

In 1890 a group of former students of Carlisle held a council for the purpose of discussing what could be done with the education we had received at that institution and which we had found useless to us on the reservation. Julian Whistler was a harness-maker, Frank Conroy and Robert American Horse were blacksmiths, Amos Long Hill and Ralph Iron Eagle Feather were carpenters, while Frank

Twist and I were tinsmiths. I had wanted very badly to be a carpenter, but was not allowed to choose my trade, therefore had never been quite satisfied. However, about fifteen of us met and decided that we should each like to open a little shop of his own, providing the Government would give us the necessary tools. This seemed to us a splendid idea for keeping the knowledge which we had gained at school and which was supposed to fit us for civilian life. So we drew up a letter stating our plans and asking for tools, and mailed it to the Commissioner of Indian Affairs. Our letter was ignored, much to our disappointment.

When my brother Henry returned home from Carlisle, it was with the hope that some day he would go on with his education. He had been graduated and had made a good record there and wanted to go to some higher institution. The family not having the necessary money, Henry conceived the idea of writing to the Commissioner for assistance. He wrote saying that he would like to attend a Chicago college and asked for a sum that would see him through the course. But the Commissioner refused, his excuse being that, if one boy be given such advantages, all Indian boys would want the same advantages and that such a thing could not be done. Tribal funds would not accommodate all the Indian boys who would at once crave a higher education. That is the most exalted opinion I ever heard an Indian Commissioner express on the educational aspirations of the Indian youth of the land, and I think his compliment was unintentional. Anyway, it was absurd, for in our Black Hills alone there was wealth enough not only to educate all the Lakota boys, but the boys of other tribes as well. Just a few days ago there passed away in this city of Los Angeles an honored millionaire who had taken his gold from the Black Hills of the Lakotas.

I have always believed that Indians should teach

Indians; that students who return from Government schools should be put in charge of schools on the reservation. Many of them are capable and would find teaching to their natural liking. Soon after I returned from the East, the Indian teachers were replaced in the reservation schools by white teachers. Some of these people were actually afraid of Indians, did not know how to live among them, get along with them, nor instruct them. Their knowledge of Indians was book knowledge, and they had come for a salary, not because they sought or cared to have personal contact with them.

I was for a time assistant to Miss Spencer, who taught one of the day schools at the agency — not that she was capable, but she was the daughter of the agent. Now, Miss Spencer was tall and slender, and perhaps to add plumpness to her figure she wore a huge bustle, but why a woman would tie a bundle to her back under her clothing we never came to understand, and we often puzzled over it. But for all our mystification, when the bustle began to travel around to the side we began to laugh.

One time before white teachers had entirely displaced Indian teachers, I had a chance to show off my pupils to a great advantage. The teachers in the district had been called together with their classes for a sort of convention. The agent said he wanted to find out how Indian children were progressing. On the appointed day about ten teachers, including myself, arrived at our classes. The agent, his wife, employees, and others interested, were there to witness the program. One teacher had her class sing a song in English, which they did very well. Other classes read from their readers in English, and it could be seen that the youngsters were learning fast. They could read readily and their pronunciation was good. It came time for me to present my class, which was then, I believe, reading in the second reader. My pupils read first in English, then I asked them to read the same words in their own tongue to prove that they knew what they were reading about. They read the translations as well as they did English. Then I asked if the other classes would translate, but this they could not do. They had been merely drilled parrot-like to read some words out of a book. I leave it to the judgment of my intelligent readers which way was the better.

At Carlisle we had been ordered never to speak our own language and I now remembered how hard it had been for us to forego the consolation of speech. I remembered how lonely we used to get and how we longed for the loved ones at home, and the taking away of speech at that time only added to our depression. Those of us who knew the sign language made use of it, but imagine what it meant to those who had to remain silent. In teaching, I remembered all these things, so not only allowed but encouraged the speaking of both languages at the same time. I would write a sentence on the blackboard in English and have the pupils repeat it over and over, each time explaining the meaning; then they repeated it in their own language. The children were so delighted with the system that they learned very fast. It gave me a great deal of pleasure too, for I knew that I was not making it disagreeable for them. I still think of those days with satisfaction and pride.

But all the while it was not hard to see beneath the surface the airs of importance which the white people put on. We were never allowed to forget that they were emissaries of the Government; that they were endowed with superior knowledge. Never once were they intelligent enough to admit that they might have learned something from us. In pompous ignorance they made mistakes, like the supervisor who used his leg for a wagon-brake. We should have been absolutely without humor had we not at times indulged in a good laugh.

Once on my way home from the East I stopped off at Omaha to visit some friends. They asked me to accompany them to their reservation home for a visit there, so I de-

cided to do so. In the group were Noah La Flesche, Levi
Levering, Noah Lovejoy, and others. We all went to the
agency store, there to separate, each going to his own
home. Someone asked me with whom I wanted to stay,
and I said I would visit with all of them, first one and then
the other, but they told me that was not the way the
Omahas did. I had supposed that, since they had all
been to school, they would do as the white man did, but
they said they intended following their tribal custom in
entertaining me and that I was to choose one of them to
stay with. Noah Lovejoy lived nearest the store, so I chose
to go home with him, while the rest of them began at once
to plan festivities in my honor. I was not to go calling from
one friend's house to another; they were all to call on me.

In a few days a dinner was given me at Noah's house.
He asked me if I had anything that I could give as presents
to the guests and I replied that I had brought a few things.
So when all the friends had arrived and the feasting had
begun, I put out my best belongings — a fine beaded
blanket, tobacco pouch, moccasins, an otter skin, headdress, and leggins with beaded strips. Every garment was
my best, but I put them all on display. Every now and
then a guest would walk over and take something that
suited his fancy. When the meal was over, all my fine
things were gone.

It was not long before another feast was announced for
me, and this time there were many more people than had
been at Noah's home. The spokesman made a speech
saying that I was a guest and that every courtesy should
be shown me. The feast began, and when it was over
I had been showered with gifts — blankets, moccasins,
garments, money, and even livestock. I had come poor
and went home well-to-do.

During my visit there I noticed that the Omahas were
not having their tribal dances and ceremonies, so I urged
them not to give them up. I did not believe that it was

right for them to forget all their fine ceremonies and indulge in nothing but feasts. So I helped them repair their meeting lodge and soon it was ready for a dance. The braves all came and danced, and again they gave me a great number of presents. The Omahas are a very generous people.

I made ready to end my visit and go home, but some of my friends begged me to stay longer, and so I did, lengthening my stay into two years. But when I left, they had established all their tribal performances once more.

I returned home again to take up my battles against agency rule. With good agents, men with humane and constructive ideas, such as Captain Brown who formerly had been disciplinarian at Carlisle and who shared the same high principles of General Pratt, we were but occasionally blessed. They were soon replaced by those willing to carry out the orders of a department that never intended that the Indian should settle down to peace and industry. The reservation became a place where people were herded under every possible disadvantage and obstruction to progress until the race should pass out from sheer physical depletion.

It was not hard to see that the white people coveted every inch of land on which we lived. Greed, human greed, wanted the last bit of ground which supported Indian feet. It was land—it has ever been land—for which the white man oppresses the Indian and to gain possession of which he commits any crime. Treaties that [have been made have been but vain attempts to save a little of the fatherland — treaties holy to us by the smoke of the pipe — but nothing is holy to the white man. Little by little, with greed and cruelty unsurpassed by the animal, he has taken all. The loaf is gone and now the white man wants the crumbs.

Worse and worse have become reservation conditions under a system that was bad from the beginning. Such a deplorable state of affairs could only continue to exist because of several reasons, mainly because of slight public concern for the Indian; because the declaration of President Coolidge on June 5, 1924, presumably made the Indian a citizen of the United States, and because the mass of people think and say, 'The Government takes care of the Indian.'

The very act of signing the bill disclosed the fact that a bonded and enslaved people lived in the 'land of the free and the home of the brave,' even though it was then more than half a century since slavery was supposed to have been wiped from the land. The bill signed by President Coolidge supposedly gave the Indian the same rights enjoyed by other men, but it was just another hoax. The reservation still remains, the agent is still on the job, Indian children are still wrested from their mother's arms to be sent away, young 'citizens' still go to segregated schools where they are refused the right to speak their native tongue, the Indian Bureau politicians still fatten on Indian money and the Indian is still being robbed. My people of South Dakota have been in dire straits, and during the past two years the old have rapidly passed away, unable to endure the cold of winter insufficiently clothed, and have slowly become undermined in health by starvation while the public sleeps on the thought that 'the Government takes care of the Indian.' The twenty million dollars public appropriation disbursed last year among the various tribes was but a crumb thrown into a starving mouth. Each Sioux received the sum of seven dollars and a half, and when I talked to the agent about it this summer (1931) he admitted that it came at a most needed time. But public appropriations never have and never will supply the Sioux people with the need to have their reservation freed from the white cattle-raiser and given cattle of their own to raise; nor can the doling of such pittances to any tribe effect the needed relief and reform.

Within a few hours' ride from this city are people living

on restricted plots of ground, waterless and inadequate to support them, as fast and defined as ever was a southern plantation, and over this group an overseer. Distasteful as this form of 'citizenship' is to friends of the Indian, it has its supporters, and one Bureau defender write me, 'If the Indians were put on their own tomorrow, without supervision and guidance, inside of a year they would not have a dollar to their names, and what would happen if all Government appropriations ceased?' There, my readers, in the weakness and arrogance of that man's words, you have the key to the situation. *The white man claims the right to guide and supervise the Indian!* Yet, from whence emanated the *right?* Who gave the white man the right to *guide* and *supervise* the Indian? Here in this city within the past year thousands of white families have been robbed of their last dollar through the manipulation of white real estate and oil promoters. But these unfortunates have not been put under *guidance* and *supervision*, have not been restricted in their rights in any manner. The stamp of thought, the white attitude toward the Indian, is epitomized in the above quotation; and this acclaimer is an 'authority' on the Indian and he compiles data for the archives in the Smithsonian Institution at Washington, D.C.

This is the picture — the scene of today's stark and naked truth — that is challenging and gripping the attention of thinking people. It is a picture which friends of the Indian wish to efface. And it is to this task of effacement that I bend my efforts, not without, however, a sense of its magnitude. Can the wrongs of centuries be righted? Are my efforts but straws to which I cling in desperation in the darkness of lies and tyranny that envelop my people? Or may I not with the burning light of truth touch a straw with flame and may I not with that spark light a fagot of thought with which to bring back to life the fires of Indian faith — the brightest that ever burned upon this continent?

CHAPTER IX

WHAT THE INDIAN MEANS TO AMERICA

THE feathered and blanketed figure of the American Indian has come to symbolize the American continent. He is the man who through centuries has been moulded and sculped by the same hand that shaped its mountains, forests, and plains, and marked the course of its rivers.

The American Indian is of the soil, whether it be the region of forests, plains, pueblos, or mesas. He fits into the landscape, for the hand that fashioned the continent also fashioned the man for his surroundings. He once grew as naturally as the wild sunflowers; he belongs just as the buffalo belonged.

With a physique that fitted, the man developed fitting skills — crafts which today are called American. And the body had a soul, also formed and moulded by the same master hand of harmony. Out of the Indian approach to existence there came a great freedom — an intense and absorbing love for nature; a respect for life; enriching faith in a Supreme Power; and principles of truth, honesty, generosity, equity, and brotherhood as a guide to mundane relations.

Becoming possessed of a fitting philosophy and art, it was by them that native man perpetuated his identity; stamped it into the history and soul of this country — made land and man one.

By living — struggling, losing, meditating, imbibing, aspiring, achieving — he wrote himself into ineraceable evidence — an evidence that can be and often has been ignored, but never totally destroyed. Living — and all the intangible forces that constitute that phenomenon — are brought into being by Spirit, that which no man can alter.

Only the hand of the Supreme Power can transform man; only Wakan Tanka can transform the Indian. But of such deep and infinite graces finite man has little comprehension. He has, therefore, no weapons with which to slay the unassailable. He can only foolishly trample.

The white man does not understand the Indian for the reason that he does not understand America. He is too far removed from its formative processes. The roots of the tree of his life have not yet grasped the rock and soil. The white man is still troubled with primitive fears; he still has in his consciousness the perils of this frontier continent, some of its fastnesses not yet having yielded to his questing footsteps and inquiring eyes. He shudders still with the memory of the loss of his forefathers upon its scorching deserts and forbidding mountain-tops. The man from Europe is still a foreigner and an alien. And he still hates the man who questioned his path across the continent.

But in the Indian the spirit of the land is still vested; it will be until other men are able to divine and meet its rhythm. Men must be born and reborn to belong. Their bodies must be formed of the dust of their forefathers' bones.

The attempted transformation of the Indian by the white man and the chaos that has resulted are but the fruits of the white man's disobedience of a fundamental and spiritual law. The pressure that has been brought to bear upon the native people, since the cessation of armed conflict, in the attempt to force conformity of custom and habit has caused a reaction more destructive than war, and the injury has not only affected the Indian, but has extended to the white population as well. Tyranny, stupidity, and lack of vision have brought about the situation now alluded to as the 'Indian Problem.'

There is, I insist, no Indian problem as created by the Indian himself. Every problem that exists today in regard to the native population is due to the white man's cast of mind, which is unable, at least reluctant, to seek understanding and achieve adjustment in a new and a significant environment into which it has so recently come.

The white man excused his presence here by saying that he had been guided by the will of his God; and in so saying absolved himself of all responsibility for his appearance in a land occupied by other men.

Then, too, his law was a written law; his divine decalogue reposed in a book. And what better proof that his advent into this country and his subsequent acts were the result of divine will! He brought the Word! There ensued a blind worship of written history, of books, of the written word, that has denuded the spoken word of its power and scaredness. The written word became established as a criterion of the superior man — a symbol of emotional fineness. The man who could write his name on a piece of paper, whether or not he possessed the spiritual fineness to honor those words in speech, was by some miraculous formula a more highly developed and sensitized person than the one who had never had a pen in hand, but whose spoken word was inviolable and whose sense of honor and truth was paramount. With false reasoning was the quality of human character measured by man's ability to make with an implement a mark upon paper. But granting this mode of reasoning be correct and just, then where are to be placed the thousands of illiterate whites who are unable to read and write? Are they, too, 'savages'? Is not humanness a matter of heart and mind, and is it not evident in the form of relationship with men? Is not kindness more powerful than arrogance; and truth more powerful than the sword?

True, the white man brought great change. But the varied fruits of his civilization, though highly colored and inviting, are sickening and deadening. And if it be the part of civilization to maim, rob, and thwart, then what is progress?

I am going to venture that the man who sat on the ground in his tipi meditating on life and its meaning, accepting the kinship of all creatures, and acknowledging unity with the universe of things was infusing into his being the true essence of civilization. And when native man left off this form of development, his humanization was retarded in growth.

Another most powerful agent that gave native man promise of developing into a true human was the responsibility accepted by parenthood. Mating among Lakotas was motivated, of course, by the same laws of attraction that motivate all beings; however, considerable thought was given by parents of both boy and girl to the choosing of mates. And a still greater advantage accrued to the race by the law of self-mastery which the young couple voluntarily placed upon themselves as soon as they discovered they were to become parents. Immediately, and for some time after, the sole thought of the parents was in preparing the child for life. And true civilization lies in the dominance of self and not in the dominance of other men.

How far this idea would have gone in carrying my people upward and toward a better plane of existence, or how much of an influence it was in the development of their spiritual being, it is not possible to say. But it had its promises. And it cannot be gainsaid that the man who is rising to a higher estate is the man who is putting into his being the essence of humanism. It is self-effort that develops, and by this token the greatest factor today in dehumanizing races is the manner in which the machine is used — the product of one man's brain doing the work for another. The hand is the tool that has built man's mind; it, too, can refine it.

THE SAVAGE

After subjugation, after dispossession, there was cast the last abuse upon the people who so entirely resented their wrongs and punishments, and that was the stamping and the labeling of them as savages. To make this label stick has been the task of the white race and the greatest salve that it has been able to apply to its sore and troubled conscience now hardened through the habitual practice of injustice.

But all the years of calling the Indian a savage has never made him one; all the denial of his virtues has never taken them from him; and the very resistance he has made to save the things inalienably his has been his saving strength — that which will stand him in need when justice does make its belated appearance and he undertakes rehabilitation.

All sorts of feeble excuses are heard for the continued subjection of the Indian. One of the most common is that he is not yet ready to accept the society of the white man — that he is not yet ready to mingle as a social entity.

This, I maintain, is beside the question. The matter is not one of making-over the external Indian into the likeness of the white race — a process detrimental to both races. Who can say that the white man's way is better for the Indian? Where resides the human judgment with the competence to weigh and value Indian ideals and spiritual concepts; or substitute for them other values?

Then, has the white man's social order been so harmonious and ideal as to merit the respect of the Indian, and for that matter the thinking class of the white race? Is it wise to urge upon the Indian a foreign social form? Let none but the Indian answer!

Rather, let the white brother face about and cast his mental eye upon a new angle of vision. Let him look upon the Indian world as a human world; then let him see to it that human rights be accorded to the Indians. And this for the purpose of retaining for his own order of society a measure of humanity.

THE INDIAN SCHOOL OF THOUGHT

I say again that Indians should teach Indians; that Indians should serve Indians, especially on reservations where the older people remain. There is a definite need of the old for the care and sympathy of the young and they are today perishing for the joys that naturally belong to old Indian people. Old Indians are very close to their progeny. It was their delightful duty to care for and instruct the very young, while in turn they looked forward to being cared for by sons and daughters. These were the privileges and blessings of old age.

Many of the grievances of the old Indian, and his disagreements with the young, find root in the far-removed boarding-school which sometimes takes the little ones at a very tender age. More than one tragedy has resulted when a young boy or girl has returned home again almost an utter stranger. I have seen these happenings with my own eyes and I know they can cause naught but suffering. The old Indian cannot, even if he wished, reconcile himself to an institution that alienates his young. And there is something evil in a system that brings about an unnatural reaction to life; when it makes young hearts callous and unheedful of the needs and joys of the old.

The old people do not speak English and they never will be English-speaking. To place upon such people the burden of understanding and functioning through an office bound up with the routine and red tape of the usual Government office is silly and futile, and every week or so I receive letters from the reservation evidencing this fact. The Indian's natural method of settling questions is by council and conference. From time immemorial, for every project affecting their material, social, and spiritual lives, the people have met together to 'talk things over.'

To the end that young Indians will be able to appreciate both their traditional life and modern life they should be doubly educated. Without forsaking reverence for their ancestral teachings, they can be trained to take up modern duties that relate to tribal and reservation life. And there is no problem of reservation importance but can be solved by the joint efforts of the old and the young Indians.

There certainly can be no doubt in the public mind today as to the capacity of the younger Indians in taking on white modes and manners. For many years, and particularly since the days of General Pratt, the young Indian has been proving his efficiency when entering the fields of white man's endeavor and has done well in copying and acquiring the ways of the white man.

The Indian liked the white man's horse and straightway became an expert horseman; he threw away his age-old weapons, the bow and arrow, and matched the white man's skill with gun and pistol; in the field of sports — games of strength and skill — the Indian enters with no shame in comparison; the white man's beads the Indian woman took, developed a technique and an art distinctly her own with no competitor in design; and in the white man's technique of song and dance the Indian has made himself a creditable exponent.

However, despite the fact that Indian schools have been established over several generations, there is a dearth of Indians in the professions. It is most noticeable on the reservations where the numerous positions of consequence are held by white employees instead of trained Indians. For instance, why are not the stores, post-offices, and Government office jobs on the Sioux Reservation held by trained Indians? Why cannot Sioux be reservation nurses and doctors; and road-builders too? Much road work goes on every summer, but the complaint is constant that it is always done by white workmen, and in such a manner as to necessitate its being done again in a short time. Were these numerous positions turned over to trained Indians, the white population would soon find reservation life less attractive and less lucrative.

With school facilities already fairly well established and the capability of the Indian unquestioned, every reservation could well be supplied with Indian doctors, nurses, engineers, road- and bridge-builders, draughtsmen, architects, dentists, lawyers, teachers, and instructors in tribal lore, legends, orations, song, dance, and ceremonial ritual. The Indian, by the very sense of duty, should become his own historian, giving his account of the race — fairer and fewer accounts of the wars and more of statecraft, legends, languages, oratory, and philosophical conceptions. No longer should the Indian be dehumanized in order to make material for lurid and cheap fiction to embellish street-stands. Rather, a fair and correct history of the native American should be incorporated in the curriculum of the public school.

Caucasian youth is fed, and rightly so, on the feats and exploits of their old-world heroes, their revolutionary forefathers, their adventurous pioneer trail-blazers, and in our Southwest through pageants, fiestas, and holidays the days of the Spanish *conquistador* is kept alive.

But Indian youth! They, too, have fine pages in their past history; they, too, have patriots and heroes. And it is not fair to rob Indian youth of their history, the stories of their patriots, which, if impartially written, would fill them with pride and dignity. Therefore, give back to Indian youth all, everything in their heritage that belongs to them and augment it with the best in the modern schools. I repeat, doubly educate the Indian boy and girl.

What a contrast this would make in comparison with the present unhealthy, demoralized place the reservation is today, where the old are poorly fed, shabbily clothed, divested of pride and incentive; and where the young are unfitted for tribal life and untrained for the world of white man's affairs except to hold an occasional job!

Why not a school of Indian thought, built on the Indian pattern and conducted by Indian instructors? Why not a school of tribal art?

Why should not America be cognizant of itself; aware of its identity? In short, why should not America be preserved?

There were ideals and practices in the life of my ancestors that have not been improved upon by the present-day civilization; there were in our culture elements of benefit; and there were influences that would broaden any life. But that almost an entire public needs to be enlightened as to this fact need not be discouraging. For many centuries the human mind labored under the delusion that the world was flat; and thousands of men have believed that the heavens were supported by the strength of an Atlas. The human mind is not yet free from fallacious reasoning; it is not yet an open mind and its deepest recesses are not yet swept free of errors.

But it is now time for a destructive order to be reversed, and it is well to inform other races that the aboriginal culture of America was not devoid of beauty. Furthermore, in denying the Indian his ancestral rights and heritages the white race is but robbing itself. But America can be revived, rejuvenated, by recognizing a native school of thought. The Indian can save America.

THE LIVING SPIRIT OF THE INDIAN — HIS ART

The spiritual health and existence of the Indian was maintained by song, magic, ritual, dance, symbolism, oratory (or council), design, handicraft, and folk-story.

Manifestly, to check or thwart this expression is to bring about spiritual decline. And it is in this condition of decline that the Indian people are today. There is but a feeble effort among the Sioux to keep alive their traditional songs and dances, while among other tribes there is but a half-hearted attempt to offset the influence of the Government school and at the same time recover from the crushing and stifling régime of the Indian Bureau. One has but to speak of Indian verse to receive uncomprehending and unbelieving glances. Yet the Indian loved verse and into this mode of expression went his deepest feelings. Only a few ardent and advanced students seem interested; nevertheless, they have given in book form enough Indian translations to set forth the character and quality of Indian verse.

Oratory receives a little better understanding on the part of the white public, owing to the fact that oratorical compilations include those of Indian orators.

Hard as it seemingly is for the white man's ear to sense the differences, Indian songs are as varied as the many emotions which inspire them, for no two of them are alike. For instance, the Song of Victory is spirited and the notes high and remindful of an unrestrained hunter or warrior riding exultantly over the prairies. On the other hand, the song of the *Cano unye* is solemn and full of urge, for it is meant to inspire the young men to deeds of valor. Then there are the songs of death and the spiritual songs which are connected with the ceremony of initiation. These are full of the spirit of praise and worship, and so strong are some of these invocations that the very air seems as if surcharged with the presence of the Big Holy.

The Indian loved to worship. From birth to death he revered his surroundings. He considered himself born in the luxurious lap of Mother Earth and no place was to him humble. There was nothing between him and the Big Holy. The contact was immediate and personal, and the blessings of Wakan Tanka flowed over the Indian like rain showered from the sky. Wakan Tanka was not aloof, apart, and ever seeking to quell evil forces. He did not punish the animals and the birds, and likewise He did not punish man. He was not a punishing God. For there was never a question as to the supremacy of an evil power over and above the power of Good. There was but one ruling power, and that was *Good*.

Of course, none but an adoring one could dance for

days with his face to the sacred sun, and that time is all but done. We cannot have back the days of the buffalo and beaver; we cannot win back our clean blood-stream and superb health, and we can never again expect that beautiful *rapport* we once had with Nature. The springs and lakes have dried and the mountains are bare of forests. The plow has changed the face of the world. Wi-wila is dead! No more may we heal our sick and comfort our dying with a strength founded on faith, for even the animals now fear us, and fear supplants faith.

And the Indian wants to dance! It is his way of expressing devotion, of communing with unseen power, and in keeping his tribal identity. When the Lakota heart was filled with high emotion, he danced. When he felt the benediction of the warming rays of the sun, he danced. When his blood ran hot with success of the hunt or chase, he danced. When his heart was filled with pity for the orphan, the lonely father, or bereaved mother, he danced. All the joys and exaltations of life, all his gratefulness and thankfulness, all his acknowledgments of the mysterious power that guided life, and all his aspirations for a better life, culminated in one great dance — the Sun Dance.

Today we see our young people dancing together the silly jazz — dances that add nothing to the beauty and fineness of our lives and certainly nothing to our history, while the dances that record the life annals of a people die. It is the American Indian who contributes to this country its true folk-dancing, growing, as we did, out of the soil. The dance is far older than his legends, songs, or philosophy.

Did dancing mean much to the white people they would better understand ours. Yet at the same time there is no attraction that brings people from such distances as a certain tribal dance, for the reason that the white mind senses its mystery, for even the white man's inmost feelings are unconsciously stirred by the beat of the tomtom. They are heart-beats, and once all men danced to its rhythm.

When the Indian has forgotten the music of his forefathers, when the sound of the tomtom is no more, when
noisy jazz has drowned the melody of the flute, he will be a
dead Indian. When the memory of his heroes are no longer
told in story, and he forsakes the beautiful white buckskin
for factory shoddy, he will be dead. When from him has
been taken all that is his, all that he has visioned in nature,
all that has come to him from infinite sources, he then,
truly, will be a dead Indian. His spirit will be gone, and
though he walk crowded streets, he will, in truth, be —
dead!

But all this must not perish; it must live, to the end that
America shall be educated no longer to regard native pro-
duction of whatever tribe — folk-story, basketry, pottery,
dance, song, poetry — as curios, and native artists as curios-
ities. For who but the man indigenous to the soil could
produce its song, story, and folk-tale; who but the man who
loved the dust beneath his feet could shape it and put it into undying, ceramic form; who but he who loved the reeds
that grew beside still waters, and the damp roots of shrub
and tree, could save it from seasonal death, and with almost superhuman patience weave it into enduring objects
of beauty — into timeless art!

Regarding the 'civilization' that has been thrust upon
me since the days of reservation, it has not added one
whit to my sense of justice; to my reverence for the rights
of life; to my love for truth, honesty, and generosity; nor
to my faith in Wakan Tanka — God of the Lakotas. For
after all the great religions have been preached and ex-
pounded, or have been revealed by brilliant scholars, or
have been written in books and embellished in fine language
with finer covers, man — all man — is still confronted with
the Great Mystery.

So if today I had a young mind to direct, to start on the
journey of life, and I was faced with the duty of choosing
between the natural way of my forefathers and that of the

white man's present way of civilization, I would, for its welfare, unhesitatingly set that child's feet in the path of my forefathers. I would raise him to be an Indian!

THE END